D0518595

THE ORIGINALS

THE SECRET HISTORY OF THE BIRTH OF THE

SAS

IN THEIR OWN WORDS

GORDON STEVENS

EBURY
PRESS

First published 2005 by Ebury Press,
An imprint of Random House,
20 Vauxhall Bridge Road, London SW1V 2SA

Random House Australia (Pty) Limited
20 Alfred Street, Milsons Point, Sydney,
New South Wales 2061, Australia

Random House New Zealand Limited
18 Poland Road, Glenfield, Auckland 10, New Zealand

Random House South Africa (Pty) Limited
Endulini, 5a Jubilee Road, Parktown 2193, South Africa

The Random House Group Limited Reg. No. 954009

www.randomhouse.co.uk

Printed and bound in Great Britain by Clays Ltd, St Ives plc

A CIP catalogue record for this book is available from the British Library.

Cover designed by Two Associates
Typeset by Textype

ISBN 009190177-4

CONTENTS

We are the pilgrims, Master, we shall go
Always a little further, it may be
Beyond that last blue mountain barr'd with snow
Across that angry or glimmering sea.

James Elroy Flecker
The Golden Road to Samarkand

Inscribed on the clock tower at the SAS headquarters, near Hereford, on which are also inscribed the names of members of the Special Air Service killed in action.

'SAS had to be developed as a concept on the basis of actual operations and performances. One of the things I could be sure of was my own defeat of craven fear, which I had to a maximum degree. I'm not arrogant. I always hoisted on board guys who argued. I didn't want psychopaths. But I think one of the reasons that the SAS concept has survived longer perhaps than might be expected is because of the fact that it was forged in hell.'

Colonel Sir David Stirling, OBE, DSO
Founder of the Special Air Service

'We of the Delta Force have built upon your philosophies, organisation and operational concepts in creating this unit. Your principles and ideas are as sound today as they were in World War Two. The common bond between the special forces of the Western world is that we all trace our root back to you . . .'

From the Commander of the US Delta Force
to David Stirling, on the occasion of his being made a
Knight Bachelor in 1990

'In a sense they weren't really controllable. They were harnessable. The object was to give them the same purpose. And that goal had to be an exacting one, because from the start we knew we would never make it as a regiment unless not only we operated effectively, but we succeeded in establishing a new role. And that band of vagabonds had to grasp what they had to do in order to get there.'

David Stirling
on The Originals

'. . . of David Stirling's greatness there can be no doubt. As a leader, a man of action and a man of ideas, he left an enduring mark on the military thinking of his age . . . There was about him, as about many great men, an element of mystery, an intangible quality, akin perhaps to what Lawrence called "the irrational tenth, like the kingfisher flashing across the pool" . . . David was a man of ideals as well as ideas. What is for sure is that when he got hold of an idea – or for that matter an ideal – he didn't let go. And this was as true after the war as during it . . . But I shall always remember him in the desert when he was young, a great soldier and a great friend.'

Sir Fitzroy Maclean of Dunconnel
at the memorial service for David Stirling,
February 7, 1991

AUTHOR'S PREFACE

This book is made from the actual words of The Originals themselves; the moments they chose to remember and the stories they chose to tell, told in their own way.

The Originals are the founding members of the Special Air Service, including the founder himself, David Stirling: the men who were there on Day One, the men who started it all. To understand why it is a privilege to be allowed to tell their story, it is necessary to appreciate one simple statistic.

The first-ever SAS operation was in the desert campaign of North Africa in November 1941. Sixty-five men took part. The operation involved a parachute jump at night. Just before they took off, a massive storm blew up. They were given the chance of pulling out, but insisted on jumping, into the night and the storm, in the full knowledge that many of them would not survive but that unless they jumped the SAS would be disbanded before it had properly begun. Of the sixty-five men who jumped that night, only twenty-one (or twenty-two, the figure is unclear) made it out to the desert rendezvous. Three months later, that figure was down to thirteen. War, and time, has since cut that number even more. In 1984, at a ceremony at which David Stirling officially gave his name to SAS Headquarters at Hereford, he made a wry reference to the fact that the present SAS refer to The Originals as The Dirty Dozen.

In addition to the men who were there on Day One, two others had 'Honorary Original' status conferred upon them. They also tell their story in this book.

The Originals is not a standard chronology of SAS operations, nor is it a history of the SAS, both of which can be obtained from any one of a number of excellent books on the subject. And it is not the standard chronology for one specific reason, which is interesting in that it reveals a great deal about the men themselves.

Except for the first operation, and what David Stirling decided to do as a result of it, the men sometimes seemed reluctant to talk about what exactly they had done, and details which other people might find fascinating seemed to them day-to-day and run-of-the-mill. Perhaps that is because The Originals were there at the beginning of the Second World War, and were still there at the end – five years of SAS operations behind the lines and five years of almost continuous fighting through a whole series of campaigns: North Africa, Italy, France, and Germany. Some events which other people might remember are simply logged with many others, or not even logged at all. Which means that those The Originals do choose to talk about have a special significance for them. It is these which this book records.

And it is for this reason that *The Originals* is different. It is the story of the birth of the SAS through the lives of an incredible band of brothers – though they would laugh at the expression – and the story of an incredible band of brothers through the birth of the SAS.

The men themselves would also wish to say one thing: that other men fought with distinction in the SAS, and that other men – and women – served with great distinction in other services.

The story of how this book came about illustrates the sort of men The Originals are, and the very special nature of the bond between them.

In 1985 I made a television documentary, *Secret Hunters*. The SAS had been formed in 1941, disbanded in 1945, and not re-formed until the Malayan crisis of the early 1950s. *Secret Hunters* revealed how for three years, between 1945 and 1948, after it had been disbanded and therefore did not officially exist, the SAS defied the government's closure order and kept going its own secret unit to hunt down war criminals responsible for the torture and murder of SAS men behind the lines.

(The unit also hunted others down, including a concentration camp guard who had pushed a woman member of Special Operations Executive live into a camp furnace.)

The programme was shown to certain influential members of the SAS – the existence of the post-war unit not being known to the regiment at that time – and as a result of this I was invited to London and introduced to David Stirling and The Originals and invited to make a television series on the wartime creation of the SAS.

The series was never made, but as part of it, and at a point when Stirling seemed ill and the prognosis was not great – though he went on to live another ten years –

we took over a small hotel in the New Forest and, with a certain secrecy and security, over a period of three days filmed interviews with Stirling and The Originals.

During those days, two things happened.

The first evening was to be a dinner, complete with piper – himself an ex-SAS sergeant. But Stirling was still uncomfortable with the idea of being interviewed (during background preliminary research he had frozen even at the sight of a small microphone) and did not turn up.

At the time, Stirling was running a company based in London – the address, not coincidentally, was 22 South Audley Street – 22 SAS. Most of those who worked for him were former members of the regiment.

The following lunchtime Stirling's deputy at the company phoned and asked how the interview with Stirling had gone. I explained that Colonel David, as he is known, had not turned up. 'I'm putting him in a car,' the second-in-command said. 'He doesn't come back until he's done the interview.'

Stirling turned up that evening, driven by one of the SAS's top counter-terrorism specialists. Dinner was excellent, though without the piper, and Stirling was courteous enough to thank us for being there. He was also generous enough to say the following words about the project on which we had embarked, and which I now hope he would also feel about this book:

> We've been approached something like twenty-five times since the war to have a film made about us, and three or four of them I've handed down to consideration to others. All the others I haven't bothered with. I kicked each of them out the window, because they weren't going to make it with the integrity we require the story of the SAS to be told. And these boys across the table, led by Gordon Stevens, I'm quite certain they'll make the story objective, and will make it ring true as well, because the story is no good unless it does justice and pushes the project. We were fighting to win the war, but we were also fighting to create a new strategic role in the British army. And I believe this will be brought out effectively, by the fact that you are pursuing this target of yours in a way which we all agree with.

The next morning Stirling looked old and cold and extremely unwell – though he was never a morning man. After one roll of film – ten minutes in duration – he rose to leave, but was persuaded to stay for one more roll, which became another, then another. Finally, Stirling turned to his minder. 'He's fucking me, Pete. Sort him.' The minder stood behind him. 'Yes, sir.' And we shot another roll. 'He's still fucking me, Pete. Fuck him.' The SAS sergeant put his hands gently on Stirling's shoulder and equally gently but firmly held him down. 'Yes, sir. One more roll, sir, then I'll fuck him.'

The other thing which happened was, at first, hard to understand. One of The Originals, Dave Kershaw, had been seriously unwell for some time. At the time of the interviews, Dave was only just out of hospital and was accompanied by his wife, who was looking after him. Midway through dinner on the first night, he excused himself, and he and his wife went to bed. One of those present was the Very Reverend Fraser McLuskey, MC. As Dave left, and almost unnoticed, he bent over Fraser's shoulder, whispered something, and gave him a small folded sheet of paper. Dave should do the first interview the next morning, we all agreed, then he should go home.

The next morning Dave did the interview. As he walked to the car afterwards, the rest of The Originals stood in a line. Dave went down the line and shook their hands. Cheerio, Reg . . . Cheerio, Johnny . . . Cheerio, Benny . . .

Cheerio, Dave, they each said.

Dave Kershaw died the following day. Don't feel guilty, his wife said when she phoned with the news, knowing, I imagine, what I was thinking. Before he died, she said, he had enjoyed one happy last lucid hour – he'd had his last drink with the handful of men he wanted to have it with. Above all, he'd had the chance to do his last job with the boys. 'You don't see it, do you?' the rest of The Originals said when I told them. 'Dave only kept going to do the interview.'

The service for Dave was the following week. The Reverend McLuskey, SAS wings on his flowing black gown, officiated. The slip of paper Dave had given Fraser at the dinner were the hymns Dave wanted sung. The church was full. Before, as they waited outside, The Originals – after a good lunch – may not have been as silent and sombre as is usual on such occasions, and were admonished by a member of the staff. It's not a celebration, he told them. You don't understand, they told him back. It is.

As far as possible, *The Originals* is in the words of the men themselves. I have added a certain amount of text, though only to provide background or explanation.

When the interviews were recorded, of course, The Originals were not in the first flush of youth. Only very occasionally, however, is there an inconsistency in their recollections of an operation, e.g. the numbers of men who gathered at the desert pick-up point with the Long Range Desert Group after the very first SAS operation. Sometimes they also saw an operation from a limited perspective rather than its significance in the overall conduct of the war. But they were, of course, the men at the sharp end.

Although this book is in the words of The Originals themselves, a number of people played their part on the road to it. Many of them are now dead, their own stories – and in several cases their secrets – gone with them. I would like to thank them all.

My very special thanks to the late Lieutenant Colonel Tankie Smith, MBE.

David Stirling, Bob Bennett, Johnny Cooper, Jim Almonds, Dave Kershaw, Pat Riley, Reg Seekings, the Very Revd Fraser McLuskey, Mike Sadler.

Maurice Buckmaster, Vera Atkins, Brian Stonehouse, Bob Shepherd, Prince Yorka Galitzine, David Lloyd Owen, Ian Crooke, Johnny Crossland, Alan Hoe, Dave Abbot, Alastair Morrison, Don Palmer, George Franks, Trevor Harvey, Pat McDonnell, Chalkie White, Ernie Bond. Eric Barkworth, Fred Rhodes, Henry Druce, Roy Farran, Alastair McGregor. Keith Edlin and Chris Dodkin. Lorna Almonds Windmill and John Almonds. Greg Dyke, Peter Williams, Pippa Cross, Fee Wood and Philip Nugus.

My thanks to the SAS Regimental Association and their archivisit, Grenville Bint, for allowing me access to their photographic records.

To those who helped, but cannot be named.

Special thanks also to Tony Kemp, a companion on the journey.

My thanks to Jake Lingwood at Ebury for giving The Originals the chance to tell their story, to Andrew Goodfellow and Bernice Davison for guiding it through, and my apologies to the guys that their story has taken so long to be told.

And one last word.

David Stirling did many things, and was misunderstood and attacked for some of those by many people. He was a fervent believer in the SAS, where it should go and the sort of organisation it should be. But he was something else. He was a painter, a thinker, and an inspirer of men. He was a visionary and a believer in mankind. Above all, David Stirling was a patriot. That should never be forgotten.

Gordon Stevens
Cornwall
April, 2005

BOOK ONE

The Beginning

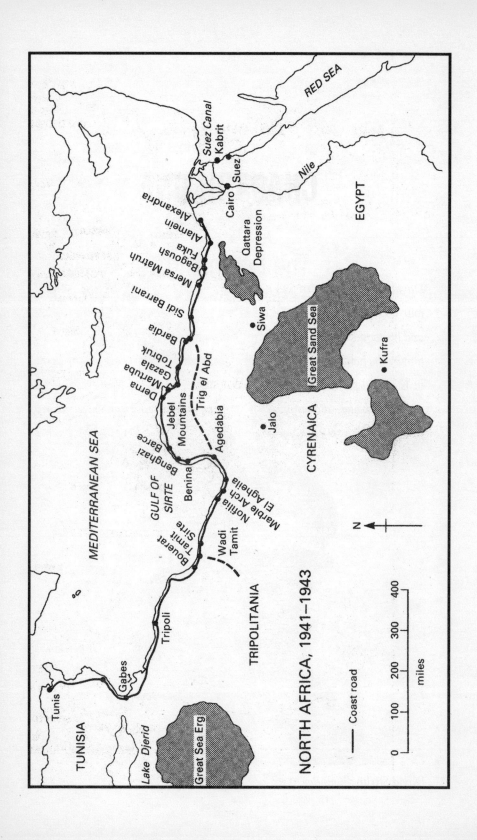

NORTH AFRICA, 1941–1943

— Coast road

miles
0   100   200   300   400

CHAPTER ONE

The Founder

*David Stirling was born into a Scottish clan on November 15, 1915, one of
four boys and two girls. His father was General Archibald Stirling of Kier
and his mother was a Lovat. When he was still a small boy, his mother took
him by the hand, past the stern portraits of his ancestors in the family home
at Kier, and paused for a moment under one place which was empty – the
suggestion being, said or unsaid, that the missing ancestor had not succeeded
in what he had set out to achieve. And what will you do in life? his mother*

David Stirling, founder of the SAS.

then asked the small boy. What will you do that people will remember?

As a child, he almost lost a leg after being bitten by an adder, and doctors wished to amputate the limb. At Kier, he spent much time with the ghillies, from which was born his feel for tactics and field craft.

David went to Ampleforth College, then Trinity College, Cambridge, where the nightlife typical of the young men of his class made inroads into his studies. He was eventually read a list of twenty-three offences, and invited to choose the three for which he would be sent down.

From Cambridge he went to Paris, where he studied to be an artist. When, after a year, his tutor told him that he lacked the necessary drawing expertise, he returned, devastated, to Kier, to decide what to do next.

By this time he was six feet five inches tall, and strong. He would, he decided, be the first man to climb Mount Everest. He enlisted in the Supplementary Reserve of the Scots Guards, spent time training in the Swiss Alps, then in the American Rockies. He was in America, somewhere along the Rio Grande near Albuquerque in New Mexico, and twenty-four years of age, when he heard the news that Britain was at war with Germany. He returned immediately and was sent to the Guards Depot at Pirbright.

It was at Pirbright that something happened which, two years later, would impact not just on Stirling's life but on the birth of the SAS. Pirbright was a mere hour from the attractions of London. During one lecture, possibly after a night at White's Club or the gaming tables, Stirling fell asleep. He probably fell asleep in many, but on this occasion he was woken by the lecturer, asking him to repeat what had just been said. Stirling repeated it verbatim.

He volunteered for, and was accepted into as a sergeant, an expeditionary force training to fight a winter campaign in Finland, which included ski training at Chamonix, but the force was never sent. When Robert Laycock planned the first unit of army commandos, David again volunteered and joined Layforce, as the unit was known, as a newly commissioned subaltern.

DAVID STIRLING

As a young man, I didn't read military history at all. My own life was devoted towards other objectives. I'd been turned down as an artist, which I wanted to be, but couldn't make it. I went to Paris to study art, but my teacher there reckoned that whereas I had all the originality in creative terms, I could never master the basic central discipline of draughtsmanship. This created a hell of a reaction in me because I was devoted towards that proposition, and so I had to go to the other extreme, and make Mount Everest my physical goal. I was in pursuit of that when the war broke out. I went into the reserve of Scots Guards, purely out of a sense of patriotism, because it did look as though something might happen.

BOB BENNETT

I was born a Cockney in the East End of London. We weren't very well off. At the outbreak of war I volunteered for the Grenadier Guards. Actually I volunteered for the air force, but they didn't seem to want to know. Sitting in the recruitment office, one of my old school friends came in, and took the King's shilling, and I chased after him and said: 'What are you joining?' He said: 'The Grenadier Guards.' I said: 'Is it good?' And he said: 'It's great.' So I enlisted in the Grenadier Guards. Two weeks later I could have killed him. I was being chased

Bob Bennett in the 1950s.

5

from reveille to lights out at Chelsea Barracks, up in London, and didn't know what had hit me.

I had very hard training in the Grenadiers. I don't regret any of it. But I felt that after weeks and weeks I was getting nowhere. I'd signed up for the war and I wanted to be involved. We were doing trench warfare. I wasn't a very educated chap, but I thought surely to goodness we're not going to start digging ditches and carry on where the '14-'18 war left off? So every time they asked for volunteers, for gunners in planes, gunners on trawlers, myself and Lofty Baker kept volunteering. In the end the major said if we volunteered again, we'd be put in jail.

Then in about June 1940, Lofty and I were lying on our beds at the barracks, and we'd heard talk about forming a Guards Commando, that we couldn't volunteer for, of course. It was a Wednesday afternoon – that was the relaxation afternoon – and in came a sergeant major that we called Shit Head Joey and he said: 'Bennett and Baker, get down to the orderly room.'

There was a great big queue of guardsmen and NCOs volunteering for the commandos. We were taken straight up the front, in front of the major, and he said: 'You're off to the commandos.' Everyone else was being asked if they could swim, drive, etc., but we were asked nothing, just told to report.

Then my soldiering started. We went to Burnham-on-Crouch, where we began intensive training. I was happy. It was hard training, very, very hard. And when we were fully trained, we went off to the Middle East.

JOHNNY COOPER

I was seventeen, in Yorkshire, and apprenticed to the wool trade. At the outbreak of war I tried to join the army but was rejected because of my age. Then I was tipped off by a friend who was living in the same accommodation that if I went to the Bradford recruiting office and took two half-crowns with me, and gave them to the recruiting sergeant, he would take me in as I was tall enough to get into the Guards. I decided the Scots Guards because my grandfather and my mother were Scots.

Johnny Cooper

I went down, said I was twenty, paid the two half-crowns, and joined the Scots Guards. The next thing I knew I was at Caterham. From there I went to Chelsea Barracks, and went through the course there, then went to the training battalion at Pirbright. Then there was a notice up about commandos going to the Middle East, and I put my name down and was interviewed by a major who was going to command the Scots Guards troop. He said: 'I think you're much younger than you say you are.' But I got away with that OK, and ended up in Scotland, and there was David Stirling, then a lieutenant. He'd just joined from the ski battalion, which was going to Finland. We did our training then went to the Middle East.

'GENTLEMAN' JIM ALMONDS

I was always known as Gentleman Jim. I don't think I was ever a vaga-bond really; I was just a chap having a good time and doing my job.

I joined the Coldstream Guards on August 6, 1932, when I was eighteen. In 1936 I joined the Bristol police and served with them until the outbreak of war. I received my call-up papers on December 1 and reported to Pirbright camp in Surrey, where I was a corporal. Life at Pirbright was rather dull, not a bit like I envisaged war would be, so, along with a few friends like Pat Riley I'd known before, in the

Jim Almonds

Guards, I decided to agitate. We tried for all sorts of jobs: gunners on trawlers, rear gunners on bombers – that seemed an exciting prospect. They called for ski trooper lumberjacks for Finland and that seemed interesting too. Eventually the real plum came along when they decided to form a Guard Commando, which we all applied for and were selected. That was the only possible outfit.

We went to Burnham-on-Crouch to commence our training, then we moved to Loch Fyne and went through all the rigmarole of assault landing training and walking through the Scottish countryside. I went out on my own and did a bit of private training, shot a stag or two. I'd been brought up in England, where everyone is so controlled by rules and regulations. The cookhouse was rather short of fresh meat anyway, so I not only trained myself, I provided something for the cookhouse.

Then this idea of personal training got me into trouble. I shot a stag and was caught, through being idle. I could have got away by going up a water course, but instead I took the lazy way and went down hill and was cut off. I was arrested and put up for court martial. Eventually the court martial was quashed, I think probably chiefly because we were due to sail, and we went in convoy round the Cape to the Middle East as part of Layforce.

REG SEEKINGS

At the beginning of war I was in the Territorials, in the Cambridgeshire regiment. I kept volunteering for different special service duties, like machine gunner on trawlers, etc, but being the divisional boxing champion, no one wanted to release me. When they called for parachutists they said to me: 'I suppose you want to be one.' I said: 'Yes, certainly.' So they said: 'Right, put your name down.'

I was acting company runner then, and a few days later the adjutant called me in and said: 'Your company hasn't put in the returns for special duties.' So I went to the company office – in a barn, on the east

Reg Seekings

coast, nobody about – and I looked in the lists, and there was nobody under Parachutists and nobody under Sea Raiders, so I put my name down under Parachutists and delivered the list to the adjutant. Two or three weeks later I was called up to go for medicals, much to the disgust of my company commander, who threatened to put me inside for meddling with official documents.

I went for the medical, which I passed with flying colours, but they were only taking paratroopers at eleven stone with skeletal equipment on. In those days I weighed about fourteen stone. The medical officer said: 'You'll hardly get through a three-foot hole.' So I said: 'Well, put me down for Sea Raiders then.'

We formed up 7th Commando, then went to Scotland and did our training, then went out to the Middle East with Layforce.

DAVE KERSHAW

When war broke out I was on reserve with the Cheshires. I'd gone to sea in 1926, done some things, fought for the Republicans in the Spanish Civil War, served with the Cheshires. The war broke out and my brother was going to join the Grenadier Guards rather than wait for any land regiment, because apart from corps units, the Brigade of Guards were the only ones who would accept volunteers at the outset of war. So he wanted to join the Grenadiers, and I thought: 'I'll come along with you.'

Dave Kershaw

At a later date I was summoned to the CO, to explain why I didn't report to the Cheshires, because I'd been posted as a deserter by them, even though I was in the army. I explained the situation and it was accepted. I got reprimanded, but it all blew over and nothing was done about it.

We were stationed at Wallington Barracks, I was a sergeant, and it was stagnation: public duties, public duties, and all the time there was a war going on, so naturally the lads were getting a bit browned off. Don't forget, Dunkirk's happened and there's a build-up to a future theatre of war, and these were all trained men, ready to do battle immediately.

Then they asked for volunteers for a Guards Commando, and practically all the garrison volunteered. Eventually seven of us were chosen and were sent to Burnham-on-Crouch. This was great, because we got commando money, as they called it, on top of our meagre army pay. Then we went to Scotland, and did some stunts – by stunts I mean training: climbing mountains, going for long walks with 50-60 lbs on your back. Then we got orders to move and joined the ship *Glengyle*, and went to the Middle East, to one of the islands, as a commando-based unit.

PAT RILEY

I was born in America, in Wisconsin, then our family came over to England. Eventually I joined the British army, but found a few difficulties joining up, so the writing on the form had to be a bit unclear and I signed up as an honest

Englishman and joined the Coldstream Guards. After four years service I left and went to Palestine; when I finished there I came back and joined the police force till the start of the war, when I went on reserve then back to the Guards where I met up with Jim Almonds and a few others.

We got very restless; we volunteered for gunners for the boats, for air gunners, and everything you could think of, because we weren't getting anywhere at all. Eventually I met Lord Jellicoe, who was looking for volunteers to form a special force called commandos. I got around me a bunch of boys, and we all went for interview and joined 8 Commando. From there we

Pat Riley

went to Scotland, went through a commando course, under Lovat's command, then finally went out to the Middle East.

CHAPTER TWO

Layforce, commanded by Colonel Robert Laycock, comprised three commando units, including 8 Commando, raised mainly from the Brigade of Guards. Its initial Middle East mission in 1940 was to invade and seize the island of Rhodes. By the time it arrived in the Middle East in 1941, however, the situation had changed dramatically. In North Africa the German Afrika Korps under General Irwin Rommel had driven the British back to the Egyptian border, leaving the coastal town of Tobruk totally surrounded and desperately holding out.

German forces had swept through Greece and Yugoslavia and, in the first-ever major airborne operation, had seized the island of Crete. Layforce covered the evacuation of British and Allied troops from the island, and was involved in a number of piecemeal actions: the holding of a section of the Tobruk perimeter, operations against the Vichy French in Syria, and raids along the coast of Cyrenaica.

DAVID STIRLING

By the time Layforce came into existence in the Middle East, because of the arrival of the Germans there, the powers-that-be didn't want to risk having casualties, and therefore unless the weather, or all the other requirements for any operation or undertaking, were absolutely alright, so that the hazards of that operation were reduced to a minimum, they wouldn't let us go. So we were involved in a series of postponements and of cancellations, and that was extremely frustrating.

I'd gone out with the usual enthusiasm for having a go at the enemy, but I wasn't going to have a go at them if we were going to have a dreary life in the desert. Life in 8 Commando was a frustration. We had a superb commanding officer, Bob Laycock, but he couldn't control events.

I thought that, to compensate a bit, I would have a temporary, but not altogether bogus, illness which got me into the very comfortable American hospital, where I was well pampered. And in a sense I was pretty ill, because I would go out in the evening, having recovered from the appalling hangover caused by the previous night's activities in Cairo, and re-establish my illness by my activities the following night. They rumbled this in the end.

I went back because I heard some real activity was looking more likely. I was received with considerable guffaws, and started training. But on one of the first training exercises, coming back from a night exercise, I tripped over one of the guy ropes to the tent I was sleeping in. I had to be taken by ambulance to Alexandria to be operated on right away. I had to have three or four stitches in my eyeball, because the fluid was escaping from the eyeball. They operated on it very expertly and no damage was done; the eye was absolutely OK. And when that was finished I went back.

But the combination of the American hospital interlude, and what they said was a deliberate effort to injure myself so I wouldn't have to go on active operations, led to some believing I should be prosecuted as a coward. I've forgotten what the actual suggested offence was, but it was along those lines. They had a committee checking it all up.

REG SEEKINGS

Our first raid in North Africa was at Bardia. Battleships took us in. Then I got wounded in the thigh and was in hospital when the Cretan business cropped up. I got out just as that finished, landed up at Geneifa depot in Egypt, along with my brother, who was in Crete but escaped – he rowed a boat across the Med. He was in hospital there a few days.

BOB BENNETT

The idea of the commando was to do landings from whatever vehicles or vessels were going. We got to the Middle East and tried several attempts at doing operations there. Lots of things were laid on, but we never did achieve anything. We tried to do landings by boats, all sorts of things, and then the thing was called off. On one operation we set off for Tobruk on a destroyer, HMS *Decoy*, and we never got anywhere. Everything we went on seemed to be cancelled at the last minute.

DAVID STIRLING

In fact, we did have one or two abortive but very exciting operations with 8 Commando, then it was decided, because of what happened in Greece and Crete, and with the fact that the Germans had appeared in the western desert, that the official forces were desperately short of recruits because of casualties, and the commandos became really without a role. The primary requirement was beefing up the 8th Army itself. So most of the commando force, Layforce, which numbered two or three thousand men, were regarded as a recruiting base and some, who had no affiliated regiment, were sent back to England.

DAVE KERSHAW

Laycock was called back to UK to take charge of some venture or other and Major Daley took over. He told us that those soldiers without representative regiments in the Middle East would have to go to the infantry depot base, and all the others would rejoin their particular units. Because there were no

Grenadiers out in the Middle East, we all went to the base depot at Geneifa. It was a period of misery and stagnation.

DAVID STIRLING

Just before Layforce was disbanded, Jock Lewes had spotted that there were some parachutes which had been landed at Port Said, which were meant to have gone to India, where they were establishing a parachute outfit. It was a complete muck-up by the shipping people. We heard about this. Jock invited two or three friends, myself included, to go along to Laycock to ask whether, as they were stranded, we couldn't use them for a parachute jump – partly for fun, partly because it would be useful to know how to do it – and Laycock said: 'Yes, absolutely.'

So we got these chutes, a dozen of them, and we managed to get from 216 Squadron one of those Valentia aircraft which were very unusual, rather unsafe, unstable aircraft, but they suited their purpose okay for this. The chutes were stat chutes, attached to a line, so we had to tie the stat line to the legs of the seating accommodation, and then jump out of the door.

REPORT OF PARACHUTE JUMP WRITTEN BY GUARDSMAN D'ARCY, IRISH GUARDS
(on file at the National Archives)

Lewes and his party first went to an RAF headquarters located somewhere near Fuka. There they discussed the details with an RAF officer who, although none of the party had jumped before, was most helpful. He showed us the parachutes we were to use. From the logbooks we saw that the last periodical examination had been omitted, but Lieutenant Lewes decided they were okay.

Next day, along with Lieutenant Stirling and Sergeant Storrie, who were hoping to do a job in Syria, we made a trial flight. The plane used was a Vickers Valentia. We threw out a dummy made from sandbags and tent poles. The parachute opened okay, but the tent poles smashed on landing. Afterwards we tried a ten-foot jump from the top of the plane and then a little parachute control.

The following afternoon we flew inland in the Valentia, which was used to deliver mail. We reached the landing field toward dusk, landed, fitted on our parachutes, and decided to jump in the failing light. We were to jump in pairs. Lieutenant Lewes and his servant Guardsman Davies first, the RAF officer to despatch. The instructions were to dive out as though we were going into water.

We hooked ourselves up, circled the field, and on a signal from the RAF officer, Lieutenant Lewes and Davies dived out. Next time round I dived out and was surprised to see Lieutenant Stirling pass me in the air. Lieutenant Lewes made a perfect landing. Next came Davies, a little shaken. Lieutenant Stirling injured his spine and also lost his sight for about an hour.

DAVID STIRLING

I was a bit unlucky. We had tied our static cords and parachutes to the legs of the seats, and when I'd jumped I must have gone horizontal in the slipstream, because when it opened my chute was attached to the tail plane, and tore an enormous number of panels away. I was second to last to leave, I was going much faster than the others because of the lack of air worthiness of the chute. Luckily it formed as a parachute, but obviously let a lot more air through, so I descended a great deal faster than my companions. I hit the ground very, very hard and really put a crater in the desert. I was paralysed, and they had to take me to hospital.

I think I was in bed about seven or eight weeks. I remember Evelyn Waugh coming in, a great chum of mine in those days, and the matron told him that they had removed one leg and they were going to remove the other the following day. And he came to see me and sat on the edge of the bed, with his usual cynical observations, and he kept looking out of the corner of his eye, because I was proud of having got movement back and was twiddling my toes, and he thought it was a bloody ghost. Then he couldn't stand it any longer; he said: 'What the hell's happening here? Matron told me you would have both legs removed. What's that twiddling at the end of the bed?' It was quite comic.

But the period in hospital gave me a marvellous opportunity – while my legs regained their power – to do some homework and write a paper on the proposals that I had in mind.

The idea came from the abortive period I spent with the commandos. The role was important but the way they tackled the role was ludicrous. It involved navy ships, army transport – they would use a whole regiment to attack one landing craft. We were involved in a series of postponements and cancellations, and that was exceedingly frustrating. And it got me around to thinking on how one could carry out the role at a hundredth of the cost. And having realised what was required, it made it all the easier to come up with a proposition along the lines of the SAS.

The proposition had hard principles.

It had to be regarded as a new type of force, to extract the very maximum out of surprise and guile. It had to be capable of approaching its target by land, sea or air.

It would exploit surprise to the greatest degree, with training in guile and night-time techniques.

The basic unit would be a four or five man sub-unit. The commando technique was such that one entire commando, six hundred or so men, couldn't succeed in tackling more than perhaps two landing grounds on the same night, and more than three-quarters of the force would be taken up with defending those who were actually operating. We preferred for every sub-unit of four or five men to tackle a full target on their own, and if they failed it would be more than compensated for by the fact that with sixty men we could attack, theoretically, up to fifteen or twenty targets on the same night.

(Later we experimented as to the best number. Originally I reckoned that five would be the right size, but that meant an odd number, which tended to make the fifth man the corporal or sergeant or the chap in command, and the others just followed behind him. We decided that the four-man module was the right number. It was psychologically easier to make them all interdependent. So we had four pairs of ears which were listening, and four pairs of eyes which were watching, which emphasises the difference between the SAS and the commandos. The commando would have a smallest unit of twelve or fourteen men – I've forgotten just how many – with a corporal or sergeant at the head of that troop. So that all the thinking and all the initiative had to be taken by the leader, and the others just followed along as what is disrespectfully referred to as the thundering herd.)

It had to be independent. As we were going to develop methods and techniques which were new in army terms, it was no good putting us under any orthodox type of Middle East headquarter department, and therefore we had to have a special status of our own. We would obviously have to have access to intelligence, because without that we wouldn't be able to determine the correct targets. And we had to have a special training centre which was well away from other units.

My whole concept was that we should be capable of reaching a target by air, sea or land, and we could arrive in an area of operation without making any demands on expensive equipment, like ships if it was a sea operation. We could use ancient aircraft, the Bombays, and be dropped by parachute and we could in due course create our own means of travelling behind the lines.

I built parachuting into the paper not because it was an efficient means of arrival at the scene of the operation, but more because it provided a good opportunity of putting the idea to Middle East Headquarters and the top management. And they could grasp the newness of the idea; it was identified by a new method of arrival. Psychologically the parachute was the ideal propaganda means of putting over the proposition of the role of the unit.

But we could, in the meantime, make use of the Long Range Desert Group to pick us up after a raid. I knew a lot about the LRDG by then, their history and how they were doing long range reconnaissance in the desert collecting information on the enemy. When I was laid up writing my paper, I was visited by Michael Crichton Stewart, who was in LRDG before that. When I first came out to Cairo I was hankering for the LRDG concept, and when I was horizontal he came to me and said that it was no good suggesting that those who were going to pick us up after the first parachute operation should take us there. But Easonsmith, with whom I made the pick-up arrangements for the first operation and planned where the rendezvous would be, said how ludicrous it was that we should be very uncomfortably parachuting in by air. But it was the only way of selling the SAS concept.

The name SAS came mainly from the fact that I was anxious to get full cooperation of a very ingenious individual called Dudley Clark, who was responsible for running a deception outfit in Cairo. I talked to everyone who knew anything about the game, but I didn't tell anyone who might have spoilt my surprise. Clark knew, because I told him. Clark was very much a pro, he had a very resourceful mind; his unit was based on misinformation to the enemy, the whole area of deception.

Clark was a very great influence on me; he'd developed the proposition that there was a full brigade of parachutists trained in the Middle East, and he did this by dropping parachutes which were tiny, they weren't proper parachutes, they were about three feet across, with something bogus at the end, around the mainly Italian prisoner-of-war camps, in the hope that they'd write back directly that we were training parachutists. It looked as if these parachutes were dropping about five miles away, but in fact they were much closer. And sure enough it was reported back that we had a major parachute-trained unit, ready to function.

Clark was quite an influential chap. He promised to give me all the help he could if I would use the name of his bogus brigade of parachutists, which is the Special Air Service, the SAS. So I settled for L Detachment SAS, and Dudley Clark was delighted to have some flesh and blood parachutists instead of totally bogus ones.

In order to capture the imagination of the top command, I also had to relate it to an operation. I wanted something to make 'em sit up and pay attention, because they wouldn't appreciate a second lieutenant having the gall to present a plan to the commander-in-chief as to how he could handle the coming campaign, regarding the most important, or one of the most important, elements in that campaign: how to deal with the German air force, which was a relatively new factor on the scene and one which was extremely troublesome.

The Germans had control of the air at the time. Our proposition, therefore, was that we could knock out the entire German fighter force in one night. I suggested that three days before the next major drive by 8th Army, sixty-five men would drop in at night, and observe for a couple of days, then the night before the start of the offensive we would go in and blow up the aircraft.

I eventually recovered the use of my legs, but was still on crutches when I went to Middle East Headquarters with my plan. I didn't tell anyone who might have spoilt my surprise, because I had to get to the generals like Ritchie and Auchinleck.

There was no way you could put it in, except to the C-in-C. Never at Middle East HQ. They were layer upon layer of fossilised shit. In the short gap between the First and Second World Wars, the great active soldiers who survived were in active command. But there was an enormous residue of staff officers from the First World War who didn't fight, who set the spirit of the administration. And it was ludicrously swollen, unnecessarily big, and wholly obstructive to anything that looked like a new idea.

There was no way I could chance giving it through the normal channels, because it would have been throttled long before it got up to anybody capable of making a decision. If it was intercepted at a lower level it would be sent upstairs with a very negative opinion attached to it. Whereas if I got it direct, I knew I could argue with a general.

So I decided to go and see the Deputy Chief of General Staff, General Ritchie. I was going to indicate I wanted to see his military assistant, because he'd been in the Scots Guards, so it gave me an alibi to go there.

Unfortunately I didn't have a pass, and I was refused admittance. I was still on crutches at the time, so I had to use my crutches as a kind of ladder to get over the wire when the guards weren't looking. Unfortunately they looked just after I got to the ground on the other side. And I wasn't able to run very fast because now I was lacking the crutches. So I had to dive into the first door – it looked like entering a burrow, and I thought that I might be able to escape the pursuit.

And, by sheer good luck, it happened to be that part of Middle East Headquarters in which the chap I was looking for had his office. But when I began talking to him, it became clear that he was the same chap whom I'd previously known in the Scots Guards at Pirbright and who'd tried very hard to get me sacked as I'd fallen asleep in one of his lectures. So when I appeared and put a paper in front of him, he was absolutely outraged.

Then he heard the noise of the pursuit, and as they came down the corridor I knew I was going to get no sympathy there, so I hopped out and into the next room, which was General Ritchie, which was another rare bit of good fortune, and asked him to read this paper.

It took him rather by surprise – it was only in pencil – but he was very courteous and he settled down to read it. About halfway through he really got quite engrossed in it, and had forgotten the rather irregular way it had been presented. There was a lot of screaming in the passage; Ritchie pushed a button, without looking up from this rather grubby pencil-written memo, for his ADC to come in. And this ADC was astounded to find me sitting snugly in the general's office. 'What's all the fuss in the passage?' says Ritchie. 'Well, there's an individual who's got in here illegally and we're chasing him – we don't know where he's got to.' 'Oh well, sit down, I've got an important paper here.' And Ritchie went on reading, didn't even look up.

And when he'd finished, Ritchie said he would submit it right away to Auchinleck, but in the meantime he would give an affirmative answer – he would like to take it up; it wasn't going to cost anything in troops or equipment. A lot of the commandos had been disbanded and were being drafted home, and I should get going in preparing a camp and recruiting the establishment of sixty-five men for which I'd asked, and that these things should start tomorrow.

'This is something we can use,' he said, addressing/commanding/instructing this chap to give me all the help possible to get going. 'This paper has real promise. It's going to make a very small demand on recruits and equipment and so on. Take Stirling next door and work out with him what the establishment in equipment and ordnance and so on would be.' And that the ADC was obliged to do – grinding his teeth as he did so. So I had to go back to his office, to one of the military police who'd been at the gates. 'That's him!' Too late, because by then the scene had changed and I'd been given official authority to get this unit off the ground.

And that was the beginning.

CHAPTER THREE

Two officers whom Stirling wished to recruit for his infant SAS also served with Layforce. One was Jock Lewes, a former president of the Oxford University Boat Club, who had originated the fateful parachute jump, and the other was Blair Mayne, better known as Paddy, an Irish lawyer but also a formidable Ireland and British Lions rugby international.

Even though he had been authorised to raise a force of sixty-five men, however, Stirling still faced problems from the hierarchy within Middle East Headquarters.

DAVID STIRLING

Two officers I wanted, and one was particularly difficult: Jock Lewes, who was absolutely indispensable to me. I didn't know how indispensable. As it turned out he was even more valuable than I'd originally appreciated. He was a chap of quite enormous professionalism, even though like me he was a non-regular soldier.

While I was in hospital, Jock Lewes went back to Tobruk. He'd become a professional raider, he'd raided every front there was a hope for, with a handful of Laycock's commando. Because of the extreme usefulness of this performance, they were kept there and not disbanded.

It was during the time when Tobruk was in a state of siege, he developed a technique of penetrating the perimeter of the German and Italian lines – mainly German in his part – that would take the enemy from behind. He developed very deep skills in that field. He had a few members of the old 8 Commando in which we'd both served, but most of them had been disbanded.

PAT RILEY

Jock Lewes was the chap in command of us.

What happened with Layforce, we fell into a sort of backwater; there was odd jobs came along – the job's on, the job's off, that sort of business. And then we finally disbanded, and we got an option of either joining Chinese guerrillas and training them, go back to your own regiment, or go with this special force.

I decided to carry on in the special forces rather than go to my own regiment. I struck a little difficulty there, because Lord Jellicoe, who was one of my officers, a very loyal Coldstream Guard, wanted us to go back to the regiment. And Jellicoe did try hard, because I'd got old Coldstreamers which were with me. But they decided they'd go wherever I went, and consequently, we went off

to these special forces. We went off into
Tobruk with Jock and were doing fighting
and reconnaissance patrols, for whoever it
may be. It was quite some experience
there.

Jock Lewes

JIM ALMONDS

I didn't know Jock terribly well until this
idea of going to Tobruk came up and I
found myself on it. It was the greater part
of 3 Troop – round about twenty to
twenty-five of us. The aim of the first raid
was to spike the guns which were shelling
our sector. It meant going out at night and
across country till we found this place.
We went out through our own lines. We
were in sangars, a deep wadi in front of us and no-man's-land on the other side
of the wadi. We went in there and the guns were duly blown. Once the attack
had gone in there was a lot of fire from surrounding troops – you could see
tracers of incendiaries, coming across like strings of sausages. They seemed to
travel so slowly, at night, as we watched them. During the action, one chap was
wounded – hit in the shoulder and arms, elbow joint had gone – and Jock said
would I make sure he got back. So I spent the rest of the time getting the lad
back across into our area.

Then we moved across to the southern sector where we did an op with the
Australians, to take out a position known as S13. S13 was a salient, sticking forward
in front of their normal positions. The idea was to straighten the line out. There
was no attempt at a break-out – there was nowhere to break out to at that time.

During the fight we got an awful pasting from the Germans. All the area was
marked down, and once we got to S13, the fire came in and we pulled out. After
the affair, the Germans granted us a ceasefire of about six hours, and they came
out and helped to pick up the dead. I suppose it was an act of humanity. Once
the thing was over, of course, we got the full force of their anger at the raid.

BOB BENNETT

Some of 8 Commando went to Tobruk when it was besieged and did quite a few
operations there. They did quite a good job in Tobruk, doing patrols at night

through the wire. 11 Commando went off to Syria; they were pretty badly done up there. But in the Guards Commando in the Middle East, very little was done. Then 8 Commando was disbanded. We went back to the Guards base depot at Geneifa and were chased around. In the Middle East at that time there were the Coldstreams and the Scots Guards, and they didn't like the Grenadiers. There's this terrible feeling in the Brigade of Guards. And we had this great big drill sergeant, who said: 'I'll give you commandos.' So we were chased all over the place.

Then one fine day not long after, Colonel David came down. We knew Stirling as a lieutenant in the Scots Guards at the time. I think that talk with Stirling was held in a big marquee. He'd come back to his own people, 8 Commando. From there he went to 11 Commando, what was left of them.

We were all called together, and he put the proposition to us, that he was forming a unit that would operate behind the lines. He realised we all felt disgusted at what had been achieved in the commandos, and he had this brainwave of small parties behind the lines. He said: 'I'm forming a unit that is going to drop in behind enemy lines and go after installations, go after aircraft, because we've got nothing out there, no air force to shoot them down, so we'll get them, blow them up on the ground. There'll be various forms of entry.' Parachuting came into it, although no one in the Middle East knew anything about parachuting at that time.

Well, this was great news. We were away from Geneifa, away from this drilling and boring stuff. People were so keen to get into the unit; they all wanted to get away from the Guards base depot.

You didn't do selection. These were all highly trained men from Guards Commando; there was never a more fit assignment of troops in Egypt; they'd had months and months of training. But when training started, David Stirling told you, if you didn't come up to scratch you were out. Simple as that.

DAVE KERSHAW

The Grenadiers didn't have a battalion out there, so we were sent to the infantry base depot at Geneifa. After a time there, of sports and various duties, there was a buzz that David Stirling was looking for volunteers to join this special service, as he called it in those days. He got overwhelmed with recruits, but then he had to interview them because he wanted the best, that sort of thing. I remember he said to me: 'What will your wife say if she finds out that you've joined this parachute unit?' I said: 'She won't know, sir. She won't know anything about it.'

REG SEEKINGS

When I got out of hospital I landed up at Geneifa depot. While I was there Stirling came round recruiting. I'd always had an ambition to be a parachutist, and this seemed my opportunity. The man in front of me went in, and Stirling asked him why he wanted to be a parachutist, and he said: 'I'll try anything once.' Stirling answered: 'Yes, and if you don't bloody well like it, you'll just drop it; I don't want people like you.' So that gave an inkling what to avoid. I just went in and said I fancied being a parachutist. I was one of thirteen selected from there.

JOHNNY COOPER

We took part in raids in Crete, and Tobruk, where Jim Almonds and Pat Riley were. And eventually, in very early '41, the commandos were disbanded and we returned to our regiments. I went back to the 2nd Battalion Scots Guards in the desert. We were up on the border, facing the Italians and the German army. One day we were in the slit trenches and suddenly the adjutant sent a message saying there's a Lieutenant Stirling wants to see you, and I went up there, to the adjutant's trench where David was sitting. I didn't even realise that he knew my name. He instilled at that stage – later on even more so – great confidence. He said: 'Do you want to do something special?' I was there with about fourteen others who he'd asked to come forward to see him. Would we volunteer for a special unit, in which you may have to parachute? He interviewed everyone. I said, 'Yes.' And that was it.

PAT RILEY

One day in Tobruk, I went down to collect some rations, and heard what you might term idle conversation about do-or-die boys being formed in Egypt, and I came back and had a quiet word with Jock, and said: 'I gather it's a do-or-die outfit that you people are forming.' All he said to me was: 'What? Getting worried?' And I said: 'No, we'll stop here as long as you want to stop.'

DAVID STIRLING

I went up to Tobruk to try and talk Jock into joining my outfit. We went very, very fast in a gunboat; they used to go up and back about three times a week, just for the central supplies. I went up and back in that, in one night. Jock was so keen on what he was doing, getting so much satisfaction out of it, so he said: 'No way.' That was very disappointing.

However, I think he overdid it, because he was hospitalised back to Cairo, an absolute wreck, because of his astounding activities. I went to see him there and got him cornered and succeeded in kidding him. He'd been operating without a halt, and never been able back to get himself back into health; they'd probably had rotten rations while they were up there. I think he'd been slightly wounded, and had some horror desert sores. He was completely and absolutely run down, but he soon picked up and agreed to join me; he didn't arrive in the first few days, but afterwards. He gradually built himself back up to being exceedingly fit again.

PAT RILEY

We came out of Tobruk on the *Glasgow* and we got down to Geneifa, and I approached Jock there, very early morning and said: 'Do you remember me talking to you about these do-or-die boys?' And he said, 'Yes.' I hadn't got all the boys this time – some of them had left, but I had sufficient, three of them. Jim Almonds was one of them, and Bob Lillie. They're the only ones that come with me. Jock said: 'I can't think of any better blokes. Get as much money as you can, and go and have some leave in Cairo or Alexandria, whichever it may be, and report in at Kabrit.' I said to him: 'How do you know all this?' And he said: 'I'm helping to form it.'

So we went off and had our holiday, and finally ended up in Kabrit. And the first man I saw was Reg Seekings. He was a chap I'd fought in the ring before the war. Twice actually. And I asked him what the hell he was doing there, and he said: 'I've joined this outfit too.'

DAVID STIRLING

The second man I really wanted was Paddy Mayne, Paddy Blair Mayne. They said I couldn't have him because he was in prison.

I knew Paddy quite well from Layforce; he had already undertaken a very well-conducted operation in Syria, but after it was over he had a slightly disturbing record because he'd found reason to knock out his commanding officer. He'd already gathered a tremendous record for fighting ability, but he felt he was being buggered about by this particular officer, and was under close arrest and doing time in the

Paddy Mayne

jail at Geneifa. I think he was awaiting court martial. Anyway, he was inside the wire. I discovered where he was through a great friend of his, and went to interview him.

He had every reason not to take me very seriously as a soldier, because he knew how idle I'd been in the prior days, in Layforce. However, I persuaded him that the proposition was a good one, and he then joined up. But I told him, very firmly, that *this* commanding officer wasn't for hitting. I knew that aspect of him, which there was no way I could put up with. So I had to do a pretty sharp bargain with him, and he was pretty surly, because he was a bit older than me.

When he listened to me, I could see his eyeballs beginning to react, which he tried very hard to hide, because he wasn't going to say yes until he was bloody sure, and I wasn't going to take him until I was equally certain that all his fisticuffs and energies would be devoted entirely to the enemy and not against me or anyone else in the outfit. I suppose that was quite a funny scene while we struck our bargain. And he always subsequently honoured that commitment. He always kept it, not always in terms of people other than myself, though. He had one or two colossal rows, one in particular with me, but he was one of the best fighting machines I'd ever met in my life. And he also had the quality to command men and make them feel his very own.

JIM ALMONDS

I got into SAS because, being with Jock Lewes in Tobruk and doing the perimeter raids there, he was obviously in touch with David Stirling, although I didn't know it at the time. And when we came to pull out of Tobruk, and went back to Geneifa, this story was circulating about the formation of a new unit at Kabrit Point. Four of us were taken from the commando troop we were with in Tobruk and put in the regiment.

DAVID STIRLING

There were certain absolute gems with MEHQ at every level, who were first rate and gave me all the help they could. But all through the first six months there were others who didn't give up obstructing, even after that original response by Ritchie to get on with it. From the start they tried to resist me. If you take the personal assistant of Ritchie, who was Scots Guards. He was hell bent on revenge, because he was rather humiliated in the initial establishment of L Detachment. He was hoping to put me under arrest at the very time Ritchie was reading the paper. I think it carried on from him. It influenced a lot of people.

They told me the best they could do was to provide me with a couple of tents and then I simply had to delay recruiting, because with the best will in the world it would take a long time to get together from spare supplies enough for us to have a basic base from which we could start our training. This we couldn't afford: we had to get down to training immediately. So I went ahead anyway. I thought we'd do what was going to be very much our way of life – but against the enemy, not normally against our own side – which was to use our ingenuity.

JIM ALMONDS
We all trundled off down to Kabrit and when we arrived, there was only a little board stuck in the ground, saying: L Detachment SAS. There was nothing else.

BOB BENNETT
All we could see was a load of sand and the Suez Canal. Not a building, not a tent, nothing. Someone said: 'Where's the camp?' And Stirling said: 'That's your first operation – you steal it.' Well, the type of chaps you had there loved that. So that *was* the first SAS operation, to go down in the dark of night to a camp near Kabrit that the New Zealanders were using – they were up in the desert at the time, in action. The camp was therefore empty. So we drove down there and we stole tents, bars, three marquees. We stole the lot. There were guards there; someone turned to the MPs and said: 'What a racket this is – our CO has us working all night.' Joked it off.

JIM ALMONDS
We pinched a piano. We raided the Royal Engineers depot for materials – cement for floors, etc. It was similar to our commando training: if you have the option of beg, borrow, buy or steal, invariably the most interesting one was stealing.

DAVID STIRLING
By next morning we had a really spectacularly effective camp, probably the best camp in the area. I've forgotten what we did with the piano.

CHAPTER FOUR

Having received authorisation to raise his new force, having somehow recruited them, and having – that word somehow again – acquired a camp, David Stirling now faced the challenge of training them, and himself, to a standard high and exacting enough for the SAS's first official operation. And in a remarkably short time. The foundations laid in those first days are still the foundations on which the Special Air Service is based today. The first principles, as Stirling describes them, are still the first principles of the SAS. And all the time, Stirling was locked in his battle with the enemy within – at Middle East Headquarters.

DAVID STIRLING

The SAS had to be developed as a concept on the basis of actual operations and performances. One of the things I could be sure of was my own defeat of craven fear, which I had to a maximum degree. I'm not arrogant. But I think one of the reasons that the SAS concept has survived longer perhaps than might be expected is because of the fact that it was forged in hell, forged behind the lines and with the running battle with Middle East HQ. That forced me all the time to be a step ahead.

REG SEEKINGS

Stirling was a very impressive man because of his height, his good looks, and his manner. He was very intense and appeared to be very, very genuine, and wanted to do something. He was very precise, he knew what he was up to. This is the big thing, this is what we were looking for all the time. We were all experienced soldiers and all of us had had a bit of action, and we were looking for something better to do. You were looking for men that you thought were better than the present ones you were serving under. And he certainly gave us that impression and as it turned out, he definitely was that type.

What he was putting forward was quite revolutionary, but I think you've got it today even. You'll get the diehards; they get a nice comfortable job polishing a seat, they don't want to upset the apple cart and rock the boat, and when anything new comes about they're anti. Which might be a good thing, because then it really makes you determined, if you're that type of man, the type of man that Stirling was – and the rest of us. 'To hell with it, I'm going to succeed, I'm going to make it go, it *will* go.' And more or less: 'You're sitting there on your backside – you haven't got all the brains, you haven't got all the ideas. We've got ideas too, and we're the people who've got to do the job, so let us do it in our way.'

People like David Stirling and Paddy Mayne, they gave us that opportunity to share in it properly. Not just the business of an officer directing operations and pulling his poor little ignorant privates along. You were treated as one of a team, and this made a big difference. That's what everybody was after.

PAT RILEY

David was trying very hard in Cairo to get this thing established. He was a hard fighter; he had a hard fight to get the unit launched. He himself is a very quiet chap, very shy. He's very detailed. He looks into things very deeply not just from the administrative side, but the operational side as well.

JOHNNY COOPER

The way that he put our unit on the map in the first place was extraordinary. I think a few in the hierarchy understood David's basic concept, but the majority were against it. Those that had faith in him were perhaps in the right places, but I would say that in headquarters, ninety per cent thought it was a waste of time. This is afterwards; we didn't know at that time.

DAVID STIRLING

I always hoisted on board guys who argued. I didn't want psychopaths. I had to look at chaps who were chaps in their own right. They had to be people who really had to be commanded, rather than those who just said 'Yes, sir,' without thinking. Each one of them had to be an individual, and there was a tremendous range of personalities.

In a sense they weren't really controllable. They were harnessable. The object was to give them the same purpose, and once they were harnessed to that proposition, then they policed themselves, so to speak. And that goal had to be an exacting one, because from the start we knew we would never make it as a regiment unless not only we operated effectively, but we succeeded in establishing a new role. And that band of vagabonds had to grasp what they had to do in order to get there. The regiment is the man and the man is the regiment.

The officers meant a great deal but the sergeants' mess were the connecting fire with the other ranks, and without sergeants who were utterly devoted to their officers, there's no way L Detachment could have done what it did. It was the foundation stone of a regiment which was going to last, and we were convinced it would last.

It's all the personalities involved which is so important: they were all vastly different, and all had a different breaking point when it came to laughter. Some were natural humorists, others we had to teach. But in any tight place, always there had to be a laugh, it removed the tension. These factors are vital in that sort of unit.

We had very tough regulations, we had far sterner discipline than any Brigade of Guards regiment, but it was of a different nature, a different type, a much more exacting type of discipline.

REG SEEKINGS

When we arrived, there was just a couple of tents up, which the Guards sergeants were using, and a marquee which was the stores. We were given a tent, picks and shovels, and told to put the tent up and dig it in. We smartly told the quartermaster what to bloody well do with his tent. He made us lug it out, which we did, and dumped it down on a bit of flat ground, and off we went. We decided the best place to go was the naval canteen down the road. We had a few beers there, came back, brought some beer back. The tent was still rolled up, nobody had put it up, so we sat down there.

An officer in a kilt came along with a sergeant and told us to shut up, we were making too much noise. He went off and came back with another sergeant and put us on a charge. We were up in front of the sergeant major, Yates, and he wanted to know who called the officer a so-and-so. He said whoever owned up would be punished and the rest would carry on. So I elected to be spokesman, and I stepped forward and told him if that was their attitude, return us back to Geneifa. If that was the type of men they wanted in this unit, who'd split on their mates, it was time we buggered off, we didn't want to know anything about them.

We were ushered outside, called back, told to mend our ways, dig a bloody hole and put the tent up. Which we proceeded to do. We'd been promised by Stirling there'd be no fatigues, no guards – and for the next week or two all we did was dig holes, fatigue work, fill 'em in. Kershaw finished up as a sergeant and we gave him a shovel and said: 'You dig, you bastard.'

DAVE KERSHAW

Being guardsmen, we were given the job of controlling the line regiments that joined us. I remember one particular regiment soldier – Seekings, who'd come from 11 Commando – and he was digging out this sixteen by sixteen square, four feet deep, shovelling the sand up. I happened to be standing by the edge of the hole he was digging, and he looked up and said: 'Don't you Guards men even do any bloody work around here?' I thought it was so funny, coming from him, because he was a powerful man in those days.

REG SEEKINGS

Eventually we said: 'To hell with this, we want to go back to our unit.' By this time there'd been another marquee put up, other people had arrived, tents had gone up. So Jock Lewes had a word with us. He told us we'd got a yellow streak a yard wide down our backs. Christ, I don't know how he survived. He said: 'Right, prove me wrong, and I'll do anything that you do, you do anything that I do.' He said: 'That's how I feel at the moment, you're just bloody yellow.' From there on we started training.

DAVID STIRLING

I put Jock in charge of training. He was probably the greatest training officer – without question I think – in the Middle East area. He improvised all kinds of training techniques, which became the foundation of today's SAS test methods and standards, in training terms. Jock was both psychologically prepared and immensely intelligent, and had a great grasp of the subject.

Paddy was very different, he was the antithesis of Jock, but he had a marvellous battle nostril – he could really sense precisely what he had to do in odd situations. It wasn't just sheer courage, it was more sheer technique. He knew how to exploit surprise. Later in the war, in Germany, when he often had to undertake operations with the enemy fully on the alert, he would succeed in wrong-footing them. What looked to be absolutely foolhardy, and would have been foolhardy in anyone else, was legitimate with Paddy, because of this extraordinary skill that he had for anticipating what the enemy would do, then taking them always using unexpected techniques, and pushing everything through at lightning speeds.

JOHNNY COOPER

We didn't see much of David Stirling in the early days because he was continually in Cairo, fighting the hierarchy about the formation of this unit. He formed the unit and we just got on with the training. I was only a private, and apart from a stage when his batman went sick and I did batman for David for about three weeks, we didn't have much contact with him. It was Jock we saw so much of, and Paddy Mayne of course.

Paddy was terrific. I didn't have a great deal to do with him until later on, but he was a tower of strength. He was an enormous chap and I think he found it quite ungainly, jumping off vehicles, etc. The lighter you were the better you came away. He was a heavyweight boxer, international rugby player. But he was very quiet, very gentle. When he was wild, he was wild, but he was very quietly spoken.

REG SEEKINGS

Stirling was busy trying to get official blessing, trying to scrounge stuff for us, get us on the map. We caught odd glimpses of him, that's all. We saw more of Paddy Mayne. He was a great one for the physical side of things. But he was a bit of a loner, very quiet. When I first saw him down at Geneifa, before we got to Kabrit, he was one of the scruffiest officers I'd ever seen. He had a huge kepi that nearly rested on his shoulders, his shorts were extra long, and his shirt sleeves were half tucked up. Later on he was very, very smart. But I saw more of him because he was my section officer. He was so big and huge, people didn't argue the toss with him. We got along with Paddy. At that stage, the only thing that impressed you was his size, and of course he had no problems with the physical side of it at all.

JOHNNY COOPER

Jock was a very quiet, unassuming chap. A complete foil to David. David was the one that did all the getting of equipment, aircraft, etc., and he spent most of his time in Cairo, whereas Jock spent the whole time training us.

We were kept to regiments to begin with, depending which commando we came from. There was quite a predominance of Scots Guards and the Guards Commando. I'd say there were more from 8 Commando than from the others. The second highest number came from 11 Scottish Commando – Paddy Mayne and McGonigle came from that. And of course Bill Fraser too. They all had their own little groups and we were very much little troops together, all training together but not en masse. Each of us had our own officers in charge, then the sergeants and the corporals, etc.

Jock was training everybody, not just his own group.

The idea was that the four-man patrol was the answer to getting round. You're not going to make the noise because you haven't got the numbers. It's no good having a platoon or troop of eight or ten. You'll make too much noise. The four-man patrol was what David wanted. So the training itself was done in the sections and the troops. We'd got to get to know each other because when you're in ops, you must know the chaps absolutely inside out. Noises he makes, noises he doesn't make, etc.

BOB BENNETT

We were doing route marches, initiative tests, all sorts of training. They were more memory tests than initiative actually. One test was to walk into a tent and there'd be a table strewn with different articles, and you had half a minute, come out, and you'd memorised what was on the table.

REG SEEKINGS

It's a memory thing – so many objects on a table, look at 'em for so long, then leave and come back and number them off. They stepped it up gradually, wanting to know the name, the make, etc., and they increased the number of objects. We did a lot of that, because it was agreed we could take no notes, everything had to be held in our heads. We couldn't write down map reference numbers, etc., so it was just memory training.

JOHNNY COOPER

David persuaded HQ to let us have the Thompson sub-machine guns, the pistols – we all had Webleys – but then we were not contemplating fighting. They were only for defence, because our job was to destroy the 109Fs.

BOB BENNETT

We had a small range down on the canal, and unlike the rest of the British Army, where you were marched on to a range and you were given orders to fire, we could go and draw weapons from the armoury, including foreign weapons – German Schmeissers, etc. – and you'd just wander off on your own down to the range, and test the different weapons. Then you chose your weapon. No one hollering and shouting behind you. So you became a much better shot. There were bangs going off all over the camp.

The physical part was very, very tough – long route marches. We started from about twenty miles and worked up from there.

REG SEEKINGS

Jock worked out how we could do dead reckoning for our march in to the target. We'd have our packs loaded with various weights, and we'd march a hundred yards, measuring the length of pace, the time it took. We'd go on a ten or twenty mile march, even thirty mile, and when we came back, it would all be weighed and we'd again pace one hundred yards, how many paces it took, to get the length of pace, the time it took, so that we could do dead reckoning on our march in.

We'd go out, after having a meal, and first do it in daylight, with a certain weight, and you'd march a measured hundred yards. You'd count the number of paces, the length of pace and the time it took. Then you'd do the same thing in the dark, in moonlight. Then you'd do a ten-mile march and immediately on return, when you were tired, before you had time to rest, you'd do it again and compare them. Then you'd do fifteen mile, twenty mile, thirty mile – all measured.

You carried ammunition and every hundred yards, when you were within a mile or two of your target, when you came to a point you definitely recognised, so far into the target, you took one bullet from one pocket and put it in the other, so you could measure the distance in.

Water discipline was another thing. We'd be working in the desert, so there had to be very strict water discipline. Even in the heat of the day we weren't allowed to drink, unless the senior man decided you could. But you were watched and you just washed your mouth out and spat it out, you didn't swallow water. Swallowing it wouldn't do you any good, only make you want more. So when we did night trips, we'd fill up with sand. That was a stupid mistake they made. There was so much sand about, naturally we weren't going to carry sand all over the desert, so we'd tip it out, and fill it up just before we got back to camp. It didn't take Jock long to twig that one and we were given bricks, etc., or explosives, which you had to bring back. It was checked out and checked in.

And water bottles too – you took out a full one and you were expected to come back with a full one. You may say why take water if you didn't use it, but the point was there was the comfort of having the water there. It was customary also if you hadn't got the water right, you had to go without. But what you'd got to train your mind to do was carry the water, and leave the damned stuff alone. Otherwise the whole effect was lost. One old chap joined us, and did everything fine, but he couldn't do without his water. On one trip I caught him with a length of tubing, pinching the water. So he had to go.

We were all given an exercise book and pencil, and we had to keep an up-to-date record of what we were doing every day and when it came to map reading exercises, with compasses, we had problems set us; they all had to be entered up. That was handed in each week. Jock spent a lot of his time checking them. We were awarded so many marks. It was practically a twenty-four-hour programme; we'd be out at night, reading the stars and familiarising ourselves with that.

And we'd simulate night conditions. This was a mistake people made. If you train men in the dark, that's fine, but they find out their mistakes in their own time, and sometimes they never do. But if you simulate darkness in daytime, with blindfolds, your mates can watch, see what you're doing. We'd put up different objects. Sometimes it was crawling, feeling, sensing objects, moving around, etc., so the instructors can see what's happening and correct a man's faults. If you do it in the dark, you can't see the faults or correct them.

This is the way Jock Lewes carried out the training – it's what made him so damned good. He was a stickler for detail and downright common sense. It was repeat-repeat-repeat of all these things. Today the tendency is to dress up everything, but he was plain and simple, the basics. But he made everything hard. The aim in training, as he told us, was to make it as hard as humanly possible, so that when you got on the real job, you found it easy. That built up confidence. As Jock said: 'The confident man will win.' Of course you'll always need a little bit of luck. This was why it was so terrifically hard.

JOHNNY COOPER

We were being bombed at Kabrit quite a lot, by the Germans. They were bombing the Suez Canal, and Kabrit was a Blenheim bomber base. They were dropping mines in the canal as well, acoustic mines, etc., as well as the bombing. We were bombed quite a few times. So we were dug in, sandbagged at the sides. There were six to a tent. We were dotted around, no regimentation or anything. Each section just dug their hole and got on with it.

REG SEEKINGS

Men fell for all sorts of reasons. At that stage we had people like Tommy Corps, he couldn't take the training. He was Paddy's batman. And Kaufman, he couldn't take it. He became the canteen manager. Something people don't seem to appreciate, when I said we drew our tent and had to dig a hole to put the tent up, we had nothing down there, but nothing. Everything had to be pinched. Eventually we got a marquee up that we could put a bar in. We managed to do a bit of fiddling and get a few beers down there occasionally. This is where Kaufman came in – he was very good at scrounging. I used to help him do deals, pinch a truck and do a bit of black marketeering. We had to do that, we had nobody helping us. We built a brick canteen, and the bricks were pinched from the air force.

JOHNNY COOPER

We didn't have any ration clerks, pay clerks, etc. Hardly any of that at all. We had Gerry Ward, the quartermaster. He had one three-tonner, three storemen, and a couple of drivers. The adjutant had a tent, but as regards documentation and lettering, etc. – don't forget, in those days it wasn't a big army. The 8th Army hadn't really materialised at that stage, so in the beginning the administration was almost nothing. We only had one non-operational officer at that stage. All the others – Bill Fraser, etc. – were all operational. So we only had a quartermaster and an admin officer. The admin was very, very small indeed.

REG SEEKINGS

I don't think the authorities really wanted to know. I think it was deliberate also on Jock Lewes's part: the food was terrible and his idea was if you wanted to be a parachutist – we weren't called paratroops in those days – you'd go through hell to be one. As simple as that. So it was bloodymindedness all the way through.

There was nothing more annoying than to come back after being out all night – perhaps covered forty miles, going like the clappers of hell over the desert – then come in absolutely buggered to find a bit of dry bread for breakfast, no jam or anything. After all this training you were as fit as hell, and Jesus you could eat a donkey. And we were getting yams! Day after day. The food was terrible.

You'd be told: 'Oh, that's for tiffin.' At tiffin it was: 'Oh, that's for dinner tonight.' This was how it went. You eventually got sloshed. I finished up having one good meal during that period, and that was because when I got in, in the morning and went up for breakfast, ravenous, and there was nothing. I wanted a bit of jam: No. Tiffin: still none. Bill Fraser was orderly officer, and I thumped the table and he said: 'You'll get it tonight, they're making jam roll. Are you satisfied?' I said: 'I suppose I have to be.' So come dinner time, we got our swill, then went up to get a jam roll. They had a poor little orderly there – I always feel ashamed of this – not only did he give me a small bit, but it was the end of the roll: there wasn't a bit of jam in it. I just picked it off the plate and stuffed it in his bloody face. Poor little bugger, it wasn't his fault. But I was so frustrated, I'd been waiting for my jam all this time, and that's all I got. So Captain Fraser quickly took me across to the cookhouse and said: 'Give this man a meal.'

I'm not ashamed to admit it, I desperately wanted to be a parachutist. The physical side was easy, but the writing, the mental side. Everybody else would be asleep and I'd still be struggling with my notes. I thought: I'll never make it.

CHAPTER FIVE

Parachuting was one of the core elements of David Stirling's fledgling SAS. It had been built into his original paper, and was included in his proposal for the first SAS operation. Parachute training was therefore a priority. However, no facilities existed in the Middle East, so, as with many other things, L Detachment had to train themselves. A request for assistance was sent to Ringway, near Manchester, where British airborne forces were being trained, but no reply was received. A certain amount of instructional material did eventually arrive, and an instructor was later sent out, but not until L Detachment was qualified and operational.

JIM ALMONDS

Parachute training was a new thing to everyone, no one had ever done it before, and there was a certain amount of nervousness about it. Just leaping out into nothing requires a certain amount of thought.

BOB BENNETT

The parachute training started – no one had a clue about that. Stirling sent off to Ringway, the parachute place in England, to get instructors out to come and join us. That request was refused. It was said it wasn't practical to jump in the Middle East because of the air currents – some feeble excuse – and they didn't send anyone out. So Stirling acquired parachutes and Jock Lewes started ground training. We had stands of scaffolding from about ten feet up to sixteen feet. We used to jump off, do front rolls, side rolls, back rolls. The clothing we were issued with was American baseball gear – helmets, knee pads, elbow pads. It was pretty good but we didn't use it for long.

JIM ALMONDS

David Stirling gave me the job of building up the camp. He'd got some designs of what he wanted in the way of a parachute structure, stands, etc., and I set to work to build this thing. We had a Sapper officer who, although he didn't take part in the building, gave me some useful tips about what to do, and we built the big gantries at the bottom, on the ground, built the tower separately, got the measurements right, then hoisted the gantries up and bolted them up on top. We finished up with three towers and a gantry joining across the top. We rigged up giant rings for the parachute canopy and some smaller towers which you could walk up, slide a board out, put a man up there, put his harness

45

Parachute training at Kabrit.

on, cast him off and shut the trap so he didn't catch himself when he swung
back.

REG SEEKINGS

The training up to that stage was a process of shaking down – a lot of PT, running,
work with poles etc. There was a lot of physical work. Then we got down to it and
we built towers and began learning how to jump from them. We were jumping
some ridiculous heights at times. This is where the broken bones came in. We had
broken arms, collar bones. We were doing guard duty all the time, which we'd been
promised we wouldn't. Not only that, the men who were sick were doing guards. So
it wasn't a case of scrounging off guard duty. If you went sick: 'Oh, he's good enough
to do guard duty.' We had men with broken arms doing it, and patrols.

JIM ALMONDS

Then we built a small railway and had a trolley on rails which would hit the
buffer at the other end, and you catapulted off and did a forward roll or
shoulder roll or whatever, to save damage. Then Lewes had the idea it would be
better to have a fifteen hundredweight truck. You stood in the back of the truck
to do a back roll, and jumped off as the truck was going along.

REG SEEKINGS

Jock got hold of a truck, the driver drove across the sand, and Jock stepped off the back and did his back roll. Then he said to the driver: fifteen miles per hour. OK. Twenty, twenty-five. He went up to 35mph. We were all worried by this time – when is this crazy so-and-so going to stop? He said to the driver: 'Drive at 30mph, I'll guarantee they'll do backward rolls.'

You stood in the back of the truck, and you stepped off the tailboard, facing backwards, so when you stepped out, that whipped your feet from under you. I thought: I'll be clever on this one, I'm not doing that, because the driver was in his glory, it wasn't 30mph – he was putting his foot down and laughing like hell. I decided I was going to bail out, I was going to be clever. So I jumped over the side, facing forward. I took two tremendous strides and I ploughed up the bloody desert with my face. I was in a hell of a state. That was the last time I tried to be clever. Paddy Mayne jumped out and you could hear his head hit the deck half a mile away. We did backward rolls after that, and we didn't need the lorry going that fast. It was done in a civilised manner after that, but it taught us a lesson.

But Jock did it himself. This was routine. When you had a man setting the example, what else could you do? Also, when we'd finished, there was Jock – I've known him to sit up all night planning and working out the next scheme.

JOHNNY COOPER

To give you an idea of Jock Lewes's devotion to everything, I jumped off and crooked my ankle, so I couldn't go off the twelve and fourteen foot jump. I was on guard one night with McKay, another of the Scots Guards, and I thought the ankle was okay, and about three o'clock on the morning I went up the tower and started to jump off to see if my leg was alright. But up came Jock. He'd been watching this with great interest. He said: 'You do your training in training time. I admire your devotion to getting yourself fit, but your job at the moment is to guard this camp.'

BOB BENNETT

Came the day of the first parachute jump. Colonel Stirling had acquired some Bristol Bombays from Kabrit airfield – flat out I think they did ninety miles an hour. They were the old pre-war, about '33, troop carriers. And it was going to take place the other side of the canal, in two lifts.

In the early days, the SAS had to train themselves.

REG SEEKINGS

Pat Riley got number thirteen chute. He came across and said to me: 'You like thirteen, don't you? Swap with me.' So I took thirteen.

BOB BENNETT

So the first plane took off, loaded up. I myself was on the second lift, standing with Dave Kershaw and the rest of the chaps, and we saw the plane circle the drop zone, and Dave Kershaw said: 'I'm sure something came out from the plane.' I said: 'Well, if it had done there'd have been a parachute.' But with that the Bombay landed.

REG SEEKINGS

The plane came back and landed. We found out that two of the lads had crashed. In those days my hair was blond, sun-bleached, and the rumour went round it was me that had gone for a burton, and you can imagine how Pat Riley felt, and how relieved he was when he saw me. This shows the calibre of the chaps and certainly of the colonel. Stirling was in Cairo at the time: he was informed, and he signalled back that every man would jump next day.

BOB BENNETT

We all got paraded, and Jock Lewes took the parade and explained that a chap named Warburton and another chap named Duffy had been killed. What had happened, they were the first to go out, and the ring on the static line had jumped over the hook and of course the chutes hadn't developed. And Jock Lewes, being the man he was, said that there's been a fault, and that it would be rectified and the hooks would be made safe, and we'd all be jumping in the morning.

Well, you can imagine everybody saying: 'Well, good gracious, what goes on? This is a right unit: the first that jump get bumped off.' We were all moaning like hell. And we all went back to our tents with a fifty tin of cigarettes, and sat up all night smoking, worrying about the next morning.

REG SEEKINGS

We had to scrounge extra chutes – they were in short supply; Jock Lewes had found ours by accident. We had to get ready, and every man would jump at dawn. And Stirling was down there, first man out. It was bloody cold too. I don't think anybody was very happy.

BOB BENNETT

The next morning convinced me that I was with the right crowd, because they were offered at that parade to leave the unit if they wanted to, and not one man left. The whole unit jumped, everyone from Stirling and the officers to the last man.

REG SEEKINGS

We jumped and didn't have one failure. We were proud of the fact we never had a refusal to jump.

BOB BENNETT

Sitting in that plane, with your turn coming up to jump . . . we knew what the cause of the thing was. As I say, you put the ring of the static line over a hook, and of course that had been left open. When we were given 'action stations', everyone was sort of tugging these static lines like mad. And everything went off perfect. We did the first jump from two thousand feet, which takes quite a long time to get down to the deck, and I thought it was a wonderful feeling, the first one, because you go through the door and you didn't have any knowledge of anything – at least I didn't – until the parachute developed. And when it did develop, I pulled a mouth organ out and started playing on the way down. The first one was the best jump ever. After that I didn't like the jumping so much.

As well as parachuting, however, there was another requirement which Stirling and The Originals had to meet. In order to fulfil their mission, each four-man L Detachment unit had to carry enough explosive charges to destroy large numbers of aircraft on the ground. What was needed was a bomb that would not simply blow a hole in the wing of a plane, but would also ignite the fuel inside. But such a bomb had to be small enough for each man to carry a number in his backpack. Various types of high-explosive and incendiary bombs were available, but none combined the two functions. The only suggestion which a range of experts came up with was too big. The Originals therefore had to fall back – again – on their own initiative.

REG SEEKINGS

During the training different people were brought in to lecture on different stuff. We had architects, builders, etc. and they taught us how to pick out structural weak points of bridges, etc. It was very well organised. No mistake about that. There was nothing slap happy. We even had MI5 people brought in. We had doctors training us too, right up to amputations. Jock was fantastic at organising all this stuff. We were taught how to use a pound of explosives to best effect. We had railway people in to teach us the best and weakest places to blow a railway. We had an oil rig driller too because that would be a target for us.

JIM ALMONDS

We had a man from the Egyptian railways, who taught us how to blow lines, where was the most effective place – points and on curves. Straight sections were usually replaced but not curves. To blow a railway line, you put a charge here, a charge there, so when it blew a train was bound to come off the rails whichever way it was coming.

There was an aircraft production man too – he showed us that with destroying airframes, it was always the same part that was to be destroyed so the parts couldn't be cannibalised and replaced. And the petrol tanks in the wings were ideal places to put bombs.

PAT RILEY

But we had a problem. It was how the hell to blow up these aircraft. We realised – or at least Jock realised – that we had to have a bomb which would explode and ignite, and which men could carry quite easily. And each man had to have several bombs, because the enemy's got many aircraft.

DAVID STIRLING

This arrogant little major came down and said no way could we combine an explosive with an incendiary element; they would have to be done separately. The most a four- or five-man module could hope to destroy was what they could carry, which would be two each. It was very elaborate and had to be tied and took several minutes to set up. We said forget about it.

REG SEEKINGS

We had some Royal Engineers down, two or three lots, because Jock wasn't satisfied with the bombs they made. The nearest they could get to a lightweight bomb weighed about five pounds – a time bomb with clock, etc. We couldn't see ourselves carrying those around. So Jock got to work.

PAT RILEY

Jock experimented with a plane wing over a forty-gallon drum of petrol, and we tried explosive after explosive. This lasted over days and weeks.

REG SEEKINGS

He got on to this plastic explosive and thermite, to give a higher flash point. He tried different distances – he'd cadge wings off the air force and set them up on drums, then put a can of petrol underneath, and put a bomb on top. Then he'd raise and lower the heights. Then he had the idea of mixing thermite and oil. We got used to hearing this bang-bang-bang going on. He couldn't set one alight, which is what he wanted – fire. But Jock persevered night after night, day after day, with the formula. Exactly how he arrived at it, I don't know – trial and error, etc. And eventually he got it. That's why it's called the Lewes bomb. I was there the night he solved it. He was going nuts – the only time I've ever seen him excited: 'I've got it, I've got it!' Everybody left their beer and went out there and he tried a few more, and that was it, the Lewes bomb was in operation.

DAVID STIRLING

I was fighting MEHQ for supplies and everything else. Everything had to be fought for in those days. I came back one day to see a lot of excitement around, because Jock had invented the Lewes bomb, which is a mix of plastic explosive and aluminium and thermite turnings which mixed into the PE, and went miraculously, combining the incendiary aspect with the explosive. It meant that each man could carry quite comfortably the wherewithal to destroy twenty-five aircraft himself.

They wouldn't believe us, so this arrogant little runt of a Sapper, very senior, came down and we set up the apparatus for him, and he openly sneered at the possibility of it working. Jock Lewes was wholly in charge of this. He put a tray of petrol on the top of a forty-gallon drum, and put the drum with three bricks below to insulate it further by the space between the desert sand and the top – through two metal thicknesses, i.e. the top and bottom of the drum, and then a tray of petrol on that.

Up it went, and off went the tray of petrol with the most splendid flare. Then I said to Jock: 'Will you demonstrate it the other way?' to make quite certain it operated regardless of whether it was on top or below.

JIM ALMONDS

The bombs were made of a pound of plastic and a quarter pound of thermite, good for creating a blaze. You mixed the two together with a little engine oil – nice little black pudding. Inside you put a two-ounce dry guncotton primer and detonator, and a thirty-second fuse. You had two means of ignition: time pencils – the shortest fuse was red, which gave you ten minutes – and a miner's igniter: when you pulled the pin out it went bang straight away and you'd thirty seconds to get away. We also had release switches, pressure switches, etc.

REG SEEKINGS

We had copper and acid time pencils. In the timer you had a lead one, so that when you pulled the pin it gradually stretched the lead, and we had different thicknesses of lead. But that was very inaccurate, out there in particular, with cold nights and very hot days.

The time pencil was just a wire holding a plunger and passing through a copper tube and a glass phial of acid. You broke that and it started to work on the wire. You'd have a different thickness of wire according to how long the delay you needed. You broke phials any way you liked. The best way was to just press them – you could twist the wire by bashing them.

CHAPTER SIX

The Originals were now ready for their first official operation – almost. As was quite often the case with David Stirling, a wager was involved.

BOB BENNETT

The big exercise before we were ready for ops was to march from Kabrit to Cairo, across the desert, to 'attack' Heliopolis RAF airfield. The object was to get into Heliopolis and put labels on these planes. David Stirling had a bet with the man in charge that we'd stick so many labels on the planes. So they had a terrific guard round the perimeter. He didn't fancy losing a £100 bet.

We had four pints of water, a piece of hessian, about a pound of dates, half a pound of boiled sweets, biscuits that we called sand channels because you couldn't bite them, the old army biscuits, some raisins, and that was about it. We conserved water, because they had planes out looking for us, so we didn't march in the day, we marched at night. During the day, you laid on the desert and you had this piece of hessian, and you just put that hessian right over you and camouflaged yourself if aircraft were about. Believe me, to do a hundred miles on four bottles of water in the desert is a hell of a feat . . . the heat of the desert in daytime and you daren't touch your water.

We had a lad called Chesworth with us and he did nothing but moan all the time: 'There's not enough water; it's time for a break; what the bloody hell are we doing this for?' Paddy got pissed off with him and decided it was time to stop it. We were on the crest of an escarpment and Paddy suddenly beckoned Chesworth to him. He picked up the bugger and held him over the cliff – with one hand, mark you – and said: 'Any more from you and that's your lot.' I tell you we never heard another peep out of him.

JOHNNY COOPER

We were in parties of four or five. I was with Pat Riley. Laying up in the daytime, we went into little clefts in the rock. It was very flat, that stretch. There are small wadis etc, but we'd find a place and cover ourselves with the hessian, because the RAF had planes going up and down. We were not all that far from the road from Kabrit to Cairo. If we'd got into dire straits, we could have got on to the road, but none of us did, except one chap who packed in. Everybody else made it. We walked all the way to Cairo, took three days, and only one man fell out. Then the fourth night we attacked the airfield. In lieu of bombs we had sticky labels. And by the morning the RAF woke up to find that two-thirds of their planes had these sticky labels on them. They were not highly amused. David won his bet.

Before The Originals went on their first operation proper, however, there was one more piece of business to attend to. The unit had adopted a name – Special Air Service – from Dudley Clark's psych ops unit; now they needed a badge and a motto, even though, perhaps, they were not entitled. As usual, Stirling ignored official channels.

REG SEEKINGS

The problem, right throughout the commandos in the early days, was that there was no common badge. Because in your infantry regiments, whether it was Guards or county regiments, there was always such a pride of unit, battle honours, all this sort of stuff. In the commandos we had no such insignia. We could only tell people we were commandos, we were specialist forces, and I think the tendency was then: Oh, it's a tough rough unit, we got to act tough and be tough and of course we used to get into quite a lot of trouble. And the same applied to L Detachment when it was first started. We were still a little bit wild, but once we got the badge, that made all the difference because there was this pride – no way that anybody was going to let that unit down. And also tremendous pride built up, because of what happened on the first op.

We had a competition for a badge, and then we reckoned we wanted a beret. Who decided on a white beret I don't know. And there was controversy over the cap badge.

They asked for designs and about a dozen went in. I'm positive that two were by Bob Tait and Jeff DuVivier. Their designs were a winged dagger, and the other a man diving through flame with the motto We Descend To Defend. As for the wings – a lot of people had seen scarabs in museums and things in Cairo, but a lot of people don't understand what it is. It's the dung beetle, and it's the hieroglyphic for the medical fraternity – fertility, longevity or something. Jock was a medical student, and that's where he got that idea from.

BOB BENNETT

David Stirling asked the regiment to devise a badge. The one they have now was done by Bob Tait, from 11 Commando. He designed the winged dagger, although at that time I'm sure he didn't call it a winged dagger. He called it the flaming sword, but it became a winged dagger over the years. And David Stirling added the motto Who Dares Wins. And the breast wings that were awarded (some wore them on their arm) were the wings of Egypt. I think Stirling and Lewes devised that between them.

JOHNNY COOPER

Bob Tait, MM and bar – he got one Military Medal with Scottish Commando, and one with us – designed it. Above every shop in Cairo, you have the like . . . with an eagle in it. He said: 'Right, we'll put a parachute in there.' So it is an Egyptian design with a parachute. And it's not a winged dagger. They're flames. The sword of Excalibur. When The Winged Dagger came out, we laughed our bloody heads off.

DAVID STIRLING

First of all there was the inventing of it, which was quite difficult, because Who Dares Wins is quite a good motto for us. I did that in Cairo, and put down a £10 bet on anyone improving on it. Randolph Churchill, who was Prime Minister Winston Churchill's son, had lots of reference books. Randolph insisted Who Dares Wins was totally rotten, and should be thrown away, that he had a much better one coming up. However, he never came up with it. But he had to come up with his ten quid. The wings were designed by Jock Lewes, the design of the badge was mainly Sergeant Tait, with Strike & Destroy, which was substituted by Who Dares Wins.

The next stage was to get it manufactured, which we did in Cairo, both Who Dares Wins and the wings. And we put them on immediately, because we had to have our own identity, and of course, it enraged the Middle East Headquarters.

But on this occasion even the top brass nose was rather out of joint, because there was no time to ask any permission or anything of that kind. So the trick was to have it recognised, in spite of their objections to it, and that was done by tricking General Auchinlech when he came down to do an inspection. I was standing at one side to him at the end of the demonstration that we laid on for him, and as he was coming up to the salute, I turned to him and he saluted the badge, so that was it. And he laughed; he was perfectly charitable about it after.

In fact, I think we gave him an honorary badge at one time. He was very enthusiastic about the unit, and so was General Ritchie. We had great support at the top level, but even they didn't like the idea of us having our full regimental regalia.

REG SEEKINGS

Who decided on a white beret I don't know. When we finished training and passed out, we were given a couple of days' leave in Cairo before the first op, and got into a lot of trouble straight away with the white beret. Particularly poor old Johnny Rose, sergeant major at the time. He was rather baby-faced and he was walking along in Cairo and an Arab started trotting alongside and saying how nice he was. Poor Rosie ran a mile. There were fights all over Cairo.

PAT RILEY

You can just imagine six-footers and what-have-you, wearing a white beret in among Australians, New Zealanders, every type of nationality out there. That brought some very great wolf whistles, which naturally were not received in the right manner. They did cause some trouble. Later, of course, we got the sand-coloured beret.

REG SEEKINGS

We were given the option of wearing the wings on the shoulder immediately, or wait until we come back off an operation and wear the wings on the breast. So we all opted that we'd wait, and come back from an operation – hope we came back – and then we'd wear the wings on our breast. And the mere fact of what happened on the first operation, you can imagine the value that was placed upon these wings.

CHAPTER SEVEN

*The first SAS operation was included in David Stirling's original proposal.
Operation Crusader, the offensive to drive Rommel back out of Cyrenaica,
was planned for the night of November 17, 1941. Its main objectives were
to relieve the garrison at Tobruk and secure advance airfields from which
the convoys to beleaguered Malta could be protected. L Detachment would
parachute behind the lines prior to the offensive and remove enemy air
power which was a major threat, by attacking the German airfields
around Timimi and Gazala, then make their way to a desert rendezvous
with the Long Range Desert Group.*

DAVID STIRLING

A lot of the training was devoted towards this particular undertaking; it was even written into the original paper, presented to Auchinleck, to get the unit started in the first place. That was the destruction of the German fighter air force, which were based on the three Gazala landing grounds and the two Timini landing grounds, which were stretched over about seventy miles of coastline. The proposition was to knock out the entire German fighter force, because they had control of the air at that time, in one night.

The proposition was to get the sixty-five men divided into five lots, and drop at night three days before Crusader, so that we could observe for a couple of days from very good cover, which you can do with a small number of that kind. During those two days we could observe precisely where the aircraft were at night time when we would attack. Then the night before the start of the offensive, we would go in, with the Lewes bombs, and blow the aircraft up.

JOHNNY COOPER

We had our last training exercise, and then we were told we were going to have our first op. It was November 15; we flew up forward to Bagoush, which was purely a desert strip. The five Bombays were there and we were put up in the tented RAF camp there. Timini and Gazala airfields were in the Gulf of Bomba. The idea was to go with the Bombays at a height we could manage, about eight thousand feet, fly out to sea and then come in from the north straight over the gulf to get our bearings, and drop us on our respective targets, about five miles past so that we could then walk straight in. After the job we'd come out to the Trig al Ab, which was just a desert track running parallel to the coast, and meet up with R Patrol, the New Zealand patrol, of the Long Range Desert Group.

BOB BENNETT

We knew how important the first operation was going to be, because all the operations in the commandos had misfired so much, and the chaps' morale was pretty low, so we knew it was very important that Colonel Stirling had to have a success, having had such a job to raise the unit. Most people in the Middle East were so anti, and thought that Colonel Stirling was mad talking about getting behind lines and doing this sort of thing.

We were flown up to Bagoush. Then the weather deteriorated, storms blew up, and they contacted David Stirling and said: 'It's terrible weather for dropping: you're going to have casualties.'

JOHNNY COOPER

Terrible met reports began coming in – very high winds, rain forecast. It was touch and go. We were wondering whether we should fly or not. The officers got together, then we all went into a tent and we were told that the winds were against us, that the operation could be put back, but that it would not be tactically sound to do. We were all given the option of opting out. Jock Lewes spoke, and then of course David spoke and he said: 'We'll go because we've got

David Stirling (left) and Jock Lewes – planning in the desert.

to go, the job is so important, the push is coming on from the wire, the whole army depends on us to get in there and knock off as many of these Messerschmitt 109-Fs as possible, which are crucifying the RAF.' And I don't think anybody opted out at that stage at all; everybody went forward.

DAVID STIRLING

There was no question of postponing the operation. I'd already indicated that being a small unit, we could parachute whatever the weather, but we didn't envisage as ferocious a gale as blew up. The Middle East command was rather anxious to see if we did postpone it. They gave us the option. However we refused absolutely.

There were two reasons that I refused. The first was that we came from the commandos, where time and again we would form up for an operation, and it would be abandoned or postponed, with all the resulting effect, not only on the soldiers involved, but also on those who were trying to make use of us in MEHQ. So I swore when I started SAS that if we undertook to take on a target on a particular night, we'd do it utterly regardless. And therefore I simply wasn't prepared to see the first of our operations being postponed because of bad weather – it couldn't be postponed, it had to be cancelled, because it had to take place on a certain evening. In these particular circumstances, there could be no question of postponement, because it was related to Zero Day, Zero Hour, for the coming offensive.

REG SEEKINGS

The men insisted. We – the men – insisted. It was very important. This is one thing you've got to remember: that we were the product of commandos, and in the commandos we had cancellation, cancellation, cancellation. And when the first job come up, in spite of all this rough weather and rough conditions, everybody wanted to jump – they insisted. Otherwise if it was cancelled, that was us finished. We were trying to get away from this cancellation all the time. There's nothing worse than to build yourself up for an operation, then it's cancelled. We wanted to get in.

We weren't prepared to worry about the casualties. It's not bravado, it's just a case of you get in and go in. If you start thinking about casualties . . . You're going into action, you've got to wash that out of your mind. You can't sit around there thinking about casualties. You don't turn round and say 'Oh I'm going to get the chop' because sure as hell you'll get the chop. You're wishing it upon yourself. You forget that side. That's a risk that you accept as a soldier, that's what it should be. We joined to fight a war; we knew what it was about.

We had a bit of time, because we were being dropped in the dark. We were treated like men going to the gallows – a slap-up meal, the whole works, by the air force. Last supper, so to speak. I bought a tin of Craven A – cigarettes were difficult to get then.

BOB BENNETT

That evening we were given a meal. It was out of this world, the RAF had laid it on, and it was like the Last Supper – that was what went through my mind: what a beautiful meal this is, what's it in aid of? I think the RAF thought they'd never see any of us again.

REG SEEKINGS

Rightly, people might turn round most probably and say we should never have dropped under those conditions. But if we hadn't, there would never have been an SAS. That is for sure.

DAVID STIRLING

So we went ahead.

REG SEEKINGS

It was very uncomfortable. They had Bombays and they only made a few of those. I think they were the first troop transporters built. But they used to flip on their backs, their centre of gravity moved feet instead of inches. They had a rear gun turret they couldn't use, so they'd used that area as a lavatory. But you had to warn the pilot before you moved, so he could take an extra grip on the thing, to stop her flipping. There was a big fuel tank to cover the mileage. It was huge and took up practically all the fuselage. We had to squeeze past it.

It was freezing cold, because the door was off. There was no heating. Very draughty. We had to pass all messages by word of mouth to the so-called rear gunner. They had a couple of holes in the fuselage, and had Vickers Ks in there. Very Heath Robinson. We went over the sea and turned in towards land, and started to get some searchlight activity. We'd expected a rough trip, but not anything like that. There was a 30mph wind blowing, then the ground fire came up at us.

JOHNNY COOPER

I was with Jock in our plane. The weather became terrible, teeming with rain, and we were in cloud. Our aircraft got into the searchlights over the Gulf of Bomba, and all this flak was coming up, it was Breda machine-gun fire, all different colours, and the plane inside was absolutely lit up. And Jock got up and just walked up and down as though he cared nothing at all. He gave you confidence: well, he's not frightened, why am I frightened? Jock said: 'Prepare to jump out.' The pilot was in communication with Jock – we weren't, of course – and we were all hooked up ready to jump, and then the pilot threw it around and got out of the searchlight, and then about a minute later, another searchlight got us, and the aircraft was hit, although we didn't hear it, hit in the wing. Then we flew out of that, and the pilot wasn't terribly sure where we were.

DAVE KERSHAW

We crossed the coast, and I looked out and my stomach turned over, because you could see the black oily swell, topped with foam, and it looked pretty rough.

PAT RILEY

As we got over the targets we got picked up by searchlights, these flaming onions were coming up one after another at us, very slowly – they looked very slow as they came – but they went like hell actually, they were really moving. We went round again, but unfortunately the pilot misjudged things.

BOB BENNETT

I was with Mayne's stick. We had containers then – we didn't carry any kitbags like they do today, just containers dropped separate, carrying explosives, rations, everything else. Terrible winds started coming up, and the pilot said that it was very dodgy and should he call it off? Colonel David apparently said: 'No, certainly not.'

JOHNNY COOPER

The weather was terrible. We said: 'Well, we're jumping blind anyway.' Prepare to go, red light/green light, and off we went.

DAVE KERSHAW

When we got the green light to go, Paddy went and all the lads followed, but it was a question of finding out where you were, because as soon as you jumped, you were blown away. Must have been 45mph wind force.

DAVID STIRLING

The sand blew over the coastline, making it impossible for the aircraft carrying us to know what height they were at, to know where the coastline point was from which they would be able to determine their dropping zone for the parachutists. And they dropped the sixty-five men taking part all over the bloody shop.

DAVE KERSHAW

As we were cascading down, the containers which held our Lewes bombs and so forth hit the ground and bang-bang-bang, they were going off like nobody's business. I hit the deck and couldn't get out of my harness, and was dragged along the ground. I was pulling on one side of the chute, then pulling on the other to try and spill the air out of the canopy. I was dragged in the sand, and it was folding the skin back, the sand was getting underneath, and I was in a shocking state. Eventually the canopy collided with a boulder or something like that, and I got it off.

DAVID STIRLING

My particular stick came down about twelve miles away from where it ought to have been. That caused total disruption. And it was a night without any moon, pitch black, so there was no way you could see the ground, particularly with all the desert blowing up, all the flying sand. Moreover, the wind was on such a hell of a scale that when we hit the ground – and we weren't dropped from five hundred feet, we were dropped from about three thousand feet – quite a few of us were knocked out and it was a struggle to get out of one's parachute rigging.

BOB BENNETT

I hit the deck and was dragged about half a mile – just couldn't get out of the chute, the wind was blowing that hard. Just dragged along with my arms up like that. And everyone was the same. It took a heck of a time to get people together – they were spread all over the place and it was pitch black. When we did get everyone together – we'd been dropped about thirty miles from the coast, in the desert.

JOHNNY COOPER

On hitting the ground, I went off about forty miles an hour. They didn't actually register the wind, but it must have been fifty or sixty miles an hour. The worst storm for thirty years. I went streaming off and luckily for me – because some of them were dragged to death – my parachute got caught in something. I was trying to knock my quick release and I was in such a state of shock, I hadn't turned it. Then I released it.

REG SEEKINGS

We were wearing our overalls with the trenching tool across our backsides, and the lift webs of the chutes caught on this. We hit the deck and the wind took over, and we went at a hell of a lick. We were trapped. You couldn't shake yourself free of the chute. I was struggling and struggling to free myself and I thought: 'This is it.' I had one more go, struggled like hell, got over on my stomach, and I went face first into a thorn bush. I could feel the blood running down, and Jesus this got my temper up, and eventually I managed to break free. My hands and arms were completely skinned, and my face was a hell of a mess.

BOB BENNETT

Everything was supposed to be done in silence, and it turned out so comical because everyone was yelling their heads off: 'Where are you?' etc. We only found one container out of all of them, so we were short of everything – water, only a few Lewes bombs. When we did get together, two of our chaps had broken ankles and we just had to leave them where they were. What happened to them I don't know. We had to go on. These two poor chaps – we had to leave them what water we could and whether they got picked up or not I don't know to this day. I doubt if they did. They probably perished. It's an awful feeling, to leave two friends that you've been with, operated with and trained with, but you had to, couldn't carry them.

I mean you were operating and you were miles from absolutely nowhere, making your way to the objective, so you couldn't do anything else about it except hope that the Germans had planes out all the time, spotting – hope that they would be picked up, by the Germans.

DAVE KERSHAW

The idea was to bury the parachutes, but to dig in those conditions was impossible. After a few moments I met Paddy, and considering he was first out and I was last, the remainder of the stick was all over the place. We were just two people alone in the desert, because we didn't know how far the stick had been blown.

So I suggested to Paddy to start cat-calling and whistling and no, he argued, there could be enemy there. I remember distinctly remarking: 'Well, if there was any enemy there, with all the row that was made with those containers being dropped and bombs going off, they'd have been at us by now.' And he eventually agreed, so we started whistling and cat-calling, and the next man I saw was Reg Seekings. Then we discovered Keith with his damaged back, and detailed Corporal Arnold to stay with him.

There was flashes going, away to our left and right, and I thought that they were our ships shelling, or our aircraft that was bombing Timini and Gazala. So I took a cross bearing on them and found out where the two lines met, and we decided to go forward. We left blankets and water with Keith and Arnold.

I was in pain now, I'd broken my arm, and they had these small cactus plants in the desert. Hawkins was in front of me, and every little bit of cactus, of course, he'd find, and walk through them, and it gave such a swish, and because I was behind him, it seemed to aggravate the pain. I said: 'If you walk through another bloody cactus, I'll bloody shoot you.'

DAVID STIRLING

The parachutes carrying the supplies were distributed all over the place, so we were reduced to two containers, neither of which had any of the explosives. So there was nothing we could do about the operation, because we only had our personal arms, and none of the raw material with which to undertake the raid. And it was much the same in the other groups, so we were utterly incapacitated by a combination of the wind and sand.

JOHNNY COOPER

Before we jumped we were told the bearing of the aircraft, so I walked back down the line, and in half an hour's time found all of us of that stick – there were about ten of us. Pat Riley was the sergeant. Jock the officer. But we'd lost our containers which had been dropped – the Thompson sub-machine guns, etc. A hell of a lot was lost, but we managed to find at least some of the Lewes bombs. Then we started to walk.

The heavens opened up, there was an electrical storm – terribly difficult to navigate, and it was pretty obvious we were going round in circles. In the end, the water was up to your chest, and Jock got us on a bit of high ground and said: 'It's now one or two o'clock, we've no idea where we are, and to get to the airfield before light now is out of the question.' We couldn't even cross the wadis – they were in spate.

PAT RILEY

We got together and set off for the target, but it bucketed it down. We ended up in a wadi and we sat there for a while and finally it was decided Jock and I would go ahead to see where the target was, because by this time we were a little puzzled. And Jock and I went on but couldn't see the target and by this time it was just absolutely pelting down, terrific, and Jock decided the explosives would be useless by this time, and we then came back.

JOHNNY COOPER

Jock said: 'Put all the explosive down, put a time pencil on it, so if we are caught, they won't see the secret of the Lewes bomb.' And off we went. And the damned thing went off in our faces. We'd gone round in another great circle.

REG SEEKINGS

This is when Paddy started to shine. There were six or seven of us left. He got us organised and we started to march clear of the drop area. One man had a broken ankle and we had to leave him. It was cold and dark, and then it started to rain – the first rain we'd seen. It hadn't rained out there for over twenty years. It came down and down and down. I couldn't believe it, the water was running down, and the next minute we were chest-high in water, a flash flood was roaring down. In the middle of the desert we had this raging torrent. We struggled away, with Paddy shouting to us, and we made a bit of high ground. Then it really opened up. We huddled together under a blanket. I've never been so cold in my life.

DAVE KERSHAW

We decided to hole up for the night and recce the next morning. We more or less got settled and then the heavens opened up again, and it absolutely belted down. In fact, we were sitting on a slope of a small wadi, and the rain seemed to run down the wadi, through our little encampment where we were sitting, and find a way between the cheeks of your bottom, which wasn't very pleasant.

We had a blanket and we spread it over and above us. There were three that side and three this side, and we'd each have a turn of pulling the blanket a bit nearer over them, consequently leaving the other side bare, and this went on for quite a time, until Paddy said something. Reg Seekings had a tinned packet of Gold Flake – I think they were Gold Flake anyway – and we smoked our way to oblivion until dawn came.

REG SEEKINGS

We had an issue of rum and Paddy got his out and said: 'Take a little sip, but don't guzzle it. If you go to sleep there's a danger of not waking up again', it was so cold. This is where my cigarettes came in. They kept us going. The blanket over our head just kept away the force of the rain – if you put your head out, the rain really hurt, it was so heavy, really battered down. All our gear had gone, washed away, bombs, the lot. All we had was the odd grenade and our personal weapons.

BOB BENNETT

So six of us were sitting there with blankets over our heads, and of course we couldn't operate, so we had to get back to the rendezvous that had been arranged. I suppose the water saved our lives that time, because we filled our bottles from the wadi. Then we started marching back to the pick-up zone, which had been arranged with the Long Range Desert crew.

JOHNNY COOPER

Dawn came and it had stopped raining. Jock said: 'Only one thing for it – Long Range Desert Group. At least we won't die of thirst.' There was water everywhere. So we started off walking. Jock up in front with Pat, with me just behind.

REG SEEKINGS

Paddy wanted to go on, on his own, he wanted to get an aircraft. We had a hell of a job talking him out of it. But we couldn't see any sense in him going off alone. There was no point getting knocked off in a hopeless cause – you couldn't knock an aircraft out with a grenade. You might if you got it in the cockpit, but what chance of that if you were on your own? So we decided it was best to start making our way back to the rendezvous. We had a pretty good idea where it was. The searchlights had helped us pinpoint it within twenty miles or so. So we started off in the direction of the pick-up. And that was tough. The ground that first day was mud, but that saved us, because it meant water. We had only the odd water bottle, the food had gone, and we just went on and on and on.

DAVE KERSHAW

After a couple of days and nights, we came to the Makele and Masous track, that cut right across our front, and we saw four or five bodies, which was going completely away from the direction that we were going. I got the glasses on them – I had binoculars with me – and it seemed that they were Sergeant Yeats with Tranfield, Boland, Calhoun, and maybe a couple more. So we whistled and I got my .45 out and fired a few rounds but they took no notice. So we carried on.

JOHNNY COOPER

I was scanning the horizon and said: 'Sir, I can see a pole.' Jock said: 'Where?' 'There. Right.' We diverted and went across, about a mile away, and it was a pole on the Trig al Ab track. But we didn't know which way to go. So Jock said: 'We'll go west.' So we did, and we walked all day long.

Nightfall came about 7.30pm, it was dark, and I was up in front and I said: 'I can see a star very low down on the horizon.' 'Oh yes? Whereabouts?' 'There.' In front of us were two hurricane lamps the LRDG had put up as a homing device. We marched straight on to them and stopped about 150 yards away, and Jock said: 'We'll all sing Roll Out The Barrel.' Then out of the dark came a Kiwi voice: 'Over here, pommies.' And there was Jock Easton with R Patrol LRDG.

DAVE KERSHAW

I kidded myself up that I was a bit of an astronomer. When night fell, Bennett suddenly said: 'There's a light over there, Dave. Tell Paddy.' Because you must remember, in those days it was Dave this and Paddy this, until we got back to camp. I said: 'It's not, it's not a light, that's Mars.' So we argued about it, and it stayed in the same position all the time, and then I realised that he could be right, that it was a light, because the planet moves east to west, and then it would disappear entirely. Anyway, Bennett proved himself right, it was a light, because when dawn broke a spiral of smoke went up from where the light was, and then of course we knew it was the LRDG. And before long we saw one of the trucks coming out to meet us, and you can bet we were glad to see it.

We had two rendezvous; we had a rendezvous to meet up, and then we had a real rendezvous at a small encampment. Stirling was at the rendezvous. He'd made it somehow or other, and then we got the full story. Quite a number had been captured; aircraft had been forced down. Of the sixty-five, apparently there were twenty-two of us left. I still say there was only sixteen.

JOHNNY COOPER

From then, our lot came in in dribs and drabs. David only came in with one. Bob Bennett came in. Paddy came in with his crew – Gunner Gulkiss never turned up. Twenty-two of us out of the whole lot arrived. We waited all the next day. The LRDG tried to find somebody else, but some went the wrong way, they were picked up by the Germans. McGonigle was dragged to death, we think; anyway he was killed. Fraser came in, of course – he was alright. Reg was with Paddy.

BOB BENNETT

We were absolutely choked that only about twenty-one had got back from the original crowd. And I thought personally that it would be the finish of L Detachment.

JOHNNY COOPER

My thoughts were: Jock's decisions, his navigation etc were absolutely professional. It wasn't my first time in action – I'd been at Tobruk, of course – but the first time in a small party. Jock was only about twenty-four, twenty-five then, David too. It was really: OK, we've had a beating, it's been a fiasco, but the weather did it all. The general plan was alright. A great pity.

DAVID STIRLING

It was tragic because there was so much talent in those whom we lost, but we still maintained our reputation – it was a good object lesson to us how to cope with bad weather parachuting. Now we had to try and survive with a small unit, which had become smaller than tiny.

CHAPTER EIGHT

L Detachment had always been small. Now it was down to a third of its original size. To most people, the disaster of the first operation would have signalled failure.

PAT RILEY

That night we lay down, under a tarpaulin – it was Stirling one side of me and Jock Lewes the other – and there was formed the idea. We were parachutists up to that time. And Stirling was struck suddenly with the idea of why not use these chaps [the LRDG] to bring us out, drop us off and walk to the target, then walk back. And he and Jock tossed this idea round between them, and that's where it was born.

REG SEEKINGS

The others started filtering in. Stirling, Cooper and me hung around there for a day or two, and that's when I got to know Stirling. He took me with him to observe and look for stragglers. We got on a high point and lay there all day with binoculars, and took it in turns, scouting the countryside. I don't think we did spot anybody. The LRDG would periodically make a run-round to the different look-out points. Their efficiency so impressed us, Stirling said: 'I don't see the point of parachuting in when this is so much simpler. And far more efficient. We can do so much more, carry stuff to fight with, do anything we want. If we could get these to ferry us out, we could walk in, whether ten or fifty miles.' And that's what we agreed as we lay out there watching. From then on we forgot about parachuting.

DAVID STIRLING

David Lloyd Owen picked us up after our first op. He had a great deal of influence, along with Easonsmith, with Prendergast who commanded LRDG, and we made a sort of pact that whatever happened, we would cooperate, because it would have been so easy to have buggered up LRDG – they could have been jealous of us doing the fighting, because they were all fighting men, but they were committed to their task of reconnaissance and information gathering. They were the masters of the desert, and David Lloyd Owen in particular helped us every inch down the road. He's a very high-grade chap. We all admire him.

REG SEEKINGS

You felt bloody sorry about it, and terribly disappointed. Not so much at losing the men in a sense, but that we had achieved nothing. The consolation was that out of it had come the big answer to our problems. So it wasn't wasted effort. We had no success against the enemy, but it put in our grasp the means of attacking in a sure manner. Air attack is very much hit and miss. There's air conditions to think about, it has to be at night, etc. Whereas you could travel overland, pinpoint your positions and make much surer of your target than you could by dropping. And also supplies. And you could come back to a reserve. It was so much surer.

In meeting the LRDG, everybody said: 'Well, crikey, if these people can penetrate this far, why the hell take all the risk and trouble, and jeopardise the operation by a drop by parachute? Why not get them to carry us in?' It was so obvious. We had no idea that we had patrols penetrating two, three or four hundred miles behind the enemy position, and it made the idea of parachuting in stupid. And so we quickly adopted that method.

JOHNNY COOPER

Twenty-one of us came out of that. We thought of the others – we didn't know whether they were alive or dead – but I think most of us wanted to continue. We'd gone through so much, so whatever happened afterwards was going to be, as you say, a piece of cake. It wasn't, of course, but . . .

David knew we must get into an operation right away, and the fact that the LRDG could be so near to pick us up, why couldn't they take us there? We'd hoof it in, do our sabotage, hoof out to another LRDG twenty or thirty miles away from the target, and do it that way. That set-up was brought about by the fiasco of that first operation. The idea was that parachuting was a method of transportation. We were not crazy parachutists – it was just a method of penetration. I didn't parachute for a long time after that. My next parachuting operation was jumping into France for D-Day.

PAT RILEY

We took off to go back and off we went and I was in a truck with Jock, and all of a sudden there was this aircraft come up behind us, very low. Of course you had a signal for the alarm, you shouted, 'Aircraft.' And the driver swerved to get out of the path of the thing, and as he swerved, of course, he overturned the truck. Jock and I were trapped underneath this truck. We were saved by the gun. There was a rear gun on the back of the truck, and this dug into the sand and held the truck up. But there was petrol, everything dripping on Jock and I. My face was buried in the sand, and Jock was close to me, we were lying side by side. Jock was very cool. But eventually we got out.

DAVID STIRLING

If I had gone back to Middle East Headquarters directly, they would, without question, have abolished us. I think they would have been delighted. As it was, they were very chuffed that the unit had apparently been annihilated, and they were going to disband us. If we hadn't undertaken the first operation at least we would have survived for another day – probably. They wouldn't have been able to disband it. So the way it was working out was first rate from their angle.

It was absolutely essential to keep quiet and not report to MEHQ. The day after, the Long Range Desert Group took me back to army headquarters. I sent the men back to Kabrit, which was our base camp, where they had to operate without being rumbled that they were there, but they got sufficient supplies together and rather on tiptoe got hold of a truck or two.

David Stirling had always been a gambler – one of the reasons he'd been sent down from Cambridge. In a letter written on the ship out to the Middle East, the writer Evelyn Waugh described him as 'a gentleman obsessed by the pleasures of chance. He effectively wrecked Ludo as a game of skill and honour'.

That last night, in the desert, hoping against hope that more men would appear, Lady Fortune smiled upon David Stirling the gambler – but only if he was bold enough to smile back and seize the chance offered by luck and the fog of war – only if he really believed his own motto, Who Dares Wins.

Though he did not know it at the time, Operation Crusader had been halted. After initial successes, it had been outflanked by the brilliant Rommel, and brought to a standstill.

DAVID STIRLING

It was two days after the offensive had started, and there was a major battle going on within hundreds of yards of the 8th Army headquarters. The preoccupation of the 8th Army was the battle which wasn't going too well, so there was no way they could really pay attention to what was a minor detail of L Detachment at that time.

So I went and saw a great friend of mine, John Marriott, who had also been in the Scots Guard and who was Brigade Major to the Guards Division. I told this chap my quandary, and that I couldn't afford to go back to the Middle East Headquarters, because they would undoubtedly disband the unit. And when we had talked out the options, he and I entered into a conspiracy and decided the best chance was for me to go down to Jalo, and he would get in touch with Brigadier Reid who was commanding a brigade group out of Jalo, which was well ahead of the line as a whole. And he felt that what was left of us could operate very effectively from that base. And that of course was ideal.

Marriott signalled to him to the effect that I'd be coming. Marriott wasn't behaving in orthodox fashion, getting in touch with Reid and sending me down to prepare for the return of the remnants of the unit to start these raids. I swore John Marriott to secrecy on it; he kept his word admirably.

During that time Middle East HQ assumed that I just hadn't reported back, and they were rubbing their hands, saying: 'Splendid, we won't be bothered by the L Detachment SAS any more.' So during that period our existence really hung by one hair.

I met up with Brigadier Reid, and he was very pleased when we told him that, in collaboration with the Long Range Desert Group, we would raid those landing grounds which were being particularly troublesome to him. So I got a message to Jock – not by open signalling, because I couldn't afford that in case Middle East HQ rumbled where I was – to bring the boys back to Jalo, so they could travel without giving away who they were and what they were up to, but equipped as far as they could be, particularly with the sabotage material, and to meet me at Reid's HQ. And two days later they turned up.

BOB BENNETT

We couldn't go back to base, not with a flop. They'd have said: 'That's it, finished.' The powers-that-be had promised help, but everyone else was anti – the HQ majors and colonels were against SAS.

So we were all taken to an oasis about five hundred miles south of Benghazi.

Just the Long Range Desert crew, and ourselves. The twenty-two that got back, including Stirling and Mayne. From there Stirling started planning operations.

PAT RILEY

Headquarters thought we were in Kabrit, whereas we were in Siwa, and Stirling started operating on his own. Stirling was very good there. That's when he came in very, very well. He worked us all up into starting operating then. It was against all rules and regulations.

JIM ALMONDS

It was essential for the unit that some success should be recorded, and recorded quickly. Otherwise, with the way fluid conditions were in the Middle East, another failure like that and they'd have disbanded it before it even got off the ground. It was very important to me – we'd only just formed the thing and I was keen to see it blossom, and with the characters we had there it was obviously going to be a very fine unit. And furthermore, it would be a profitable unit as far as expense is concerned. If the object could be achieved of destroying aircraft on the ground with just two or three men and a little bit of explosive, then it was obviously a worthwhile project. And if it brought help to beleaguered Malta and the troops at the front . . . Because our airpower was practically nil out there.

No after-action reports exist for what happened next. LRDG took The Originals back into the desert, in a series of airfield raids. Some were successful in attacks on enemy aircraft; where no aircraft were found, other installations and road systems were attacked. On one airfield, Paddy Mayne wrote his own place in SAS folklore – out of bombs, he climbed onto an aircraft wing and ripped out the instrument panel with his bare hands.

BOB BENNETT

Bill Fraser went off with a party, with Bob Tait, and Philips, and they got the largest number of planes ever – thirty-seven aircraft. Paddy went off to Tamit and they got twenty-four aircraft.

I'd left Paddy to go over to Jock Lewes – we'd swapped the sections around a bit – and we went to Agheila but there were no aircraft there, and it was decided we'd pick a fresh target.

On the way out from Agheila, we marched for miles and how the hell we got back to our rendezvous I don't know – only through Jock's navigation. Kershaw was there. We stopped about 7am, drunk our water, we were all gasping, and we had very little water, and someone said: 'Oh, no water.' And Jock handed his bottle down to him and said: 'Have a sip.' Then Jock said: 'Pass it round. You've got no worries, in twenty minutes we'll be back at the rendezvous.' And we were. He had hardly touched his water. There's only one man in millions like him. You couldn't just sit down and talk to him. You just respected him as the No. 1. It was the same as with Paddy Mayne, he had the same effect on me. But Paddy used to get lost, he couldn't navigate. Then he'd give you the compass and say: 'There you are, you've done it again, you've lost us.' We'd say: 'You old bastard.' But you'd got faith in these people.

We blew a few communications, then the next night we took a big Lancia truck we'd captured, a ten-tonner, with a 20mm gun on the back. We took that on to the main road and the Long Range Desert crew trucks with us, going down the road and Jock said: 'Light your cigarettes up. This is right behind the lines.' So we all lit up and the Germans were coming up the road, taking no notice.

We found there was a halfway house the German used, so we were going to do that up. We did shoot it up and place bombs on trucks, and we took an Italian prisoner back with us. He thought we were Germans, and as we were amongst the trucks, he came up to Jock with a cigarette. So Jock gave him a light. The chap said: 'Italiano?' And Jock said: 'Inglesi, guv.' And stuck a pistol in his back and said: 'Get on the truck.'

We'd also captured a couple of prisoners – they were absolutely useless – with outdated weapons. One, a Libyan, was called Ali. We'd split into parties by then and left them with the other party. Eventually we took them back to Kabrit; Ali was put in the canteen there. He drunk himself silly. Completely alcoholic. He loved it. He worked away in the canteen, and the boys liked him. I should think he passed out, he was in a terrible state. The Italian was passed on for information, but Ali didn't know what day it was.

DAVE KERSHAW

Stirling detailed Pat Riley to take me into the casualty clearing station in Jarabub to get my arms done. And this is the only time that my jacket, plus the jumping smock, had been pulled back fully to show the extent of the injuries. The CCS bound it up and we went back to Kabrit and I went to hospital at Cairo to get treated. Then I managed to get cleared by the hospital and I was back at Jalo. And then it came through that Paddy had got over forty planes on the ground, so obviously there was jubilation. We're back in business sort of thing. Stirling came in then with his little gang, and he'd managed to find some planes. So everybody now was quite happy that the unit wasn't going to fold, because with a haul like that, they'd be stupid to say no more.

I went off with Jock Lewes. I had Rose with me, Bennett, Baker and Chesworth. It was an ambush type of operation. We got to the road, and there was a kind of valley and then it climbed up and the road was beyond that. Not knowing what was the other side of the top of this little dip, Jock sent me off to recce it to see if it was alright to carry on down. Anyway, my training came to the surface, and I zigzagged one or two times, but at least it was what we were supposed to do, and got to the top of the hill. And of course there was nothing there, but beyond it on the other side of the road there was a three-ton Lancia loaded up with stuff. What it was, of course, we didn't know.

We waited to see if there was any trucks or convoys coming along which we could enjoy ourselves with, but nothing happened. It was turning quite dark now, and we decided to have a look at this single three-tonner. It was loaded up with incendiary bombs, so we put bombs in between the track of each wheel, fore and aft, and as many bombs as we could in the cargo itself. Then we came back to where we were hiding up, and after half an hour or so, things started going off. Talk about Guy Fawkes night, a lorry load of incendiaries up in flames.

We decided then to go back because we had another job in the offing at Agheila. We had a Lancia which we'd brought over the desert with us, to fool any Italians or Germans we might encounter, because them seeing an Italian truck, they'd think we were friendly. So we get to Jalo, and the LRDG are there, and we contacted them and they went off ahead of us with the Lancia at the back.

JIM ALMONDS

We were allotted a Lancia which had a 20mm Breda mounted in the back, and we set off with Jock to do an airfield at Agheila. When we got there we discovered that there were no planes. So we turned the situation round into a strafing thing, and we ran up the road, where the convoys were too heavy and too many for us, so we left them alone. When the opportunity occurred you shot them up. But the chief target we came to that night was the roadhouse which is a staging post for enemy convoys along the route. We pulled in the car park alongside the other trucks outside this place – most of the drivers were inside having a brew up or whatever – and some of the boys got off and went round, and put the bombs on the trucks that were standing in the car park.

DAVE KERSHAW

We got to this laager, where all the Italian and German trucks were all stationed, and decided that this was the place to have a bash out. We scouted round some of these trucks, while Bennett and Captain Fraser was putting the Lewes bombs on the trucks. The men – Italians, maybe a few Germans – were sleeping on the floor alongside the trucks, so we had a shoot out with them – tommy gun and all that business. Jim Almonds had a Breda on the Lancia and as we started to open up, the force at the top of Agheila started firing back at us with the heavy stuff, so Jim promptly got his Breda going.

JIM ALMONDS

The idea was, on the signal, I was to open up this Breda and shoot up the cafe. The great snag came when we tried to use the Breda. Although we'd tested it in the day, the drop in the temperature was so great that the oil in the mechanism was sluggish and thick. You cocked the old gun and squeezed the trigger, and it just went forward too slowly to fire the round. When your gun fails to work it's a terrific let-down; you're not virtually helpless because you have alternatives, but it's a great loss. I mean, not achieving the job you went to do really. So we were left without a main means, so we used the small guns we had. Shot the place up.

DAVE KERSHAW

I had a bit of fun – well, I call it fun, but I realised a few moments afterwards it wasn't quite as funny as I thought, because I opened the door of one of the Italian trucks and a blue flash came, and it missed anyway. I had my .45 in this hand and I had the tommy gun slung by the belt over my shoulder and I just held the .45 up and pressed the trigger. I must have caught him right on the bridge of the nose because his face opened up. At first it was a pat on the back – that I'd won and he hadn't – but afterwards when I remember seeing what an inside of a man's face looked like, it wasn't pleasant.

We carried on, shots and bangs all over the place, and we decided to leave the Lancia now, because there's no further use for it – it had done its job – and in between the Lancia and the tail end of the LRDG truck, they'd mined all the road. So we had to come round the side of the road, get on their trucks and disappear.

On the way back to our turn-off to reach our rendezvous, we passed a white Italian truck, with little cubicles in it, and some of the lads said it was a passion wagon – you know, they used to take the women up front to let the Italians enjoy themselves, but there's really no proof of that. But as we passed we just gave it a few bursts, just in case there was somebody enjoying themselves when they shouldn't have been. We picked up with the LRDG and exchanged all kinds of conquests, because it was a matter of getting back to camp, or the rendezvous, getting the Indian rum out, which we certainly had plenty of, and comparing notes with each other. So that was the end of that job.

BOB BENNETT

Christmas came up, and it must have been on Christmas Day, the LRDG shot a gazelle and we made base that evening, and the New Zealanders cut this gazelle up. We made a little fire in the sand, and we had gazelle, and rum and lime – we had a very, very nice Christmas.

Then I rejoined Paddy and we went back to the same places that Paddy had been with Reg Seekings and others and got twenty-four planes, and eight days later we went back and got another twenty-four off the airfield with no bother at all, except that we were only using twenty-minute time pencils and these weren't efficient enough, because we were still on the airfield when they started going up.

When they went up, they went, and you had great big volumes of flame, and so we started running. We ran in a southerly direction to get out of the airfield, and of course you couldn't see anything with the light behind you, and we suddenly heard Italians challenging, saying: 'Avanti.' And Paddy was a man that if you walked behind, there was no fear at all. He could take on anything. And Paddy, in his Irish German, said, 'Freund,' which they didn't believe, and they started shooting. So we just ran through, throwing grenades and firing, and managed to get through and back to the rendezvous.

JIM ALMONDS

After two or three days we set off again, to the airfield at Nofilia. The LRDG trucks took us up into a position where we were equidistant between walking into what we called Marble Arch near Tripolitania, where Bill Fraser and his party were going, and walking into Nofilia, where Jock Lewes's party was going. The LRDG dispersed and hid up and we walked in, a good twenty miles. At the end of the airfield was a ber – an underground water well, cut out of the solid rock and set in a depression so any rainfall that comes will flow down into it. The idea was we were going to lay up there during the day, with the exception of two of us who would go up and keep an eye on the airfield and see what was happening with the planes.

It was quite dry – it had been dry for months, probably years. In the corner, among a pile of stones there was the skin-covered skeleton of a fox, which had obviously died, unable to get itself out of the ber, because as a man, you could reach up and you could take hold of the side, you could pull yourself up and get out. But this fox in the past had gone down there in search of water, and when the time came to get out, he'd discovered that it was incapable of jumping up high enough to get back through the aperture. It made quite an impression on me, thinking about its struggle, because life is always sweet and it would obviously carry on until it was too weak to jump any more. And I often thought about that fox. Many times. I felt deepest sympathy for the animal. The desire to live, the desire to see things through.

We lay there during the day and watched the planes, where they dispersed to, and at nightfall we went back and picked up the others and went in on the field. We found the first plane quite easily, put a bomb on it; found the second, did the same; then we walked around and around and never found another plane. The two planes went up in flames and we decided to get out of it and started to walk back.

On the way back we saw an aircraft. We crouched down till he'd gone by, then when we got back to the LRDG trucks and as we were about to get on board, a Messerschmitt 110 came over. He did one sweep over us and had a look and when he came back we could see he meant business. Everybody could see it was coming in. He came in just above the ground and some of the shots from that plane went right through the drive shaft underneath the truck. They were equipped with cannon as well as machine guns. It was coming in at that sort of altitude.

I took a Bren gun and Bob Lillie took a box of magazines, and we bailed off, because there was a steep little knoll there, and it was good enough protection, that knoll, so he couldn't actually hit us. The truck didn't go on fire the first time. I got off with the Bren gun, and Bob Lillie and I went to the knoll, and as the plane came in, and went back out, I think we killed his under gunner. But on the second pass – I didn't realise it at the time – he hit Jock Lewes. Jock was sat in the truck. I don't know why he didn't get off, just don't know why. He was the only one on the truck. All the rest of us were behind the knoll.

As the plane finished his run, perhaps out of ammo, the Stukas began to arrive and they systematically set every truck on fire, with the exception of one.

You could see these columns of smoke starting to rise. We spread out then, because you can't hide from a Stuka like that; they can dive bomb and blast you out from behind anything. So we scattered and I lay the rest of that day, we all did, curled up on the ground, no cover except little bushes. I thought: You've got to make yourself look as least like a human being as possible, because they kept firing at things they thought were people, spurts of sand coming up. Eventually they decided they'd done it and sent a reconnaissance plane, that went over very slowly, surveying the scene. They thought they'd got everyone.

Then night came, and it was then I realised Jock was dead. He got hit through the knee, and it severed the artery and smashed everything up; it was such a mess where the bullet came out. There was no way of trying to do anything with it. He was dead long before I knew. Bob Lillie found him and buried him, just Bob and perhaps an LRDG man.

We started to gather together again. The damaged truck came to life; we got it going. We waited for the other party who went to Marble Arch to turn up, Bill Fraser and his lot, but they didn't, so we thought we couldn't stay there till daylight, we'd have to make a move and set off, all of us in one truck – the LRDG personnel plus our party.

REG SEEKINGS

We were waiting for Jock's lot to come in, and eventually Bob Lillie, Pat Riley, Jim Almonds got through to us, with the news that Jock had been killed. This was a severe blow for us. Jock was outstanding and very difficult to replace, on training, his ideas, etc. He was a very close friend of Stirling's too. Stirling was very cut up about it. A debate was going on whether it was worth carrying on. He spoke to Brough, Cooper and myself about it. I said it meant we had something to fight for, get our own back, that we owed it to Jock to see the thing was a success.

DAVE KERSHAW

We were a unit. If anybody got killed, that was the end of it. There was no shedding tears and getting handkerchiefs out or drying your eyes and thinking: There's my best pal, I'll get the Germans for this. None of that. You took your chance and that was it. No 'I could be next'. Not a bit of it. That's all rubbish, that is. No 'If your name's on the bullet you'll get it'. It's a matter of if you're in the road of the bullet you'll get it. I didn't go for anything like that. We were given a job to do, and we simply did it. If you came off best, all the better it was for you.

JOHNNY COOPER

Everybody was the same. It was a blow, but in a war you've got to expect casualties. We were killing enough. The reaction was we'd lost one of our best officers, one of our best men. Everybody was upset. But when a thing is done it's done. He was very unlucky, he got this 20mm from a Messerschmitt. Caught them before they could get away from the vehicles. He was the only casualty. All the vehicles were set on fire. They managed to patch one up out of the five, took bits off this, bits off that, to get them back. Absolutely marvellous.

DAVID STIRLING

The successes gave L Detachment enormous self-confidence and a feeling of exhilaration which I very much shared myself. And of course it led to great puzzlement in Middle East Headquarters, because they had lost track of us, they'd forgotten about us in effect, and yet they didn't know who the hell was destroying these aircraft up front, and it was only when they got a despatch from the 8th Army that they realised that L Detachment would be coming back for recruiting and a considerable expansion of establishment. That, of course, hit them rather hard. But it made us feel very happy.

REG SEEKINGS

We'd lost two thirds of our men on the first job, all good men, lost them through no fault of their own, and I think we all felt that we owed it to them to really make something of it. And so this tremendous pride grew up. Particularly as they'd given us the option of either wearing our wings on the breast – if we waited until we come back off an operation – or putting them on a shoulder immediately. So we'd decided to go on the op, then come back and wear the wings on our breast. It was a good move because it had added value then. The mere fact that only a third of us – roughly a third of us – came back, you can imagine the value that was placed upon these wings. All the men we lost, they never got the chance to wear it. So that decision was a good one, built up tremendous pride. And so we adopted the lot. We had our wings, our cap badge, and off we went to Cairo on our first leave.

BOOK TWO

The War in the Desert

'I shall always remember him in the desert when he was young, a great soldier and a great friend.' Sir Fitzroy Maclean at the memorial service for David Stirling

CHAPTER NINE

On their return from the first operations, David Stirling and Paddy Mayne received DSOs, and Stirling was promoted to major and authorised to raise another six officers and up to forty more men, although this remained a paper figure for some time, with Stirling having to fight hard to recruit more men and even to prevent L Detachment being swallowed up by headquarters bureaucracy and reorganisation.

One headquarters ploy, for example, sought to amalgamate the various small clandestine units under one commander. In the memorandum on the subject, Stirling was singled out. 'Some unit commanders such as Stirling want to be absolutely independent and directly under GHQ. Our experience in the past has proved this very unsatisfactory.'

Amongst the officers Stirling sought to persuade to join him was Fitzroy Maclean.

During the 1930s, Maclean had served as a diplomat in Moscow. As well as attending some of the Stalin show trials, and despite the rules restricting travel to a few miles, Maclean had undertaken a whole series of incredible journeys – his goal was to take the golden road to Samarkand – brilliantly described in his book Eastern Approaches. *When war broke out, Foreign Office regulations prevented him from enlisting; Maclean therefore took the only route possible. He resigned his civil service post, stood for Parliament, won a seat as member for Lancaster, immediately joined up – Winston Churchill described him as the only man who had* used Westminster as a public convenience – and ended up in Cairo.

Despite his successes, or perhaps because of them, David Stirling still had to wage his war on two fronts – the enemy under Rommel, and the enemy at Middle East Headquarters.

It was during this period that one of the legendary teams of SAS folklore was born: Seekings and Cooper. Seekings was a former boxing champion from East Anglia; Cooper had lied about his age to join up. Whenever possible, Stirling chose these two to accompany him on operations. Cooper is often described as Stirling's driver; he was not. Stirling always drove himself.

BOB BENNETT

When we got back from Cairo leave, we had to get ready for the next operations, and they came fast and furious. Pat Riley went all round Syria, the Middle East, recruiting. So it started growing a bit from there, and went up from the twenty-two survivors. We had people over fifty years old. One chap named Richmond put boot polish on his hair to get in. And a Major Mellor, a Belgian – he was about fifty-four or fifty-five when he did his first parachute jump at Kabrit. He was a wonderful man. He'd been operating in the Jebel country round Benghazi, in the hills. He'd lived in Egypt before, and had been operating with the Arabs. He was going into Benghazi dressed as an Arab, and getting information. He was a fluent Arabic speaker. Same as Fitzroy Maclean. Speaking the lingo is the key to that sort of work.

REG SEEKINGS

We had to decide how to award the wings to the new people. It was decided by the colonel that three successful operations would be the criteria. But I said: 'The successful ops are the easy ones.' And he said: 'Yes, but we can't issue it for failures.' But it's true that failures are the hardest. I don't suppose the others were really easy, but success makes anything seem easy.

The tough thing to handle was this feeling of individuality. When you're with a small party, when aircraft came in to attack, they weren't attacking a regiment of thousands of men, it was you as an individual, they were gunning for you, and that made it very personal. That's what caused some people to crack, because the tension was tremendous. You weren't just one in a mass. When we were with our own people in small parties, the individual was under attack.

Another thing – I'd operated en masse with the army, and I'd say: 'To hell with this, let's get back to doing our own thing.' My fear of being in a mass wasn't being killed by the enemy, but being buggered up by stupid people who weren't up to the standards of training, guts and leadership we were accustomed to. They'd get us killed.

It was from that day that the fear of an RTU – Returned To Unit – became real. Most of us were youngsters, twenty years old, etc., and to come back from your first op and wear your wings on your chest, with the old cap badge, it was a good feeling. But that fear of an RTU was with everybody. It was made absolutely clear that if a man was returned to unit, it was because he couldn't make it, he was in disgrace for not making the grade. I'm talking about being RTUed after you'd been accepted into the unit. Not failing in training, that's to be expected.

RTU was a fear with everybody. Even with my reputation and my decorations, sergeant major, well respected, right up to the end of the war, it was always there, at the back of the mind, that if you really stepped out of line, there was gonna be an RTU. And it was made obvious right from the start by Stirling and later on when we'd done some recruiting, that it was no good a man joining us, getting returned to unit, and going back to his unit and saying: 'Oh hell, I had enough of those, I didn't want anything to do with them.' So we made it quite obvious, if a man was RTUed, he'd been RTUed for one thing: he was useless. So he could never boast about it.

DAVID STIRLING

It's very important that when we are recruiting people and we're having to do it in a very rough way sometimes, that we never hurt the feelings of anyone in being RTUed. The important thing – two important things – is that we get the right guy, and secondly that the guy who isn't selected isn't damaged in any way by not being selected. And we were very careful, and I know that today's regiment is equally careful. By and large it's a question of training and leadership. We were in a hurry to recruit so we had to have an eliminator, because we didn't have the facilities, in terms of time, to do our training slowly. We had to rush at it, and the operations we were doing were outside the normal army experience. It was vital that they learned quickly.

REG SEEKINGS

You've got to have people working as a team, like Johnny Cooper and myself did. You've got to have people who are in complete harmony with each other, and you go to a lot of trouble to select people and iron out any of their problems. If there's a bit of bitchiness about anything you move 'em round and find a section in which they can fit in.

Just because they can't fit in one section, it doesn't mean that they're useless. I would turn round and say: 'Look, the man's been through the mill, he's done just exactly the same thing, he's been selected, he's the same type of person as yourself, surely you can bury your differences for a couple of weeks or so.' And that often happened. Very often again, you got people who were anti each other to start off with, but after they'd been through the mill and come under terrific fire and had a real rough time, they came back the best of pals. It makes a big difference – guts, courage, is the big thing.

If you look after your pal and he's doing the same for you, then you're happy. It's the man out on his own I'm always sorry for. If you can instil into people to think about their mate... Working in a small group everyone has to get along with each other, particularly operating for long periods of time. If it was only a short op, you can bury your individual likes and dislikes for a period of time. At least you know he's got guts, etc. But over a long period of time, you've got to have people who are pals working close together. That's very important.

It became hard when the unit got larger to keep that, the right combination of comradeship and discipline. In a small unit you get the respect quicker, because you can see what each other is doing. In the larger unit you're often only working from hearsay. The larger the unit gets, the more you become a glorified regiment – that's the big trouble.

When John and I first met, we hated each other's guts. I was the country yokel, he was the public schoolboy, and we nearly fell out after the first job. We got back to this oasis, notorious for its flies – can't remember the name – we were cold, and had been sharing blankets and bedding and kipping down with these New Zealanders. At the oasis we were on our own and were issued with a couple of blankets. I drew mine, put them down, went off to talk to somebody else, and when I came back my blankets had gone. Naturally I went round checking the number of blankets everyone had, and woe betide the bastard that had extra. I came to Cooper, and he said: 'Oh bloody well lie down'. I said: 'You get on your feet, you bastard, and I'll knock your bloody block off. Big bloody mouth. I've had enough of you.' That was the only time we really flared at each other. Then much to my disgust, when I got back I found I'd been transferred into his stick. He was originally with the Colonel and Brough. We were unhappy, I'm telling you. We didn't speak, looked daggers at each other all the way up on the job.

It was the night of the Sirti attack. We came up against sentries, etc. Well, he'd got guts, I'd got guts, and we just clicked. We came out of that, that night, we'd been shot up, convoys stuck by the roadside – you could say we'd been in a bit of action – and as dawn came up, John and Brough and I got talking about that night, how exciting it was, etc., and then John turned to me and said: 'What do you do when you're on leave? Why don't you join Jim and I and Mac?' And I said: 'Fine.' And we've been close mates ever since.

JOHNNY COOPER

I suppose it was a case that he kept me alive. Reg was very strong and I was very weak. I was perhaps more scared than he was, but I would never let myself down in front of him. I think that was the relationship. And then slowly he made me stronger. His personality is something that you've got to live with for a long time before you realise how strong it is; he gets into you.

REG SEEKINGS

We set up a real team. When we first met we had a dislike for each other. I'd done a good job with Paddy Mayne, and as a result of his report, Stirling grabbed me, so I was going to be married up with a man I didn't like. But after we had an action, there was mutual respect all round. There was a man there that you didn't have to worry about your back, and vice versa. There was never any need for instructions or anything like that, we had a complete understanding with each other, we were very confident in each other. So you could do a good job, and I think that's why we'd done a good job, because of this complete confidence in each other. People do run when things get tough, it's a natural reaction. So it's a great thing to have a man behind you or alongside you who you know you can trust, and whatever happens he's not going to beat it.

We didn't have to worry about whether we'd got support from one another. It was automatically there. We didn't argue the toss about whether there was something to be done or not. 'Right, let's get on with it.' We enjoyed life. Neither of us was frightened to speak up for ourselves. The Colonel will tell you that. And from there, things just developed. There wasn't a lot of bullshit about a job. We'd just get on and do it. We'd talk things over. When you talk about the two of us, you've got to include Stirling as well, because he more than anybody really got us going.

When we were up there in the desert, it wasn't a case of officers and NCOs, we were all mates in this together, and one idea was as good as another. We depended on each other. Stirling overhead us talking once, and asked if he could come along with us. He was prepared to be just one of the party, on my idea. We used to say things like: 'Oh Dan Dare would tackle that.' One night Stirling heard us talking about a job, and Christ, it was on. Although I was only a private, a farm labourer, all that went by the board.

But it was no good doing things by the book. The enemy knows the book better than you do. It's your job to defeat the enemy, so you know more about them than about your own side. So you've got to use your imagination and do something unexpected.

CHAPTER TEN

For the next months, most SAS operations took place in the moonless period of the month. As always, they would be along the thin stretch of North African coastline, attacking from the great Sand Sea inland where no one else dared venture.

The SAS operations from this point reflect two essential things: the unswerving will of Stirling and The Originals to be behind the lines, attacking the enemy. And, even though he was authorised to raise more men, David Stirling's drive to ensure that his enemies at Middle East Headquarters did not interfere with L Detachment.

They also reflect the changing fortunes of war and the ever-shifting positions of the front lines, of attack and counter-attack. Thus one raid is on the German airfield at Bagoush, captured by the Germans in one of Rommel's offensives. The Originals had taken off from Bagoush on their first ill-fated mission.

In January, 1942, when the remnants of L Detachment had finally come back from their first successes and David Stirling had received authorisation to raise more men (at least on paper), the balance of war had tilted again, Rommel was in retreat, and the 8th Army confidently expected to take the key port of Benghazi any day. Always the strategic thinker, and never one to let an opportunity go begging, Stirling reasoned that the Germans would re-route their supply lines away from Benghazi, and through the much smaller port of Bouerat, three hundred miles to the west. He therefore proposed attacking Bouerat and destroying shipping and facilities there.

For the operation, Stirling took a relatively large group – Seekings and Cooper, of course – and included two members of the Special Boat Section, the SBS, another 'private army', set up by Roger Courtney, who had been in 8 Commando with Stirling. They took with them a folding canoe (a Folbot), and limpet mines for blowing up ships in the port.

Much to his chagrin, Paddy Mayne, just promoted to captain but the only other experienced officer left, was to remain at base to supervise training of the new recruits.

The Long Range Desert Group would deliver and collect them. It would also be the first time The Originals came across the machine gun, normally used in aircraft, which they would later make their own – the Vickers K.

JOHNNY COOPER

David knew we must get into an operation right away. David saw Prendergast, commanding LRDG, and said: 'If you can get me within twenty miles...' Prendergast said: 'Oh, I've got people at five miles.' Watching the road, just lying there counting vehicles going west and east, and tanks, etc. We'd hoof it in, do our sabotage, hoof out to another LRDG patrol, twenty or thirty miles away from the target, and do it that way. That's why they were called the Desert Taxi Company.

We left Jalo with G Patrol of the LRDG. The run in was fairly uneventful, except the Folbot got smashed when we hit a pothole. Mike Sadler was navigating. At Wadi Ramit we had to manhandle the trucks down a defile, and as we were doing this an Italian aircraft picked us up and called in the bombers. The convoy split up and we spent the day under air attack, but no damage was done. We had a wireless truck with us, so David could get up-to-the-minute intelligence, but they disappeared and we never saw them again.

Mike Sadler took us to within a mile of the target, then we split into teams and went in at night. The port area was deserted, but there were no ships. We planted our bombs in the warehouses, the sentries must have been asleep, then we found a fleet of giant tanker lorries and put bombs on those as well. Occasionally we'd bump into another of the parties in the dark. When we'd used up all our bombs, we sat down and waited for the explosions, then we slipped away to the rendezvous.

But as we were coming out we came into ambush. It was the Vickers K that saved us. I was the first to fire the Vickers K in action. The LRDG had it, and we had decided to take it along. It was on the LRDG truck on the right hand side, mounted in the front corner. I just let rip as soon as I saw what happened, and kept on spraying. Reg was at the back with his Thompson sub-machine gun.

The driver was an LRDG chap, Gibson; he put his foot down and drove us through. He got the Military Medal for it. Stirling was on the back of the truck, and he said to me afterwards: 'Young Cooper, that's a marvellous weapon.' It had a high rate of fire. I mixed tracer and explosive bullets in it. But it was an aerial machine gun, so after sustained firing, and you're not up in an aircraft with the cooling system, it soon became overheated. But then our actions were very short and sharp. We were in, bang-bang-bang and out. You didn't hang around in the middle of an airfield with five or six aircraft flaming.

DAVID STIRLING

I had to leave somebody behind who was really able and capable of starting the new training course, so I left Paddy. When I got back he'd been in his tent three days drinking, so I knew what everyone was expecting.

I went in. Paddy was surrounded by bottles, reading James Joyce. The only thing he wanted to do, he said, was write. The only thing I wanted to do, I said, was paint. So I sat down and we talked about writing and painting.

The raid on Bouerat not only ensured that L Detachment was operational again, it also set the pattern and style of operations for the next months.

JIM ALMONDS

We had no transport of our own, so we used the LRDG. Meet up with one of their patrols, who'd take us to within twenty miles or so of the objective, then they would laager up, camouflage themselves and we would walk in with a rucksack on our back, bombs inside, arrive during the night, try and observe through the day what was happening on the airfields – where the planes were put at night, etc. – then after dark we'd approach the planes.

REG SEEKINGS

The first few days of an operation were easy. You relaxed, lay on top of the truck, got some sleep, just had a good time. We used to stop at set periods, have either a brew-up or your evening meal, camp down. There was nobody, there was no Bedouins, there was no nothing. So there was no danger whatever. But as you got nearer the target, so then the tension started to rise. First you got within bomber range, then you got in fighter range, where the fighter sorties fly out and spotter planes were liable to pick you up.

Then you'd move more into the coastal belt and you started to get a bit of scrub and stuff like that, then the tension would start building. You'd move in till you thought: that's near enough. You've got to think about the patrol, not just yourselves, and also getting back. So sometimes we'd march in fifty miles. It depended upon the terrain, depended upon how the LRDG patrol leaders felt, what chances he wanted to take, just how far you would actually be dropped in.

And the first ops, naturally they were easy, there wasn't sentries on the alert. I mean, you wouldn't expect aircraft to suddenly start blowing up and a party of men start shooting you up, if you were three hundred or four hundred miles behind the line. The war was never going to touch you. And of course when it did erupt it really shook them up. They tried various means, but there is no defence against a small party, three or four determined men, getting in.

BOB BENNETT

We had khaki drill, which was an asset because everyone wore it. It was standard kit on both sides, even the Germans. So you could be behind the lines and not look any different to the Germans. Right from the beginning we were all issued with Italian rucksacks. God knows where they got them from, but they were wonderful things. You had your belt on with your compass, pistol, etc., and your rucksack would be packed with water, etc. When you went and did a job you had your escape kit – your belt and a small haversack with Lewes bombs in. It was all very light and made it so easy to go in and get rid of your bombs.

JOHNNY COOPER

With the bomb, we were worried that because it was white, it might show up on the plane, and a chap could go up and knock it off. In the end we covered them with oil to make them black. It was just an ordinary canvas, little string bag. The bag wasn't waterproof, no reason for it. And of course the detonator, the primer, came out and was attached to the time pencil. There was a little safety pin – you pulled that out, then you squeezed the end of the time pencil and the acid activates on the wire inside and when that breaks, the plunger goes forward and hey presto. The plastic explosive would detonate, and the thermite inside made the flash, which made it an incendiary. It was pliable, just like Plasticine.

REG SEEKINGS

Later, before the Benghazi raid, we'd been led to believe they'd found a bomb of ours, and the question arose about attacking to get our bombs on. They started to put sentries on each aircraft, to stop us. There was no good getting into a fight and putting a bomb on to have it taken off and thrown away. So we thought, if we've got to attack at any time or we get involved in any shooting, then we must be able to have them instantaneous. So we put a ten-second fuse on. We thought that would give us time to pull it out, rush in, put the thing on and clear off at a run.

BOB BENNETT

On the Messerschmitts, the 9Fs, you just pulled the window back, put it in the cockpit, or stuck it on the wings. It was best in the cockpit. On the big planes they used to bomb Malta, you had to throw them up. The wings were about twelve to fourteen feet high. The bombs were in a little canvas bag and just sticking out was the safety fuse with the time pencil on. So you pulled your pin out, lit the acid tube at the end of the time pencil, and just lobbed the bag on top of the wing. Paddy and I did fifteen of these at Benghazi.

Whilst Stirling and The Originals were in the desert, Rommel had launched his Afrika Korps in a massive counter-attack to retake the key port of Benghazi, and the British 8th Army was in retreat towards the Egyptian border. The Long Range Desert Group had even pulled out of its base at Jalo, fearing that it would be overrun.

The next moonless period, when it would be easier to access targets, was in March; it was decided, however, to mount a series of raids on the enemy airfields in the Benghazi area. Stirling also saw the possibilities of attacks mounted against Rommel's vulnerable supply columns, but he also saw the importance of Benghazi itself. But Benghazi was large and well defended.

As well as planning operations, Stirling was still fighting his battle with Middle East Headquarters. In late February, it was agreed that after the next operation, L Detachment would be brought up to the strength of two troops, each of thirty men, including officers, and retrained as a parachute unit, to be operational by May 1.

If Stirling was having trouble with Middle East Headquarters, however, he also faced problems with another source of recruits. A group of Free French, led by Commandant Bergé and already trained as parachutists at Ringway, wished to join him. But the French authorities were less than happy for them to come under British command.

DAVID STIRLING

I heard there was a party of French trained parachutists in Beirut, but I was told by Middle East Headquarters there was no way I could get hold of them. It was General de Gaulle's custom never to allow any of his soldiers to be commanded by anybody except a Frenchman.

I went to Beirut – I never told anyone this bit of it – and I got enormously sloshed with Bill Astor. Bill was very good at showing one round the nightclubs, so I was really done in the next morning when I went up to do my recruiting act with de Gaulle; I think in my hangover I might have mistaken de Gaulle for Catroux, because General Catroux was out there at that time.

He said: 'Positively no.' I said under my breath, but loud enough for him to hear, that he was as bad as the bloody English in Middle East Headquarters. His ears pricked up. He said: 'You're not English?' 'No,' I said, 'I'm a Scotsman. I'm surprised at you, General, for not allowing your chaps to join what is going to be their own unit.' So he revised his opinion and finally released them, after asking a lot of pertinent questions.

The French SAS were very active. They arrived in a different uniform, but they adopted our SAS badge, and everything else. They were totally incorporated into the SAS, and except for the language bit, they were the same as us, and extraordinarily brave. They had a tremendous national need to prove themselves; there was a tremendous amount of thrust and muscularity about their efforts. It was their keenness for combat, in which they rather erred on the side of over-gallantry – because we had to be crafty rather than just brave – and we tried to indicate to them that it was rather a disgrace to be a casualty, because after so much training had gone into them and after so much operational experience, it was very important for them to survive. Just how important was that training was displayed by one squadron I had which I was obliged to use before it was properly trained, and they had something like sixty casualties in one operation, simply because they didn't have the training. The other squadrons doing more or less the same thing, if anything in a more hazardous area, had perhaps one or two casualties altogether. It did indicate the extreme importance of the training.

It was during this period that Stirling acquired what became known as the 'Blitz Buggy' – a Ford shooting brake, with the windows and roof removed, twin Vickers K aircraft machine guns at the rear and a single Vickers at the front, and modifications for desert operations including a water condenser, sun compass and large extra fuel tank. The Blitz Buggy was painted olive grey, to look like a German staff car, with the monthly enemy air recognition panel on the bonnet.

In mid-March, with Seekings and Cooper with him in the Blitz Buggy, and the rest of L Detachment and The Originals in trucks of the Long Range Desert Group, Stirling mounted a series of operations in and around Benghazi. With him, Stirling again used two men from the SBS, with a Folbot.

The technique for approach into Benghazi was simple. Stirling simply drove in, with headlights, and parked near the harbour. The actual port area, however, was wired off and guarded, the water was very rough, and the Folbot was, as in the previous op, damaged. Rather than plant bombs and jeopardise any future visits, Stirling withdrew. The raids on airfields near Benghazi also proved disappointing, except for Paddy Mayne, who destroyed fifteen aircraft at Berka Satellite.

Back in Cairo, Stirling based himself in his brother Peter's flat, and continued planning. On leave, The Originals stayed in a small hotel in Cairo run by a man who bore the name 'The Honest Greek', who kept their pay packets in his safe.

Recruitment was still a problem – other fighting units were unwilling to give up their best men and officers – so Stirling continually trawled for likely candidates. One was Captain the Earl Jellicoe, son of the First World War admiral, who would not only serve with distinction, but who would lead a vibrant and colourful political life after. Another – an unlikely addition, but Stirling was clearly aware of the need for friends in high places – was Randolph Churchill, the son of Prime Minister Winston Churchill. During this time, Seekings and Cooper were promoted to sergeants.

Then they and Stirling returned to unfinished business – Benghazi. What happened is not mentioned in any official documents.

JOHNNY COOPER

We were going to motor into Benghazi and destroy all the petrol tankers which were lying in the actual basin. We had the Blitz Buggy, stripped down, and camouflaged with the German band across the bonnet. It was about a 25 horsepower, very powerful thing.

For training we went to Suez, and paired off – Fitzroy Maclean with Reg, and myself with David. We went down unannounced to our own navy and also to the dockyards in Suez. We had these inflatable rubber boats, and we motored out, pulling the oars, of course, and put the limpets on the boats. And then the next morning informed them. Of course everybody was very, very angry with David Stirling. Apparently we could have been shot, because we didn't tell anybody, and we didn't know at the time they were throwing five-pound depth charges into the water at different periods, and if we'd been anywhere near, it would have taken our rubber boat and us and everything else.

Training over, we came up with the LRDG from Jalo. We had to go with them for petrol, because the Blitz Buggy really drank the stuff. We ended up on the top of the Jebel, overlooking Benghazi, and prepared for the operation. Reg was very unfortunate. He was priming the limpet mines, and it wasn't his fault, but somebody had done something with a detonator, and this went off and he had very bad damage to his right tommy gun arm. In other words he couldn't actually go on the operation.

The operation comprised a chap called Olsten, who had been the brigade major in Benghazi and who knew all the streets, he was our guide. We had Fitzroy Maclean as the linguist, and David Stirling. That was the front of the car. The back of the car would have been Johnny Rose, who was the mechanic to look after the car, Reg in the centre and myself on the right. Bcause of this accident to Reg, Randolph Churchill took the centre place at the back.

The night in question we motored to the top of the escarpment, waiting for daylight to disappear, and as the moon came up we motored first onto this little track which came down to Benina airfield, which we were to raid later, and then a tarmacadam road straight into the town. At the top of the escarpment David turned round: 'Cooper, you're the youngest, get up that telegraph pole.' Because they had the telephone lines on it, and we had a pair of these old crushers, and I shinned up the pole and cut the telephone wires, ping-ping-ping. Down back into the car, and I was sitting on the right hand side of Randolph Churchill, and he nudged me and said: 'Sergeant Cooper, you must have a drink.' And he handed me a water bottle, the sort with the beige cover. I pulled the cork out and of course it was navy rum. Well, the smell that came out of that bottle. David Stirling turned round, grabbed the bottle, and said: 'Captain Churchill, on SAS operations we do not drink.' And he threw it into the desert at the side of the road.

We motored down the road, past the German aerodrome, then came to some lights. A barrier was down, across the road. David said: 'We'll leave all this to Fitzroy.' There was an Italian sentry guard all across, and Fitzroy, who spoke so slowly in his own dialect – he was a Scot – actually rattled this Italian off and they opened up the gates. They were all armed. And we just motored through.

We got near to Benghazi and we started to have a hell of a screech. It was the wheel alignment, affected in the desert, which was not good on this beautiful concrete surface. And the next thing we knew two vehicles were coming towards us with lights on, and they turned and came in behind us. We said: 'God, they're after us.' So we went up at the rate of knots, with David driving and Olsen saying: 'Left here, right here.' We got into the centre of Benghazi, and David said: 'It's no good, we shall have to blow the car up, they're after us.'

We went down this very narrow side street, and we could see a sort of opening, a derelict house, with a garage at the back, and we drove straight in.

Fitzroy got out and Olsten and David. 'Cooper, put a bomb on the car.' We had a lot of Lewes bombs in the back, and I put a bomb right in the centre, right over by the gear stick. We disappeared down this side lane, and we'd only gone about five minutes from there and we decided we'd try and hole up in the bombed part of Benghazi and then try and walk out, because we were going to lose our car.

The suddenly the air raid siren 'All Clear' went. So Fitzroy went out and contacted somebody in the street – there'd been an air raid and these were air raid wardens who were chasing us. So David said: 'Cooper, get back to the car, get the bomb off!' I rushed back to the car and pushed the safety pin on the time pencil, so we were OK.

Then David said: 'Right, we'll offload.' And we offloaded one rubber boat, which I carried on my back with Fitzroy. David had gone down to the wire by the port, and came back to say: 'I found a hole.' So we went through the hole and got down to the water and Fitzroy was sort of unfolding the boat, and I got out the pump and pumped like hell – it wouldn't inflate. Would it hell inflate. And then from the first large tanker, we had: 'Chi va la, chi va la, chi va la!' Fitzroy was answering: 'Mi Italia, Mi Italia, Mi Italia.' We were being challenged from one of the boats we were going to put a limpet on.

So Stirling then came back and said: 'We've got to get the second boat.' All the way back to the car, get the second boat, get it down to the waterside, try to pump it up. Neither of the boats would work. Perhaps they were on the side of the Italians, I don't know.

Dawn was breaking. So Stirling said: 'Right, we'll go up.' But we had to get past the sentry. I had a polo neck sweater on, I had a stocking cap, shorts, and desert boots, and that was all. Fitzroy was more suitably dressed, and David actually had a bit of a bush jacket top on. So we just marched, the three of us, up to the guard room, Fitzroy in front, who was going to get us through. But instead of getting us through, Fitzroy said in Italian: 'Turn out the guard. I want the guard commander. We could have been saboteurs here, and here you are – your security is bad in this dock!' And all the time David, who was alongside me, was saying in English: 'Sergeant Cooper, why doesn't he make a move on.' Anyway, we walked through and we got back to the car just at daylight.

We went into the house above where we'd parked the car, and looked across the road – there, on the other side, right opposite, was the headquarters of the SS. So Fitzroy got into the front room, to listen to any Italian. Randolph Churchill was guarding the back stairways. Myself and Johnny Rose went down to try and rectify this track rod problem with the Blitz Buggy. Then at midday,

The Blitz Buggy – David Stirling at the wheel, Johnny Cooper beside him, and Reg Seekings behind.

David Stirling said: 'I'm doing reconnaissance, I'm going for a swim.' He had khaki trousers on, a pullover, a lovely big black beard, no headgear – he put a towel round his neck, and walked straight down to the docks in broad daylight. He looked so much like a British officer, you know, we thought that's the last we'd ever see of him.

About two o'clock, Randolph was on the stairways, Rose was working on the car, I was in the front room with Fitzroy, and a sailor came up the street, went in through the front door – which we had not opened – and went up the stairs. Randolph put his head round – he had a ginger beard – and the sailor saw him and did a quick run down, went out the front door and straight across the road towards the German headquarters. This is it, we thought. But he hit the road, turned right and ran down the street. He was obviously a sailor looting.

About three o'clock David came in, full of confidence. He said: 'I didn't have a swim, the water was muddy, but I've identified two German E-boats, which are parked right alongside the quay. Nightfall comes, we'll go down there, we'll motor round. Olsten, you know how to get there.'

'Oh yes, I know all the roads.'

'We'll go there, we'll throw the bombs into the motor torpedo boats, and drive home.'

We got the car out and on the approach it was still screaming a bit, but Johnny Rose had done quite a good job in trying to rectify the track rods. Anyway, we motored right along the quay, the front, the esplanade, and there we saw in the distance these two boats right alongside the quay. We stopped the car right alongside, got out with our bombs, went across, and about four Germans stood up from both boats. We were holding the bombs, and trying to look as though we weren't . . . Anyway, we ran back to the car, got in and motored off. And of course all the way back all we could do was to giggle, because everything had gone against us. But lady luck was certainly on our side. We motored back and we got rid of all the bombs on a petrol dump before we got to the airport, and we went back through the same Italian roadblock, with Fitzroy blasting away.

That was the first escapade with the Blitz Buggy. It was a laugh from beginning to end.

CHAPTER ELEVEN

Shortly after the second Benghazi raid, David Stirling was involved in a serious road accident. Overtaking a convoy while driving from Alexandria to Cairo, he hit a lorry and his car landed in a ditch. Stirling escaped with a broken wrist, but Fitzroy Maclean spent three months in hospital and Randolph Churchill had to be invalided back to England with a back injury.

Despite this, Stirling continued to plan operations, and carried on his battle with Middle East Headquarters. He was also already developing desert sores as a result of running the unit singled-handed as well as taking on Middle East HQ, the operations branch of which now wanted L Detachment to be used in a tactical role, to seize and hold ground with other forces landing by sea or advancing across the desert – totally against the strategic role for which Stirling had created the SAS.

Incredibly, at the beginning of March, although L Detachment had been strengthened by fresh recruits, Stirling's Originals were down to three officers and thirteen men.

To compensate, he proposed drawing on two new parachute battalions being formed in the Middle East, plus each infantry and motorised battalion in the Middle East. He also suggested he could draw more men from the SBS and the Middle East Commando, later known as 2 Special Service Regiment. This proposal met with little success.

He did, however, recruit another exceptional group thrown up by the fog *of war the Special Interrogation Group (the SIG), led by a Captain Buck, which comprised a small number of Jewish immigrants to Palestine, all of whom spoke German. Buck had also recruited two Afrika Korps men who had been taken prisoner.*

DAVID STIRLING

The men were the raw material, they were the people who did all the operating. We always believed – as I think a lot of regiments do nowadays (didn't used to then) – that the real engine room of any effective military organisation is the sergeants' mess. If it isn't, there's something wrong with the regiment. And it was particularly true of the SAS. I always put my officers under sergeants when they first arrived, to get their hand in.

JIM ALMONDS

Sometimes the SAS had to leave their own men in the desert. Of course you sometimes thought: That person could be me. That thought was uppermost in the minds of everyone. You knew the risk you took and knew that it might be you. The idea was that you did whatever you could for someone you couldn't rescue. You left them with a gun and ammunition and you left them with whatever water you could spare. After that, it was up to the person themselves – or fate.

A brutal decision, but it was a decision which everyone knew when they joined. It's quite obvious you cannot travel with somebody who's seriously wounded, over probably a thousand miles of desert, bumping about in a truck. It's not possible. And furthermore, you can't be hampered with a person who is wounded that seriously on an operation, because it puts your operation in jeopardy.

Sillito, he walked 110 miles back to Jalo with only a corned beef tin, which he frequently had to fill with urine while it lasted, to drink, and as it was a continual repeat performance, it would get thicker I suppose. But he made it.

DAVE KERSHAW

First of all you had to have guts. There was no hooligan element about them. Loved a bit of fun, liked the booze. If there was any women going they'd have them. But at the same time very strict disciplinarians. I'm not talking about parade ground discipline, I'm talking about being told what to do on these jobs. I'd had a taste of the army previous, with the Cheshires and the Guards, and although I say I was a good Guardsman, I hated too much polish on your boots and being turned out impeccable, just to stand outside Buckingham Palace gate and be stared at. Don't forget, there's a war on, and that's what you went into the army for. And humour. You couldn't go around, even when you were in battle, with a long face and scared.

BOB BENNETT

Bill Duffy – only a Guardsman, with wings on his chest. He was with a corporal, Duggy – he was Irish Guards I think – and Bill said to the corporal, 'We'll go into Shepheards Hotel.' Duggy, who was a golden gloves boxer before the war, said: 'We can't go in there, it's officers only.' Bill said: 'Come on, we're going in.' Bill was always immaculately turned out. They were drinking in the bar and the colonel of the MPs walks in, sees two tapes, and immediately gets his sergeant to arrest this corporal and there's Duffy standing there, with just SAS wings. And this colonel bought him drinks till 2am. That same chap, Duffy, walked out of a prison camp in Germany. Good-looking man, got on with a German nurse – she got him a uniform and he marched out of a POW camp. Came back to the regiment after that. What a character.

We were confined to a boat in the Middle East, before Sicily, and Ginger Jones, who was tortured in France and managed to escape, was at the bottom of the gangway, on sentry, and Bill Duffy said: 'So we're confined to the boat, this calls for a colonel.' He had a flat cigarette tin full of ranks. So he gets out his colonel's pips, puts them on his immaculately pressed khaki drill, and walks down the gangplank. Ginger Jones is his best mate. Ginger says nothing, he ignores him and off goes Bill. Naval officer comes up and puts Ginger on a charge for failing to salute an officer.

REG SEEKINGS

I picked up Arabic in the bars. When we went out there, the bars were open twenty-four hours a day, until Monty came out and closed them down. You'd go on leave there, sit in a bar, and you could stay there for a week if you wanted.

Only move to the loo. They fed you full of prawns, cheeses, etc. There was an old sah major who was barman in our favourite bar, an Egyptian. I was trying to learn Arabic, and every time I went to Cairo and went in there, he wouldn't serve me unless I asked for it in Arabic. That helped a lot. So I picked it up quite well, though not as well as my brother.

My brother was in commandos, did the rough trip in Crete. He got himself a base job, and then I found things were getting rough up the front and they were going to whip all these ex-commandos and combat troops out of these cushy jobs and put them on the front line. So I saw the colonel, who said: 'Get him by all means.' So I went down and got him and my mate and just put them on the jeep and brought them back to camp. We never even told the CO down there what had happened to him or anything. I suppose they're on record in certain places as missing, perhaps even as deserters, I don't know.

They didn't get a chance to do any real training at that stage because things were bad out there then. This was when we were planning to go to Kenya, had this big convoy.

We wanted as many drivers as we could get. My brother had never driven anything in his life, but he told them he was a driver, and volunteered to drive five-ton trucks. He was accepted and they eventually reached Hellfire Pass at Bardia. You came down a cliff face, and naturally the Ities and Germans would put it under fire, so you had to run the gauntlet down there. Bob Strider was co-driver, and they got to the bottom of the pass and Bob lost his nerve: 'You take it up there.' My brother said: 'No, go on, you're the driver. I can't drive, I'm not a driver. I just volunteered so I could get up here.' Bob said: 'So did I, I've never driven anything in my life.' But he managed to get it in gear and he crawled up Hellfire Pass.

Stirling himself was not averse to a little poaching of staff when it was necessary. One of those he poached was the Long Range Desert Group navigator, Mike Sadler, who had navigated on the first unofficial L Detachment raids after the disaster of the first parachute operation. Although, technically, Sadler is not one of The Originals, the others voted him an honorary Original.

MIKE SADLER

I went to Rhodesia before the war, from school, and I was there at the start of the war. Being very keen, I volunteered for special service, just before the start of the war, and found myself guarding Germans in an internment camp. I

Mike Sadler

was learning to be a tobacco farmer, and my boss managed to pull a few strings and get me out of the army again at that point, in order to continue farming. As soon as I got back to the farm, he said he was going to go and join up. I wasn't going to have that, so I left again and rejoined the artillery. After a bit of training we went up through East Africa, up to Kenya, and then into Italian Somaliland. We did the Italian Somaliland campaign, and from there went into southern Abyssinia, and were then brought back and sent up to the Western desert.

At that time I was a section sergeant. I had two guns. I suppose there was something about mathematics and angles and things, connected with the artillery, which perhaps predisposed me, when I eventually got to the desert, to have an affinity for navigation.

We did a period of anti-tank activity, which was not very exciting because there was a lull in the war at the time. Then, as a result of a local disagreement with an officer in my outfit, they were quite glad to release me.

On leave in Cairo I met one or two people from the Long Range Desert Group, and particularly one of the patrol commanders, a chap called John Oliver, and he undertook to get me into the LRDG, as an anti-tank gunner. After very brief training I then set off down to Wadi Haifa and then across to Kufra, which was at the time the principal LRDG base.

On the way there, I was fascinated to see the process of navigation going on. I sat up at night and watched the procedure, and when I got down to Kufra almost the first thing anybody asked me was – 'Do you want to be a navigator?' I didn't at the time realistically know why, but I said I did, because I didn't particularly want to be an anti-tank gunner by then. I thought navigating would be a much more interesting project.

We were doing road watches and reconnaissance patrols and things of this kind, up to the coastal area, and the SAS were just starting their first parachute operations on enemy airfields, and the LRDG picked up the survivors from the first operation. T patrol, I think it was, picked up the survivors from the first operation, and then the Rhodesian patrol picked up the survivors from the second one. I was with the Rhodesian patrol, so we met some of the SAS at that stage. And then shortly thereafter, David Stirling concluded that if we could pick them up, we could also deliver them probably more accurately than the aeroplanes could. And so very shortly after that we took a patrol of SAS out on airfield operations in Sirte and Wadi Tamit.

This actually conflicted with the fundamental job of the Long Range Desert Group, which was just as important in a way. It was long-range reconnaissance, trying to find good going for the army, for regular army left hooks and this kind of thing, and carrying people up into the Jebel Akhdar, near Benghazi, to find out what was going on, and maintain the road watch at Agheila. Once the SAS started operating, the Germans in particular became sensitised to activities in the desert and this made the LRDG's reconnaissance function much more difficult, because hostile reactions to SAS operations naturally rebounded on the LRDG.

I was a completely new boy as far as the LRDG and navigation and all that was concerned, but I was quite lucky and I got a feel for it and became reasonably good at it, and David eventually wangled me out of the LRDG into the SAS, so I became a navigator for him.

I don't think the SAS were any different from other people in a sense. I think they developed into different people. They were certainly on the whole fairly determined and fairly tough and prepared to develop a degree of physical toughness and resistance, but mainly because they became persuaded that this was a good thing to do. I think there was a sort of ethos attached to the regiment, which was consciously built up by things like parachuting, and by some of the exploits that people carried out, and the reactions to difficult circumstances – people who did long walks to get back from operations and succeeded. And people got the feeling of belonging to something special, and wanted to prove themselves, to be worthy of it. I think this was certainly one of the major influences.

REG SEEKINGS
You were never finally selected for SAS until you'd been in action. That was the final test. It's an unknown quantity. You can train a man up, but you can't say how he'll react in the field. But a man that can undergo this hard mental and physical stuff and suffer without complaining, he's the most likely chap to survive. One chap there, he was one of the leading boxers in the world and would take on any amount of men with his hands. But the first bullet that went

past his ear, he'd completely had it. It's the people who think about it who are most likely to succeed. It's a matter of conditioning yourself for it. If you're one of those who go in the pub and say: 'Give me a rifle and I'll go and shoot these buggers' – they're the sort of people that fold up.

I always say this: everybody has the same degree of fear, it's the degree to which you control that fear that counts. And that's training.

I was most afraid of being afraid, of being a coward, afraid of not being able to face people, face my father. He was a good soldier, and I couldn't have faced him as a coward. This is where pride of unit was so important – how could you face your mates if you went under. I can look the King of England in the eye and say: 'I'm as good as you, mate, and probably better, because I've proved it.' Any man who says he doesn't know what fear is, is no good to anybody. He's so bloody thick it's not true. Training is so important. Like Jock Lewes said: 'When you find out that things are easy and you're confident, that will contain the fear.'

Also little gimmicks, superstitions – we always carried a little talisman.

I had an expression I used: 'Though I walk through the valley of death, I shall fear no evil.' That was always my expression when we got in a tough spot. Even when I was shitting myself. Chaps used to laugh, and it broke the tension. The British soldier is a good soldier in adversity, particularly Cockneys, because of the sense of humour.

MIKE SADLER

Paddy Mayne was a great chap. I mean he was physically terribly tough, and he was a very nice and kind fellow, most of the time, although he could be roused to be something else. But he was a kind-hearted man, very considerate for other people. Unless he was having a bad day, as it were. I mean, once he had gone beyond a certain point, drinking, he became somebody quite different.

As far as operating with them was concerned, one always had a slight feeling that David was to some extent preoccupied with the affairs of the regiment as a whole, and with lessons to be learnt from situations, and not always so much with the operation immediately in hand, because he was looking at the bigger scene. Whereas I always felt that Paddy was probably not taking a consideration of the large scene so much, but he was concentrating absolutely on the operation in hand. He was undoubtedly a very good fellow to operate with, because he gave a great sense of confidence that he was focused on this operation and he knew exactly what was happening in it. David obviously did too, but he didn't give you this same feeling.

BOB BENNETT

Paddy was another one in a million. Paddy was a great big six foot four inch international Irish rugby player that played for the Lions pre-war, and he had no fear whatsoever. I really think that he loved every second of it.

DAVID STIRLING

Paddy had one or two colossal rows, one in particular with me, but he was one of the best fighting machines I'd ever met in my life. And he also had the quality to command men and make them feel his very own. That's why I'd enraged him on one occasion, when he was due to become second in command – no way that I would make him second in command – and appointed somebody over his head, a very good guy. He was outraged by this, and when I explained it to him, he understood. But it was the first time I told him that he'd get a squadron. I wasn't sure enough that I was going to get my battalion establishment until about then. Then I had to act fairly quickly.

MIKE SADLER

David was not at all the standard picture of an army officer. He was such a quiet fellow that one was never quite sure whether he was actually speaking to you or not. But he had a tremendous personality and a tremendous ability to win people over to his point of view. Even when one had been on some particularly depressing operation and got back saying, 'I'm never going to go on anything like that again,' he'd only got to speak to you for five minutes to persuade you to go almost immediately on something else. He had a wonderful gift of influencing people.

JOHNNY COOPER

We wanted theodolites, and Colonel David said to me, 'Take this bit of paper,' and I opened it up, and it was signed by General Smuts, Churchill, Auchinleck – the whole lot. 'To whom it may concern . . .' Anyway, I went to wherever it was, and they said: 'No, sorry, Sgt Cooper, you can't have the equipment.' I said: 'How about this little bit of paper, which says everybody will help.' I got the only two theodolites.

DAVID STIRLING

I managed to get this piece of paper, when I was dining with Smuts and Churchill and the rest of them, and I asked for their autographs, and then I wrote in – above their autographs – whatever I wanted. And it was a very useful piece of paper. But in a sense it was authentic, because Churchill was terribly pleased with the SAS. We used to chuck his son Randolph out of aircraft, which he thought was immensely good for him, and he thought we'd given him good training. And he was very much with the SAS.

As well as seeking to strengthen L Detachment, however, Stirling was also having to fight off other bids to take over the still-fledgling SAS. On occasion, the strain began to show.

DAVID STIRLING
The local arm of Special Operations Executive, SOE, in Cairo was getting to be a lot of bother, because they were always trying to take over my outfit, saying we'd make a very handy operation team, at their discretion. I had to resist that. At that time SOE was fairly active, but we were operating quite separately from them.

Their front men were extraordinarily gallant, but they did have some rather heavy HQ, who weren't particularly active but directed the operational chaps in the field. Whereas in the SAS, those who were directing were those who had plenty of operational experience. Anyway, the whole role was quite different.

I resisted them taking over. I had to be careful. SAS was one side of the strategic pyramid, operating militarily, sometimes out of uniform but basically in uniform, only that uniform was pretty tattered at times. On the other side of the watershed was the non-uniformed operations, and I was absolutely determined always to keep SAS out of the control of SOE, because it had been poaching across the watershed. Our functions were quite separate and quite different.

We had liaison with one or two of their blokes in the desert who collected quite useful information for us. But I didn't want to have anything of them when it came to the command.

I'd had a bit of practice, because Major Orde Wingate made a blitz to take over me. He did it on rather different lines. He wrote me a long letter after he came back from Ethiopia, inviting me to join up with him, or saying he'd like me to go under him in some capacity. But again his technique of organising guerilla attacks was quite different to mine and to the SAS. He didn't understand the SAS. So I refused absolutely. Then he got going and – a form of conspiracy almost – I was always out in the desert for three weeks and only had one week back in Cairo, fending off those who were trying to take me over, because the middle regions of the Middle East command were layer upon layer of fossilised shit. They didn't like anything new.

They'd got accustomed to Wingate by that time, but they hadn't become accustomed to this amateur soldier, D. Stirling. When it got to the higher levels of Middle East Headquarters, up to the level of the direct influence of Ritchie and Auchinleck, they protected me. But I didn't want to have too much resource to them because I had plenty of other things I had to go to them about regarding effective support by ordnance and all the other things we were after.

JOHNNY COOPER

Stirling was pushing himself too far. He had migraines, he had this blacking out. On many operations, he would come back to Cairo – we were sent on leave and he'd recall us to go out again. At one stage he was covered in desert sores, and he should never have gone out. He just had the sulphur tablets, no proper medication. He wouldn't see doctors, he wouldn't go to hospital, and then he'd go out again.

CHAPTER TWELVE

In May 1942, the 8th Army was dug in along the Gazala line, on the defensive. The strategic island of Malta was threatened with starvation unless convoys could get through with food and – militarily important – ammunition. But the convoys were being decimated by German submarines and aircraft.

Malta was the key to the Mediterranean, the only threat to Rommel's vital supply line, which now stretched from North Africa back to Italy. If Malta fell, the Germans would have massive freedom of movement in the entire Mediterranean.

Two crucial convoys were scheduled to run the gauntlet, one from Alexandria and the other from Gibraltar, in the moonless period in mid-June. Unless at least part of the convoy did get through, it was feared that Malta might be forced to surrender.

In line with this, David Stirling submitted a plan to mount a series of raids on the night of 13 June, to attack the North African airfields from which many of the planes scheduled to attack the convoys would take off. He would mainly use the Free French. He himself would be accompanied by Seekings and Cooper; Paddy Mayne would lead another small team. A subsidiary raid against airfields in Crete would also be carried out by French Commandant Bergé, Lord Jellicoe, and three members of the Free French.

But there was something else.

The Originals normally primed their bombs only when they were actually at the target. On this occasion they would prime them before they went in. On this occasion there was also another not insignificant change of orders by Stirling. Normally, the men themselves were the priority; if anything went wrong, they should get out. Even if no planes were blown up, it was vital that at least one aircraft was found with a bomb on it – because that grounded all other aircraft on the airfield. On this occasion, Stirling therefore ordered that, even if the rest were killed, himself included, one man had to get through and put one bomb on one plane.

Ironically, on June 2, Middle East Headquarters issued an instruction saying: 'It has been decided that Major Stirling, L Detachment SAS Brigade, will not take part in active operations with his unit until further notice. The reason for this decision is to enable Major Stirling to train other officers who will be available to take his place should he become a casualty.'

The same day another signal was issued: 'This letter is cancelled.'

Stirling was under massive pressure and suffering from severe migraine attacks – though he told no one.

REG SEEKINGS

Cooper and myself had got back to Kabrit from another operation and all of a sudden it exploded into a hive of industry, everybody going off and looking for jobs, and for once, Colonel David didn't have time to properly brief Johnny and myself. He always briefed sergeants first. But this time it was so busy that he gave John and I so much to do on different things, we were running around getting things organised, helping people, giving advice and this sort of stuff, and in the middle of all this, it suddenly quietened down and we were on our way. And even then things were a bit hectic because Stirling was continually on the radio, getting messages out, because we knew that we'd got parties stretched all along the Med, the Dodecanese, Crete, Sardinia, and we'd dropped parties off all the way up the coast.

Stirling was so busy with the radio messages – which we didn't like, because we were always frightened of being traced, because the Italians were very good, their radio communications and stuff, and once you've been caught on that sort of thing, you were careful. We knew something was really on, because otherwise he would never have used so much radio traffic.

And as we got near the job, I said: 'What the hell's all this business about attacking with determination?' This is the instruction we'd heard him give: 'Attack with determination.' So we said: 'Well, what is this?' He said: 'Yes, Reggie, this is perfectly correct.' And he told us that the next morning the convoy going to the relief of Malta would be in a crucial position. And if it didn't get through, Malta would have to surrender.

He said: 'At midday tomorrow, if we haven't succeeded, Malta falls. They haven't got any ammunition, no petrol, no nothing. The navy couldn't do any more, and the air force, they couldn't do anything, so I've accepted the responsibility.'

He said: 'If I go down, you and John carry on. Don't worry about me, just go. If John goes down, you go. Get that bomb on, get one, that's all we ask. Doesn't matter if we get wiped out, you get a bomb on.' If we got a bomb on, as you know, all the aircraft were grounded.

And also, a thing which we'd never done before, at midnight, everyone was to press their time pencils, prior to going into the attack. We were going to go in with live bombs. 'So that's why we go on,' he said. 'It doesn't matter, as long as we get a bomb, that is the thing. Malta's more important than we are.' And that was that.

DAVID STIRLING

On this occasion we did give different instructions. The Malta convoy was vital in terms of an objective. It fitted into our strategic type of operation. The thing was related to a timetable. Crete was the furthest away, but the aircraft there had the longest range, the others were much closer to Malta. Certainly there were other aircraft that would have been protecting or bombing – we attacked fighters as well as bombers. There were aircraft available to them from the Italian bases, which were much closer. We couldn't do anything about them.

JOHNNY COOPER

We were driving along in the Blitz Buggy, with an LRDG patrol, when suddenly there was an explosion and I ended up in the back seat on top of Reg. We'd hit a cluster of those bloody thermos bombs, small anti-personnel mines, dropped by the Italian Air Force. One of them had blown off the front wheel and messed up the front suspension, so we left the Blitz Buggy to be recovered later, and went on with the LRDG.

They dropped us off and we went on to the edge of an escarpment, about a thousand feet above the airfield, looking down on the coastal plain toward Benghazi. We lay up in some scrub and bushes and checked our compass bearings for the night approach.

At last light we went down the escarpment; it was quite difficult, criss-crossed by small wadis. We had a raid laid on by the RAF at about midnight as a blind, and eleven o'clock we ended up in the middle of the aerodrome. David said: 'We'll sit down and wait until the raid starts.' And we sat down and he started to lecture Reg and I – there were only the three of us – on deerstalking. Anyway, we had our lecture and the bombing started.

REG SEEKINGS

We all had our watches synchronised. Midnight, we pressed the time pencils, and Stirling said: 'This is a big moment in our history, all the way all along the coast, right into the Med, now everybody's pressed their time pencils.' So we pressed all the time pencils before we actually went into the hangars, and all we had to do then when we got in was to pull out the safety pin. Half-hour delays on them, so we had to get mobile and hope that the acid wasn't stronger than they said it was.

JOHNNY COOPER

We each had twenty bombs. We moved forward, and came to a dug-in dump of fuel aviation, about six feet deep and extending over quite an area. We left two bombs there, and moved on, and came to some roads. We could hear German sentries walking in hobnailed boots – there was an apron fence round the side, and we were on sand.

We got up to the first hangar, and the door was only about six inches open. 'Right,' David said. 'We'll open it.' And he got in and pushed, and we managed to get through. Reg stayed outside with his tommy gun, and David and I went in. The hangar was full of German planes, Stukas and Messerschmitts, in there for repair. David went left and I went right, putting on our bombs. Right in the front was this beautiful Messerschmitt 110, with its tail down and its propellers up and its nose pointing out. I went forward, and I was putting my hand up onto the wing with a bomb, and there was a tap on the shoulder, and David said: 'That's mine. You go in the corner and take those JU-52s out.' Then we went to a second hangar and dealt with the aircraft there. Reg found a mass of spare aero engines and highly technical-looking equipment, and took care of them. This accounted for all our bombs.

Then David went up to the guardhouse, Reg kicked the door open, and bowled a grenade in. As we walked away from the guardhouse, the first bombs went off, but because they were all squeezed at the same time, it was boom-boom-boom. What three men had done with twenty Lewes bombs each . . . The whole thing just boiled up because there was so much petrol, oil, lubricants.

We got to the perimeter fence and started to climb the escarpment, and David got this migraine. It was just about dawn and as it broke, we had to get a hold of him, because he had this terrible, terrible headache. By that time the pall of smoke from the airfield was covering Benghazi. We climbed to the top of the escarpment and found a place to put David down. Reg stayed with him, and I walked on, met up with the LRDG and then came down and picked him up and away we went.

BOB BENNETT

On the Malta thing I went with Paddy, and Jock Byrne, and Johnny Rose, four of us. We went to Berka, south west of Benghazi, and the intention was to get the planes to stop them bombing Malta. We got fifteen of them. All the activity alerted the Germans, and we spent the night dodging them. We ended up in the middle of a German camp, so we split up. Jock marched for days and days and finished up captured. Rose made it back. Paddy and myself got back to the escarpment. The only reason we got linked up with the LRDG was that one of them came down looking for a chicken from the Bedouins, so we were picked up.

REG SEEKINGS

That's the story of Malta. I think it's mentioned in our battle honours. At least some of the convoy got through.

DAVID STIRLING

We destroyed about seventy aircraft on that combined effort. A lot of the convoy was destroyed, but some got through. We maintained there was no way they would have got through, therefore we regard what we did on that raid as saving Malta. It's a little difficult as a storyline when probably two-thirds of the convoy were destroyed. But I'm quite certain, with the other seventy aircraft, they would have without question done in the other third. Not all the seventy aircraft were relevant but most of them were, and they were in striking range of the convoy. I know at the time we regarded it as a major success and we were congratulated on making it possible to get those ships in. I personally view that as one of our major successes.

As with many of the stories of David Stirling, there is, of course, a sequel. After pulling back from the airfields, Stirling and Mayne decided to borrow a Chevrolet from the Long Range Desert Group, drive back to view the mayhem and destruction they had wrought, and shoot up anything worthwhile. With them they took Karl Kahane, one of the Special Interrogation Group men, a Palestinian Jew who had served several years in the German army, who was to talk them through any roadblocks.

JOHNNY COOPER

We borrowed an LRDG truck to go into Benghazi. It was G patrol, Gus Holliman, and it was his latest replacement, a brand new vehicle. We drove to the German roadblock, with Karl, from SIG, in the back, and the Germans surrounded us. Karl spoke to them in German, but they knew that we weren't who we said we were. We all had to be quiet but Paddy kept saying something in Irish. In the end, they opened the road block and we drove through. But as soon as we were past, they started after us. We blasted a NAAFI, went round in a circle, then headed back up the escarpment, chased by armoured cars. Paddy was driving. We were jolting around – Bob Lilley was in the back. Suddenly he shouted: 'There's a bomb gone off!' We heard the time pencil, and then you've only got thirty seconds.

I went over the top of the bonnet, Stirling and Paddy went this way, and Lilley and Reg and Karl in the back that way – we destroyed a brand new LRDG truck. Bob had heard the click of the time pencil, you see. The wire had been eaten through. Obviously the safety pin wasn't in position, and that click, snap, is a little cap which sets fire to the Bickford fuse, which is only about a foot a minute. So you'd got thirty seconds. We didn't half scarper. Then vroom. We took photographs of it for the LRDG. We weren't very popular.

CHAPTER THIRTEEN

Stirling and The Originals arrived back in Cairo at the beginning of July, 1942, in the middle of what became known as The Flap. Rommel's Afrika Korps was attacking. Such was the fear that he might overrun Egypt within days that the air was full of the smell of burning documents.

For the SAS, it marked a significant period.

If Egypt fell to the Germans, Stirling decided, he would shift the base of the SAS's operation south, to Kenya, and continue his war from there. For the present, the German advance meant that their supply lines were stretched, so he would go immediately on to the attack.

But the beginning of July also marked a massive change in SAS tactics, important not simply in the short term, but key to the regiment in the long term. Until then, the policy had been to mount raids during the moonless period of each month, carried in by the Long Range Desert Group. Stirling felt that this was wasteful, that they should establish a self-contained base inland from which to mount nightly operations. But to do this, they would need their own transport.

There had arrived in Cairo a handful of jeeps known as Willy's Bantams. The silver-tongued Stirling acquired a number of these, plus some three-ton Ford trucks.

In the hands of anyone else, the Willy's Bantams might have seemed just a mode of transport. In the hands of the SAS, they became unrecognisable. But to David Stirling and The Originals, they also meant a massive step towards one of the key principles in the paper which Stirling had written whilst still partly paralysed in hospital – independence.

In early July, with the Germans less than forty miles from 8th Army headquarters in Alexandria, Stirling led a thirty-five-vehicle SAS convoy, including some of the new massively armed jeeps, and also including the French SAS, on a series of raids aimed at enemy airfields. This was timed to coincide with an Allied offensive. Stirling, in the Blitz Buggy, which had been retrieved and repaired, was also required to radio back intelligence on enemy movements and positions. The route was difficult and Stirling was forced to send some vehicles back. One of the airfields they were to attack was at Bagoush – the airfield from which The Originals had taken off on their first disastrous operation less than a year before. The operation was a partial success – some airfields were attacked, others were found to be empty.

Independence meant a classic period of SAS desert warfare for The Originals. But The Flap also helped SAS – and The Originals – in another way.

BOB BENNETT

One thing SAS did, when we came off ops and went to Cairo, you had a 'Part 2' pay book which registers the pay you've drawn. What we did, we had two pay books. That was easy, that was arranged with our pay chap. So we'd come back, be paid by the regiment, say three months' pay, then we'd go into Cairo, spend our three months' pay, then go to Abasia barracks with the other pay book, and the major would say: 'Where do you come from?' We'd say: 'We just come down from the blue, the desert.' And he'd say: 'Where's your Part 2?' He'd look at it, see that the last payout was way back. So he'd say: 'Well, I can give you twenty pounds.'

The only thing that saved us was when the Alamein thing was on, and the army was in retreat, the Germans coming down at a rate of knots towards Alexandria and Cairo, and they got all the documents out in Cairo and burnt them all. They couldn't burn them fast enough. Otherwise we would have been found out.

REG SEEKINGS

Cooper, Stirling and myself went on op after op with the LRDG. It was then the jeep made an appearance. Stirling, with his usual techniques of persuasion, had managed to get hold of one or two. This gave us the idea of being fully independent. We were very happy with LRDG, but now we could operate on our own. So we started to get three-ton trucks, and formed into a self-contained unit.

DAVID STIRLING

Creating our own transport was an essential step towards achieving our regimental status. When we left the LRDG, that's when we really began to exercise our muscularity as a regiment, although LRDG always reckoned that we became less competent after that. That's not the case. Our capability was immensely enhanced by having our own transport.

I had to decide on that, because we had to be viable on land and sea. We had to have our own transport on land. Obviously on the sea we depended on a vehicle. We would never operate except by submarine or by some minor naval facility which wasn't going to cost much if it was sunk.

Even as professionals in the desert, though, we weren't nearly as efficient as LRDG. We had two totally different philosophies. They would never leave a vehicle behind; that's always been a disgrace in their eyes. What we had to do was get to what we were trying to destroy and back, and to hell with the number of vehicles we abandoned and used as spare parts. We cannibalised freely. This horrified LRDG.

BOB BENNETT

David Stirling managed to get the fastest firing guns in the Middle East. They were off an aircraft, the twin Vickers – fired about a thousand rounds a minute, with drums. They were formidable. You only had to open up to see the enemy get down. Terrific guns. You loaded them with one round of armour-piercing, a round of tracer, armour piercing, ball. A fantastic gun. Then on the back of some of the jeeps we had a Browning .5, which I never believed in a lot. It was a bad weapon. A good weapon if it was working, but it had too many breakdowns.

PAT RILEY

The firepower coming from a jeep was absolutely terrific. Personal arms – well, if a chappie liked a weapon, a Luger or a Beretta or just the .45, he carried that. So you didn't say a troop consisted of so many .45s or tommy guns or whatever, it consisted entirely of what that man wanted himself. Of course, you had three men to a jeep, and in the jeep you had the Vickers K and the Browning. On the jeep itself, you had the petrol carrier and two tanks on it, the water jug, the condenser and the armour-plated windscreen in front, and initially we had smoke bombs for when we wanted to run away. We very seldom did that, we walked away mostly. It was a thing with Jock Lewes's training: never run away, because once you start running, you've stopped thinking.

REG SEEKINGS

I'd originally picked up a Vickers K from a crashed light bomber, and got it working. It was very impressive. It was decided to get hold of some more: they would be ideal to mount in pairs on the jeeps. I played a part there. I wasn't a tradesman but I had ideas. We'd got a workshop to work for us, a big Irishman commanded it, just outside Heliopolis. I went back with a letter from Stirling to the quartermaster-general, Jeffrey Smith, I think. I was only a corporal at that stage, possibly a sergeant. I went up and saw this general, got on well with him, and he gave me a letter, to supply me with anything I needed. I played hell with a lot of colonels in ordnance depots with this, demanding this and that. 'You can't have that! Who the hell are you? Get out!' Then I'd flash this letter and that way I got all the Vickers Ks from one place, all the magazines, all the compasses from another depot and finished up with not only getting the jeeps but we wanted a minimum of two spares on each jeep. So we cannibalised other jeeps, brand new from America, and they were standing up on blocks, we had the wheels off them. This was the power Stirling had with people.

I was down in these workshops for a week or two. The springs were breaking because of the heavy gun mountings; the recoil put tremendous strain on them. When we'd asked them to reinforce the springs, they did them the wrong way round. That's why Stirling sent me. We had this workshop going day and night. Operations were planned, but I wasn't there, I was arranging the jeeps and getting them sent up. I wasn't happy about it, of course, although I was happy that we were getting some work done, and I could see what was coming out of it.

I'd told him what I wanted, and his men were working on it. I knew what I wanted, but didn't know how to do it, but they did. I was there to put them right on anything. So we got the bits of armour, windscreens from Hurricanes to give us cover, etc. We put a bit of armour on the radiator. We weren't worried so much about the men, but with the radiators – Jellicoe had found this out, he got back quite a distance, carrying all the men, with the radiator plugged up with plastic explosive – so we put the armour plate over it to protect it. We fitted them with condensers and racks for carrying stuff.

When it came to camouflage, we got an idea from the LRDG. They had a very gaudy camouflage, but it was very good. To people who hate the desert, it's just dull and brown, but for those who like it, there's tremendous colour in it. I loved the desert.

The workshop camouflaged a vehicle, and I said, 'No, that's not true.' And this chap turned round and said: 'Sure and be Christ, here's the tools. Do it yourself.'

When I'd done it, he laughed his bloody head off. He said it was something from the fairground. It was in pink, blues, greens, yellows, all pastel colours.

We worked it all out and got one finished, and took it out on to the tank firing range at Abassea to try it out. They've got a big tank ditch there, a big embankment behind it. So we took this jeep out there, stopped and got out, and I said to the major, who'd come with me: 'Don't look behind you.' We walked a hundred yards and turned round, and you should have seen his face. He said: 'I can't believe it. I can hardly see the thing. If I didn't know it was there, I'd miss it. Right, I've changed my views. What next?'

I said I wanted to test out the new springs and the gun mounts. He was sitting on the back, legs over the side. I said: 'You'd better get off, sir, because I'm going to try and jump that trench and see how far up the embankment I can get.' 'Oh,' he said, 'I'll be alright.' He didn't have any idea what I was really going to do. He thought I was just going to go along, trudge up there and into the trench. But I took the jeep right back and built up speed, so I was going flat out, way of 60mph. It was the only way you'd jump anything. I hit this thing, we got nearly to the top, we came down and I turned round, and he'd just hit the deck, white as a sheet. Huge chap, lean raw-boned Irishman, absolutely white. He said: 'Sure I suspected it. Now I know, you're bloody mad. Mad as a hatter.' He'd lost all the skin from his armpits down past his ribs – what a bloody mess. I said: 'I'm sorry.' 'No, it's alright.' It must have been giving him hell. He said: 'Are

David Stirling and SAS jeeps, ready for the desert.

there any more like you?' I said: 'Plenty of 'em.' We got absolutely wonderful service off that man after that. No arguments, nothing. They went to town and we really built up those jeeps. They'd come and pick up a batch and take it up.

When we went on our first big do, it looked then as if Cairo and everywhere was falling – and we had plans to go down into Kenya and carry on the fight. So we packed up everything, got a lot of five-ton trucks. This is where the trouble came in. We asked for second-hand trucks and they thought they were doing us a good turn by giving us new trucks. I had to convince them that we had to have things that were well run in. You can't run new trucks on hard trips like that. We lost a lot of new trucks because they'd hadn't been run in.

That time, when we stripped everything out of Kabrit, John took half the trucks, and I took half. We were responsible for the packing of the trucks, all the organisation. This is how the Colonel used to work.

JOHNNY COOPER

On operations we had three-tonners. On some operations we made a dump. The heavy section of the LRDG, their big ten-tonners, would take the stores out to a prearranged spot, because we had astro-navigation, and dig in the water, petrol, rations, etc. On shorter operations through the Qattara Depression, when we went round and did all that damage around Mersa Matruh and the big attack on the landing ground there, we had our own three-tonners which took the supplies. The jeeps drank petrol, so we had two extra tanks in the front, two long self-sealing tanks in the back, anything up to four jerry cans. But the three-tonners would take the petrol.

We could motor in okay, self-supporting, so we could split up, but once we got in to operate and to get out again, we had to refuel. We had the Bombay land at prearranged places, bringing supplies in, but we didn't have any air drops as such.

Loading was a case of petrol and water, they were priorities. Then you went for food. Each man had an escape kit which was slung on the side, in a small haversack, just emergency rations and water again. But it was very much up to the crew. Reg and I would pack our jeep, David did the driving. His batman would bring his stuff up and say: 'This is David's gear.' He was very good, he didn't bring much stuff. We went in the same clothes, came back in the same clothes. We didn't take any toilet things, only a toothbrush.

JIM ALMONDS

We started out from camp more or less smart. We wore shorts and socks, desert boots, a bush jacket, head gear, carried a beret or something rolled up, but not normally worn. We didn't carry tin hats or anything. As the time went on your hair became longer; it wasn't possible to wash; beards grew until you were disreputable, scruffy-looking people. The longer you stayed, the worse it became. Economies on water were very tight – it's not easy to come by, of course. When you do find it, it's often brackish.

BOB BENNETT

We'd go in our own jeeps, and either you did a job in the jeeps, or you left them somewhere and the men walked in to do a job. You knew exactly where you were. We didn't use headlights. We did very little travelling at night, only on ops. You moved by day until you got near the area, then you didn't move at all. You walked from there.

PAT RILEY

You had an alarm system which we shouted: 'Aircraft!!!' And you sort of hid out. We tried not to fire at any time. This was a give-away. We just stood still and hoped that nobody saw us, and that does happen. We carried hessian, to hide under. It was the colour of the desert; you pulled it over you and just kept still. Then the aircraft either started on us, round us, or it didn't, and then we moved on again. But there was always a watchful look-out all the time.

BOB BENNETT

In the daytime, we just sat round the jeeps, or under the netting in the shade. You just did nothing until it was time to move. But the desert's a lovely place to drive in – coming from Benghazi then, over the escarpment, dead easy. And you've got the stars.

The worst drive we did was near Alamein time, when we had to get right round the lines, we had to go south following the Nile right down. Then we went across a thing that was impassable, the Qattara Depression. Going along the Nile – good God! Even during the day, the sand that was being thrown up, and all you could hear was bang, bang, bang, all the way down. It was diabolical. In the desert you were spread out in arrowhead formation. We only operated in threes on these jobs.

Some of the Originals posing with an SAS jeep.

PAT RILEY

When we stopped – you know, one's got to eat some time – we had in those days a square can the petrol came in, that's before the jerry can was invented. And we used to use these cans, empty of course, and put MacConachies and God knows what into it – a lovely stew. I'll never forget the taste of them. It was marvellous. Then we'd come to the area of the targets, and we'd drop off and start on the march in. Then it was really a question of keeping your eyes open, your ears open. The villages were a nuisance, the dogs barking.

We had Arabs working for us – they were very useful – and then we had Arabs who were not working for us and it was difficult sorting those out. Then we would go into the target and sort it out the best we could.

MIKE SADLER

The first problem with navigation in the desert is that the desert, a lot of it, is fairly featureless. There are very large features, like the Great Sand Sea and up near the coast there are wadis of varying kinds. There are also different kinds of desert. But by and large there's not much that you could recognise as a feature, and in those days, certainly down in the deep desert, there were no tracks until one got up to the coastal areas, so it was rather like being at sea. You had to travel in straight lines and know which direction you were going in, and you had to be able to fix your position just like a ship at sea, by taking star charts and by plotting a course.

You travelled in a series of zigs and zags, keeping a record of it all in a notebook, the bearing that you're travelling on, the start and end of the leg, and you carry that on for probably two or three hours, perhaps up till lunchtime if one was driving through the day, and then when everybody was brewing up and so on, the navigator plotted all these little legs onto a map. One of the problems was there were no features to put on the map, so the maps consisted really of latitude and longitude lines in many cases, with a few rather vague features on them like 'camel track' dotted across, which you could never recognise for certain.

There was one feature on the south side of the Great Sand Sea, called Howard's Cairn. This was a feature marked on these printed maps, and it was a pile of empty petrol cases, with a cross on the top, a sort of signpost on the top, from which – the first time I saw it – there was a dead bird hanging. But that was the sort of feature one had. And the Great Sand Sea was marked on the appropriate chart, in a very vague sort of way, but the sand dunes were moving all the time, so you couldn't really produce an accurate picture of them.

The oases were marked, they were firmly established as positions, and the coastline was marked, and the main roads, so everything that we did was related to those features and to the problems of picking them up.

REG SEEKINGS

In the early days, it had meant quite a long walk; the LRDG couldn't go down the escarpments and hope to get back in one piece. They were our lifeline so we had to protect them. They were often willing to come in further than they did, but we were capable of walking. But when we got our own vehicles, the mood changed. We had attacks on aerodromes. Sometimes we just faffed round the perimeter. Railway lines, you'd keep your jeep back a bit, go in the last hundred yards on foot, place your bombs.

The LRDG had established dumps and we could call on those. But when we went on the big jobs, we sent Dave Lee out with a convoy of trucks and he established dumps for us, because we couldn't carry everything. The problem was getting back. So there were dumps all over the desert. At one place the LRDG even built a swimming pool – you could relax in the middle of nowhere.

Most of the time we were loaded to do the complete journey. This is why you needed well run-in trucks. Everything was grossly overloaded. We'd carry food, water and petrol. Specially water; you couldn't depend upon finding water. The oases were few and far between. We also carried ammunition; we needed quite a lot of that. It was quite an operation. And we fed well. We got on to the LRDG ration scale: it was different from the ration scale of the rest of the army. They had tinned fruit, etc.

They were really twenty-four-hour things, these patrols. You were covering as many miles a day as you possibly could, depending on the going. Sometimes you could camp at night and still see the morning breakfast stop, the going was so bad. When we went on the big Tamit raid, I think Stirling had a bet with someone that we wouldn't make it. There was a great plain, littered with rocks big enough to lift, all festooned about. It was after that trip we always took spare tyres, because we were continually mending punctures. You can imagine, walking in front of the truck in relays, moving rocks out of the way. We'd go on for a day or two like that. Then at night we had to sit down and mend punctures. And sometimes all you finished up with was a spade to get tyres off with. It was really rough going on those jobs. Good fun.

We'd dress according to the weather. It gets terribly cold in the desert, particularly in the winter months. A bright sun, but you need every bit of clothing you've got. Heavy battledress, overcoats, balaclavas, gloves, mitts. In the heat of the summer you were just in khaki drill, with a sweater and jacket, and a jerkin to put on at night. It was always cold at night. You'd turn broadside on to the wind, throw a tarpaulin over the side and get down, dig a hole usually, so you got below the surface. The wind could be bitterly cold. In the winter the whole stick would sleep together, all curled up under the same tarpaulin. We'd just scoop a bit of sand out, not really digging. That also softened the sand up a bit. And the tarpaulin helped retain some of the heat of the day – sand loses heat quite quickly.

Some jobs you could travel two, three or four hundred miles. At times, with a bit of luck, you could really motor, particularly with the lighter stuff, mile after mile. When you got into coastal areas, that cut down the mileage, because the country was broken – scrub and stuff – and that slowed things down. And also running into opposition, so you had to keep an eye for that too – frequent stops to check the position, have a look around. Another problem, as you were getting in nearer, even on good going, you tried to keep your speed down because of dust. Particularly in the mornings and late afternoons, the dust would hang.

BOB BENNETT

They started putting fences up at Benghazi, Benina, etc., but it never stopped anyone going in. Paddy Mayne and I watched the sentries walking up the road and we just holed up until they were so far up the road, then we crossed to the other side where the planes were, in against the trees, the big bombers, and just went down throwing the bombs up. When we'd done the fifteen, we just looked out for the sentries again, crossed the road and melted into the desert. By the time they went up we were a good three or four miles away, pretty near running to get out. Then you could watch them all go up. We did things you'd never do normally. We were lucky to have very few casualties. We had some, of course, but not nearly as many as we should have had. The thing I've found in life, the harder a thing seems – as far as SAS was concerned – the easier it was.

We used to go in very, very confident, with the leaders that we had, like Colonel David and Paddy Mayne, and the esprit de corps of the chaps, who had been together for a long, long time and had been so highly trained, we never thought of anything going wrong at all. Take going in to one of these airfields. The fear didn't start until you were coming out. Fear is a hard way to put it. You had so much faith in the people you were with that no one anticipated that anything was going to go wrong. I always found that after you'd put the bombs on – you were confident up to then – then it was get out and get out quick, and it used to hit you a little bit. It used to hit me anyway, always coming out. But never on the going in part.

REG SEEKINGS

The most difficult thing was getting out, clearing the area. Getting in, you had to be careful, of course, but with good luck and reasonable skills you wouldn't alert the enemy. Sometimes we got picked up and that's when things got a little bit dicey. But if you'd a clear run, going in was easy. Coming out was the problem. You had to clear an area. Fighter planes had a limited range, so you put your foot down, and a couple of hours' hard driving, you'd just about clear. We didn't worry so much about bombers. You could hide from a bomber; they were slower; you could fight them off. But you couldn't with fighters. That was what worried us. Once they pointed their nose at you, it was rough. You'd be going like hell to get away from fighters, and praying the breeze would blow your dust puffs away. We used to make for the Sand Sea, the real desert, because aircraft never seemed to bother much with that. Whether they were frightened of crashing in there or not, I don't know. But you never saw much air activity once you got into the Sand Sea. Once you were eighty to a hundred miles away, you were pretty safe.

If it was coming up to dawn, and you weren't going to make it, you'd just find a suitable place and spend the day there. Camouflage down and lie quiet. Their system was to seek out likely-looking cover, and dive bomb it. This could go on all day. So you had to be cagey in choosing cover. You had to stay away from prominent colours. You'd use just ordinary camouflage nets, and we'd use vegetation if there was any. But you had to be careful. The big problem in the desert is casting shadows. You had to break up the shadows. If you didn't, you were sure to draw fire. You had to try and fit in to the surroundings, and most of the time we did pretty well. The only times we got caught was when we were taking a chance, usually our own fault.

JOHNNY COOPER

When we got away from the target, we'd motor like stink as fast as we possibly could until there was about an hour left before dawn. Then we'd backtrack, split up, anything up to a thousand yards between vehicles, camouflage up, then go back up the tracks, brushing them out. Tracks are a giveaway in the sand: in early morning you get a dew, by midday all tracks look the same. Then you all left your vehicles, you took your water, your maps and everything, and you split up into little funk holes away from the vehicle.

REG SEEKINGS

We got into the habit of swinging the trucks round in the opposite direction. Our pilots told us this was the thing to do, because they report back which way the enemy is facing. You had to try and kid them, particularly in an area that they could have sent patrols to. It worked on many occasions. The identification we had for our own aircraft was flares. The patrol commander carried the orders of the day, with a list of what flares to use. Once or twice that worked against the opposition. A lot of it is bluff; that's why you need good quality, determined men.

We'd look for wadis with overhangs, where you could camouflage up, or scrubby bush. I was perhaps a bit different from a lot of them, but I would take an isolated bush, put my foot down and ram right into the thing, get right in, then I'd go back, brush out my tracks, way back. I might select a bush and make a dummy run round to confuse them.

So getting out, you had to clear the fighters. Either that, or a method I adopted later, you could lay up close to the target, let the air activity die down and a day or so later creep out. But generally speaking, particularly if it was good fast going, we'd get moving, put your foot down and make sure that you're just a bit out of fighter range. At least the fighters could only make about one pass at you and they'd got to return to base to refuel. Fighters' range in those days was very limited. I should imagine, I suppose about seventy miles. On flat desert it was easy to make that.

The other problem was armoured cars – you couldn't play around with them. Those Italian six-wheelers could really move; hell of a job getting away from them. Never seen the tyres changed so quick as when they were chased by armoured cars. The truck didn't seem to stop.

MIKE SADLER

One of the great worries was that we'd get pinned down by aircraft, and a land patrol would come along and so one would be between the devil and the deep blue sea. So our technique was to camouflage the vehicles as well as we could, really well – I mean, you could dig a jeep down into the sand so that it was almost flat, threw hardly any shadow, and put nets over it – and then we would get away to a decent distance, and sit beside a bush or something of this kind, and pray for the evening.

REG SEEKINGS

When you got experienced and you'd got a good nerve, you could see the fighters coming in, and if you saw full width of wing, equal width of wing each side of the fuselage, you knew that you'd had your chips. But if you could see a little bit more one wing than the other, you knew he was going right or he was going left. You knew exactly where the fire was going.

The slow ones, the CR-42s, they could turn on a sixpence, they had one machine gun I think in the rear, and he, a rear gunner in a two-seater, was the dangerous one, because he could just stick over the top of you. You couldn't play around with those. But with the fast fighters, you could dive and get for new cover, and as I say, you had time before they actually opened fire to move your position too, if you watched 'em. Probably it wasn't everybody that would do that. They'd rather get their head right in the sand. But you can.

Generally we didn't take prisoners. I don't mean by that that we shot them out of hand.

We left them to their own devices. But this one had been taken, and we were caught by some 202s. We were in a little gully and as they went round in their circuit, these 202s, which incidentally were damned good, this Luftwaffe prisoner – he wasn't a pilot, he was ordinary ground crew – was guarding my back and I'd see them coming and I'd shout: 'Come over here, come here!' And he'd shout: 'Kom zere, kom zere!' We were running backwards and forward, looking after each other. We were in complete harmony. The only thing he disagreed with was when I saw the Savoy crosses on there, and just for a second I'd mistaken them for German crosses, and he wouldn't have that. They were Italian.

Once when I was operating on my own, I used a local tribesman. They were a Sudanese family that had trekked up there many years before. I ran into him by accident; we'd stopped near him one night. When he found out who we were, we took him into our confidence when we saw we could trust him, except we didn't really tell him we were British, we left him guessing a little bit. But we said we didn't want to be seen, didn't want aircraft to see us. He was a very intelligent youngster, and he'd get his flocks out and drive his flocks out over our back trails. That was very, very handy. So on our raids round there, we'd put in a few extra miles to get back there, because we knew he'd get his flocks out first thing in the morning.

BOB BENNETT

We did a series of raids, lots of little raids – George Jellicoe, Stephen Hastings and Madders. We had three jeeps and we were going to attack an airfield and Kershaw and me had been up there before. We knew the Germans were patrolling so far in from the coast. Lord Jellicoe, who was in charge, kept going on and on in daylight, and we kept saying: 'Look, stop here, have a brew-up and wait till it gets dark, then we'll go further.' But he wouldn't take any notice. Eventually we ran straight into it. Messerschmitts came over. We dived off the jeeps. Luckily no one was hit. You got as far away as you could from the jeeps. They did two jeeps in. Then it got dark, and the one jeep that wasn't actually set alight, the radiator was full of holes. We took plastic explosive from the Lewes bombs to plug up the radiator holes in the jeep, and nine of us got back to base. That jeep was a fantastic vehicle but for it to get us back, holed like that . . .

CHAPTER FOURTEEN

L Detachment at this stage numbered around a hundred men, most of whom had been through basic training.

But as well as having more success recruiting, the SAS was about to change in another way.

As well as giving the SAS independence, the new jeeps also gave them something else – flexibility, and a change of tactics.

JOHNNY COOPER

David's great triumph over the Germans was the fact that he was always one jump ahead. Creeping in and doing the jobs in the early days, obviously the Germans had to increase their security. They started putting one man on every plane or three men on every plane, and then of course they started putting wire barriers round the outside and putting defences. That's why we changed our tactics, going in with the jeeps and multi machine guns, which we did in the latter stages, still crippling a lot of aircraft, which was very valuable to our effort. The creeping in was okay at first; after that we had to change tactics otherwise we would have taken a lot of casualties.

DAVID STIRLING

We changed our techniques, obviously we had to, because the enemy in the first place used to just defend the perimeter, which was very easy to defeat. The next stage they spread their aircraft at night against fighter and bombing air force attack. But we became more important on the ground because we were far more destructive than the RAF. So they concentrated their planes, and that was no good because it made it easier for us. So they spread them all with individual enemy posts at each third aircraft. That wasn't very successful, because they were firing at us and didn't know if they weren't firing against themselves. The whole thing got so muddled. We were clear what we were doing – they weren't clear at all.

When we came in with our jeeps it just made a nonsense of it. But there was no other defence they could really deal with, except going into the desert and finding where we were. But they didn't do so because they didn't have self-confidence in the desert proper, beyond thirty or forty miles from the coast.

Although we were known for destroying aircraft mainly, we destroyed just as much of value in terms of communication facility, firing into command posts and petrol supplies, etc.

The mass jeep raid wasn't really characteristic. It was a tactical op, strategic in nature, with nobody involved in it except ourselves. It was a question of collecting together all the jeeps for a marvellous feu-de-joie at the airfield. It was great fun, and it did in the German-Italian assumption that our previous techniques were the only ones we were likely to use.

When we got the first jeeps, Paddy went in on the traditional scale and failed to destroy all the aircraft, mainly because the Lewes bombs had their detonators attached to the bomb before going in, and the whole thing became impregnated with damp and they simply didn't go off. A dull fizz with no explosion. So we went in with my cut-down Ford car and two jeeps and destroyed the aircraft which Paddy had failed on. So that was immensely successful. Then I planned the big jeep op.

I left all my chaps out there in the desert. We were supposed to have two Bombays, though only one made it, into a landing ground about four hundred miles behind the lines. They took the wounded and unwell back to Cairo and I came back while the jeep force was coming up. Then we went and did the mass raid.

JOHNNY COOPER

David said: 'Right, we'll have a rehearsal.' We were about sixty miles from the coast, and that night we went out on to this bit of land, a flat bit we could find. We had ten or twelve jeeps in two columns either side; Paddy was in charge of one and George Jellicoe with the other column. David, Reg and I were in the centre with the Very pistol. We just blazed away and then we fired the Very lights, changed the course left, change right, green/red/so and so. The rehearsal was even more terrifying than the actual attack.

MIKE SADLER

We went in at night. I was navigator on the attack. We had a long journey to get up to the neighbourhood of the airfield, and we had to stop something like twenty miles short of it, in order to get an astronomical fix, so we knew exactly where we were in relation to it. So the last twenty miles would be made on distance and bearing.

We stopped for a fix, in the dark, and then drove on up, stopping from time to time, and David would come and say: 'Where are we?' I'd give him an idea, and he thought that we should be there, that we should have arrived.

At the last occasion he came to ask me where it was, I said: 'I think it should be about a mile ahead.' And just at that moment, they switched on the landing lights, and they stretched right across the front of us, just about a mile ahead, I should think. Really gave one quite a boost.

JOHNNY COOPER

When we got on to the actual aerodrome, we'd all thought that they must have heard us or seen us and of course they hadn't, it was too far away. We just roared into the airfield. We had the Very lights in the centre. We went down the apron with all the German aircraft parked, with the twin Vickers firing all the way down. We motored down and we turned right, went to the bottom, turned round and came back again, and then suddenly there was a hell of an explosion, and we stopped. David shouted: 'Seekings! Get out and see what's going on.' So Reg got out, and of course there was a hole right through our engine, we were knocked out, one right through the bonnet. 20mm cannon. And Stirling said: 'Why won't it go, why won't it go?' And Reg said: 'Well, don't get out and look, but we haven't got an engine.'

We baled out on to Sandy Scratchley's – he'd just had his rear gunner killed – and we put a Lewes bomb under the jeep. The photographs that morning were thirty-eight aircraft destroyed, and the Germans were already dragging the wrecks away with their Caterpillars. We were the only jeep to be hit. Fortunately we weren't hurt, but it was act of God perhaps that we were missed.

MIKE SADLER

My role, after I'd navigated them in, was to stay on the south side of the airfield while the raid took place, to be a focal point for people to come back to if they got knocked off a jeep or anything like that, or their jeep was knocked out. We were to wait there after the raid, until shortly before daylight, in case anybody did make their way back to the jeep. So once the raid was over, they dispersed and we stayed on. This was a worrying experience, because one knew that there would be a hornet's nest round in the morning. We were greatly relieved when it began to get light, to find that there was quite a thick fog. So we set off to the south, and after a while found ourselves driving down a track, and we drove through a column of Germans who were presumably out looking for us. We approached them from the rear and drove past them, and they took no steps.

They must have thought that we too were Germans. And we just drove on into the desert at an ever-increasing speed, until the sun rose, in fact. I suppose we got on several miles more and then we camouflaged our vehicles in a little wadi, and settled down there – Jim Almonds was there as well – and prepared to spend a very unpleasant day.

One of the great worries that we had in these situations was that we would get pinned down by aircraft and a land patrol would come along. And we were picked up on this occasion from the air by a flight of Stukas who dived down several times at us, but they didn't fire, thank goodness. And then they flew away. And when we stood up to have a look round, we saw the reason – just the other side of the ridge we were hiding against, there was a German recovery team collecting broken-down vehicles out of the desert, so I think they must have associated us with the German recovery team. We were very lucky to get away from that one.

As well as The Originals, a number of French SAS also took part in the jeep attack. On the way out, however, three of the French jeeps were attacked by Stukas. All three vehicles continued to operate, but one Frenchman, Andre Zirnheld, was killed. The French SAS buried him in the desert. Andre Zirnheld was one of the first to join the French SAS. He was an intellectual, with a strong sense of duty. A 'militant' before the war, he had taught philosophy, joined the army as a sergeant but, frustrated with inactivity, he joined the Free French, then the French SAS. Among his possessions, his French colleagues found a poem which he had written. It is included here as a tribute to the SAS who fought and died in the desert, and out of respect to a man whom The Originals considered a brother in arms:

> I bring this prayer to you, Lord,
> For you alone can give
> What one cannot demand but from oneself
>
> Give me, Lord, what you have left over,
> Give me what no one else asks you for
>
> I don't ask you for rest,
> Or quiet,
> Whether of soul or body:

I don't ask for wealth,
Not even for success, or even for health perhaps,

That sort of thing you get asked for so much
That you can't have any of it left

Give me, Lord, what you have left over,
Give me what no one wants from you

I want insecurity, anxiety,
I want storm and strife,
And I want you to give me these
Once and for all,

So that I can be sure of having them always
Since I shan't have the courage
To ask you for them

Give me, Lord, what you have left over,
Give me what the others want nothing to do with

But give me strength too,
And strength and faith;

For you alone can give
What one cannot demand but from oneself

CHAPTER FIFTEEN

After the jeep raid on the airfield at Sidi Haneish, near Fuka, Stirling planned to remain in the desert and continue his raiding; four groups were sent out to attack German supply dumps and transport lines, and requests were made for re-supply by air. Stirling had already requested another thirty jeeps. Then he was ordered to return to base with his entire force. The Bombays he had requested would bring only enough fuel for the jeeps to be driven back to Kabrit; the majority of the men would fly back. Stirling protested but Middle East Headquarters was adamant.

The latest Allied offensive along the Alamein line had failed, Churchill had ordered a change of command, and Montgomery was now in command of the 8th Army.

After his previous trips to Benghazi, Stirling had submitted proposals to destroy, once and for all, the harbour facilities there. One suggestion was to take a small naval party and scuttle a ship across the harbour mouth. Stirling had discussed it with a Colonel Hazelden, and whilst Stirling was in the desert, Hazelden had sold the idea to the planners at Middle East HQ, where the project had developed into a large-scale assault, which violated every principle of SAS – a force of over 200 men, including soldiers from other units, and a convoy of forty-five jeeps, three-tonners, and two tanks to force their way through roadblocks. The route also meant travelling 1,400 miles. In return, the offer was that Stirling's unit would be expanded and that he would be given free rein to attack German supply routes along the coast.

Whether the unit would be expanded by MEHQ is another matter, but whilst the Benghazi raid was being planned, Lady Luck again intervened on Stirling's behalf. At the time, Winston Churchill was in Cairo. For no apparent reason, although the previous involvement of Churchill's son Randolph may have something to do with it, Stirling and Fitzroy Maclean were invited to dine with the Prime Minister and other luminaries at the British embassy. After the meal, Stirling enjoyed a private conversation with Churchill. The following morning he received a note from Churchill's private secretary asking for a short note 'on what you would advise should be done to concentrate and coordinate the work you are doing'. Stirling replied immediately. That evening, he again dined at the embassy.

Then he turned his attention to Benghazi.

DAVID STIRLING

They bribed me. I put in a plan before I went out on the previous operations. What I aimed to do on the following operation was to destroy all the petrol depots and all the facilities back to Benghazi. That was the crucial point from my angle, to destroy all the supply depots between there and the frontier area at Bardia, to frustrate the Germans' capacity to mount the offensive. Because they were coming in to attack at El Alamein.

JOHNNY COOPER

To my mind, it wasn't a typical SAS operation – we were too big, too many outsiders, the length of approach. We even took two Honey tanks down to Kufra – they never started the operation. The idea was to get at the naval craft. We had all sorts of people, naval people, submariners – it wasn't an SAS operation, more of a commando combined services thing. They knew we were there – it was said there'd been a leak back in Cairo and so they knew we were coming.

REG SEEKINGS

There was a lot of controversy about this, because it was an operation on such a large scale. The main party going into Benghazi was more like a regimental or brigade attack, and a lot of people disagreed with it. But the thing was, we had a job to do, and that job was to occupy the rear echelon and draw the troops from the front line. So anything we did, didn't matter how we did it – I think myself was justified.

But the bloody thing was leaked. No two ways about that. They were waiting for us. If it hadn't been leaked, we could have walked in as we'd done before. We weren't picked up by reconnaissance going in, but they KNEW we were coming in. Not the exact day, there are too many imponderables to decide that, but they were alerted. There was too much talk in Shepheards Hotel in Cairo, and places like that. Some people even felt that they'd been deliberately leaked, which I don't think for one minute it had, but it certainly appeared to the ordinary soldier that something had. But it was picked up from headquarters people talking out of place. We had one or two loose mouths in those days, not too bright.

JOHNNY COOPER

It was a feat getting to the area. We had 1,200 miles before we got to our target – we went right down the Nile, then crossed to Karga, still in Egypt, then across the border and down to Kufra. We took that from the Italians. From there we had to go right through the Sand Sea, right up to Jalo, and retook Jalo. Then up to Benghazi.

REG SEEKINGS

It was the toughest job. A big job. It was fantastic how we moved a force like that. There was such a lot to do; we'd been held up by this and that. We were working right up to the minute the convoy moved off – loading magazines, which was a big job. And also we hadn't got supplies up. We had bombs to make up – a tremendous amount of work. So we had to work against the clock.

We moved out, we drove all that day, practically all night, and stopped in the early hours of the morning for a couple of hours' sleep. We had to have sentries, not because of fear of attack, but to make sure somebody was awake. It was hard going. When Stirling said 'Move' we moved, whatever was happening. That's where I got the reputation of being a rough tough so-and-so. I kicked men on to their feet, belting them. They were falling asleep.

One night, it was midnight. I'd got my lot down. And come what may we were moving. They made me orderly sergeant that night and I made a roster and called the chaps up. 'Oh, I was on last night.' I said: 'I couldn't give a monkey's whether you were on five minutes ago, you're on now. OK? Anything you want to do about it?' 'Oh, well.' I said: 'Don't argue with me, boy. I'll flatten you, fast. Get on duty. I've got no time to mess around.' And that's how we carried it out. Crude and cruel, but the only way to do it.

So we had a roster and big Pat Riley – well, he can handle himself. We got to know each other in a boxing ring. Pat and I both had our own vehicles and we got the job – self-appointed – of marshals. We just saw the convoy stuck together. It was fantastic to see people driving there, asleep. How they didn't prang, I don't know. How many vehicles in the convoy? I don't know, a lot –

sixty or seventy perhaps. More. They nearly all got burnt out. We stopped here and there for a quick nap, otherwise it was just drive-drive-drive. Stirling drove us on – it was really hard.

He'd radioed back, vehicles proceeding in such and such a direction. I went round and found Pat. He'd dropped off to sleep. So I woke him up and shot off, and for about an hour I circled this bloody great convoy, and couldn't find Pat. Where the hell is he? Eventually I caught up with him – he was going in the opposite direction!

JIM ALMONDS

Everyone thought it was too big to be successful, although it was very well laid on – they went to endless trouble to ensure that. We had a plan of Benghazi, a plan of the harbour, and we all had our own tasks. David Stirling gave me the task of getting down first and foremost into the town as quickly as possible, to the cathedral mole, a stone jetty, in the harbour, and take over a tugboat which was tied there. I was to take this tugboat to the outer mole where there was a ship tied up, and block the harbour by warping the ship round across the harbour mouth and scuttling it. It would have sealed the harbour off, because they were bringing in supplies for Rommel on the front. In the jeep I carried all the charges ready made up, limpet mines and so on, for all parts of the ship.

PAT RILEY

The thing was to get through this little gap near Siwa. We wanted to strike that when the sun was at its height. In other words, you got mirages going all the time, and consequently you couldn't be seen. We did this, but we were picked up by aircraft as we got in, nearer to the target, and for some unknown reason – we should have dropped to it, really – that aircraft didn't attack us. It just circled from a distance around and we went on quite unaware of what was happening.

I'll always remember the picture of going along towards the Jebel. It was rather like one of these Gold Rush jobs, you know, where the horses are racing to get to the target first. There was a fort. Bob Mellor, who was a Belgian, and Johnny Rose were sent to take it, which they did and that gave us a clear passage to get down. An Arab was guiding us down the Jebel, and finally we went into Benghazi.

REG SEEKINGS

We made our way with a lot of difficulty through the escarpment above Benghazi. We got there and made our way down. Bob Mellor had been given the job of taking the fort there, and this is typical of how the colonel worked: he gave him twenty minutes to capture the fort. He took it, but in the process got hit very badly two or three times in the guts. We got him out and back.

JIM ALMONDS

Our approach into Benghazi was to be camouflaged by an air raid by our people on the town. When we finally arrived at Benghazi, a lot of our stealth had been blown because we had this little scrap with a fort before we got into town, and the air raid which we were going in under the cover of had long since finished – in fact it was getting dangerously close to dawn. We arrived at this lane leading up from the desert into the town, and then it became barbed wired either side, so you couldn't turn off the lane, and eventually we came up to a road barrier, which was a single pole across the road. And David Stirling went forward with Bill Cumper.

REG SEEKINGS

The SAS drivers were all picked for their ability to drive fast without turning the jeep over and the first few were going to go straight in. I was going to take the lead and tear round the streets, blasting up the town, to make the Ities and Jerrys really get their heads down.

Then Bill Cumper went forward, and those famous last words he actually did say: 'Let battle commence.' A real Cockney was Jim. And battle did commence good and proper.

JIM ALMONDS

I was in the leading jeep because I had to get down to the harbour. I had on the back a person who lived in Benghazi and knew the town well. He was going to guide me down to the cathedral mole. David said: 'Are you alright?' 'Yeah, OK.' 'Right ho, carry on.' So I drove on down the road, with the lights on, and in the front I saw another roadblock, which was two concrete pillboxes and a big heavy chain stretched across between them. I suppose I got to within about forty to fifty paces of this when the firing started and my jeep was hit; it was out of action. Later I'm told it burnt out. And with all that explosive on board, it wasn't a safe place to be.

BOB BENNETT

There was an avenue of trees and we were advancing with the armoured jeeps, three-tonners at the back, and all of a sudden all hell let loose. What had happened, they were waiting for us in ambush position. Jim Almonds' was the first jeep through and he was hit. Everybody was trying to get out then, jeeps going everywhere. Paddy had lost his jeep. Bill Cumper had lost his. Bill was the coolest man you could ever meet. With all this shooting going on, he's lying on his elbow, saying: 'I don't know, somebody runs over my foot and now I get shoved off my jeep.'

REG SEEKINGS

A chap named Drungeon, and another chap, they were in a jeep. I was talking to him when the first bursts of fire hit him. He was knocked off the jeep, I went down with him, and that's when they thought I'd copped it as well. The armours had gone through the roadblock, the fire hit Jim, turned him over, set his jeep on fire immediately. I got Drungeon up and it'd gone all through his hips, shot his penis off. And Doug Beard had his arm blown to hell. I loaded those two up into the vehicle.

Stirling was out directing things, smoking his pipe – he never smoked it, just chewed good pipes up much to my disgust. I used to smoke his tobacco, never got the chance to pinch a pipe off him – and I said to him: 'What are we going to do?' He was a bit niggly with me, and I said: 'Well, I want to know. Are we going through?' I didn't know whether we were still going to push it. He said: 'No, get the convoy turned round and we'll have a go another day.'

PAT RILEY

Jim Almonds was up in front, and all of a sudden his jeep went up in a burst of flames, and I saw Jim sort of collecting himself the best he could and running for it. They had been waiting for us. And we had a right good old scuffle as we tried to get ourselves out of it as best we could. Stirling was in the middle of it. I was a sergeant when I first joined SAS, then Yeats, the RSM, went in the bag. And in the midst of all this, with the vehicles and everything burning all round the bloody place, Stirling said: 'You're my RSM from now on.' I said: 'Well, let's get to hell out of this first.'

REG SEEKINGS

My driver was a chap named David Lee. His father was superintendent of police in Shanghai: born and bred out there, he was, a gentleman. Beautiful cultured accent. Errol Flynn wasn't a patch on him. Davie would not show any fear. He must have experienced fear, he was an intelligent man, but he wouldn't show it.

Never back down to a German. Air attack or anything, he would not take cover. I said to Davie: 'Take the wheel, I'll take the guns, let's get the convoy turned back.' His guns were still firing like hell: they were masked behind blankets, you couldn't see them properly. I said: 'Turn round, for Christ's sake, I didn't say attack.' He said: 'Don't get a flap on, I'm turning round' – and drove right up in to the area where the enemy guns were, reversed and drove back.

JIM ALMONDS

I didn't see that the jeep was on fire. The rear gunner bailed out, I don't know where the guide had gone, and there was Maggie McGinty and myself in the front of the jeep. I said to Maggie, 'Give 'em hell, Maggie,' and he opened up with his Vickers, and all hell broke loose from all sides. Fletcher, the rear gunner, went under the barbed wire fence. I said, 'Bail out,' and told Maggie McGinty to get back as best he could to the main party behind me. Everybody was firing by this time – the place was alive with strings of tracer and so on. I dashed through over this fence.

REG SEEKINGS

We turned the convoy round, got it back, and just as we were leaving the area, I saw a movement out of the corner of my eye and there was Bill Cumper – scuttling along on hands and knees. I shouted to him and he said: 'You're a mad lot of bastards, this is no place for me.' I loaded him on the back of the vehicle and he was with us till dawn broke. I saw a truck we'd left during the night – the sump had gone – and I said to Dave: 'Let's go to the truck and blow it up.' Poor old Bill, he said: 'I trained you too bloody well – forget the bloody truck and get us back.' I said: 'No, we must blow it up.' So we did.

JIM ALMONDS

I got under this fence and was looking for Fletcher, and I found him – he was hiding under a tree in the shade, because there was still a bit of shade cast by these trees. I then noticed that the party had turned round, best they could, in this lane, and the sound of the vehicles was dying away.

There was a section coming forward, extended order, with an officer and I said to Fletcher: 'We'd better move quick.' We both had a pistol. I said: 'I think the chances are fairly hopeless but I'll leave it up to you. I can stand up and say, "Here we are", or . . .' He said: 'Do what you think's best.' I said to Fletcher: 'Well, if they catch us like this' – they were advancing in extended order, searching the ground – 'If they catch us like this in the tree, we're going to be shot or bayoneted before we've got a chance to do anything. Our only chance is for me to stand up, if you're agreeable, and say, "Right, we're here", and we'll see what happens.' That's what I did. I stood up and said: 'Here we are.' In English. And they closed in and the Italian officer in charge of the party pushed the bayonets aside and said 'Stop' and we were in the bag.

PAT RILEY

Greasy Bird was hit. I picked him up and got on the jeep. As we got to the Jebel, the aircraft were coming over us. I took Greasy Bird off the jeep and ran to look for cover, to get the hell out of it. We were staggering along, and all of a sudden Greasy fainted, and he couldn't have fainted at a better time. Down I went with him, and at that point an aircraft came in and he certainly gave us a reception. But anyway we got up the Jebel eventually. The French put up a good show there; the French were with us, they put up a hell of a show.

It was a dramatic scene happened there. We had three parties that went up; there was a medical orderly with each party and a doctor, Dr Pleydell. It was decided that with all the wounded we'd got, the best thing we could do was to send them into Benghazi or get them taken in some way or other. Stirling and Doc Pleydell had obviously been talking together, and it was decided that one of the medical orderlies would stay behind and go in to the German or the Italian, whichever he came across first, and would say that these boys were wounded, and would you take 'em in.

You can just picture the scene really. All the trucks that we had there were burning all round us, and Pleydell got these three orderlies round him and they were to draw straws for who stayed behind. And this chap Ball drew the short straw. We cannibalised the vehicles and tried to get all the petrol and stuff we could, then we left him on the jeep, which we could ill afford, and we asked him to give us some time to get away, and we set off as best we could.

REG SEEKINGS

I was running around picking up stray survivors and whatnot all over the place, and by the time I got back to the main base, back in the escarpment, they had been bombed up. For several hours they had nothing less than twenty aircraft of different descriptions overhead. Paddy had taken the main group out, and he'd had to leave the wounded, some very badly wounded chaps, behind.

They left a medical orderly there, and the medical orderly's instructions had been that when it got dusk, he was to go in and try and make contact with a German or Italian patrol, and bring them in. But what he had done, he had put up a sign, a Red Cross sign, marked a big one out, using sheets and material, and made this on the hillside.

I came in with – I don't know what I had, a dozen-fifteen men I'd picked up – and we needed vehicles, we needed petrol and supplies. The place was littered with unexploded bombs and time bombs, all sorts of things, burnt-out trucks, and from the burnt-out trucks we managed to siphon off quite a lot of petrol. These jerry cans, they'd expanded like big footballs, but when they'd cooled down there was still petrol inside. And we were getting all this stuff out. This is when I really came across the wounded, and amongst those was two or three officers, new to the game, good chaps, and also one chap, a sub conductor as they call them in the REME, he was a friend of mine from this workshop. He had actually taken leave to come up, because the army wouldn't let him come up there officially, so he used his leave to come and attach himself to us. I done the wangling on that. Unfortunately during the night drive in, we was behind all the time, and he got thrown off and got a broken thigh, and during all this attack he was laying there helpless out in the open, and he got hit by cannon fire in the other leg, and he was naturally in a very bad state.

I got hold of this orderly and told him if he didn't bring the damned Red Cross in, that I would shoot him. That I'd got all these men safe and sound. I'd got to get them out, and I needed time. And what he was doing, all that would happen was the bombers would pick it up and they'd come in and they'd carry on their bombing if they saw activity in there. They couldn't land from the damned aircraft anyway, and he was to obey instructions. Well, I was called back by I think it was a major, and he said: 'Sergeant, you've got men here that are dying if they don't get help.' And this friend of mine, he said: 'That's right, Reg.' 'We'll die if we don't get help quick.' So I had to turn round and make the hardest little speech I'd ever made in my life.

I said: 'I'm sorry, you've had it. You're just numbers. I've got twelve to fourteen men there. They're fit, they're ready to fight another day. If I can get 'em clear, they can carry on fighting. You can't. I'm sorry.'

That was the hardest thing I ever had to do in my life. And I walked away, and my pal started to call me Sergeant then. He was disgusted with me.

I hated doing it, absolutely hated it, but it was my job. If you're doing a hard job and a tough job, you've got to be hard and tough yourself. You've got to make yourself callous, otherwise you're not going to survive, you'll go round the bend. You have to make these hard decisions. Which is more important? These men were maimed; it was going to be dicey whether they could survive being picked up and carted a considerable way out of the hills and on to transport. Whereas I had this, say, dozen or fourteen men, I forget the exact figure, but it was a minimum of a dozen. I had those, and that's a good fighting force. After all, what's it all about? Winning a war, isn't it? So you've got to do these sort of things.

And as I walked away, the major called me back and he apologised and said: 'You're perfectly right, Sergeant. I'm sorry, my apologies, carry on.' And my pal then apologised. So we went on and got all the stuff together, and that night when dusk came on, we moved out and a day later we caught up with Paddy Maine and saved the men.

JIM ALMONDS

The next day we were put on a flat truck and paraded round the town, to show the people what happened to people who attempted these sort of raids. I thought we were in a bad way. We were chained up, two hands chained down to one foot. There was not much you could do. They made a tableau out of us – a caribinieri standing behind with the muzzle of a gun against your head – presumably a morale booster. For them, not for me.

We were kept in that condition for about two weeks. I was getting a bit worried because they didn't say we were prisoners of war. They didn't say anything.

They interrogated us at HQ, a couple of battalion officers firing questions at us. Their method of interrogation varied enormously. Sometimes we were browbeaten and bullied and threatened, and so on. I just gave my rank and number and that was it. They really got annoyed about that. One night they changed tactics: 'Oh, you look a bit of a mess, would you like a bath?' 'Yeah, rather.' So I had a hot bath, they laid on a meal, cigarettes, etc. And although they didn't get what they want, I got a jolly good meal out of it. Then we were questioned again then put back into the lean-to shed they kept us in. Another man was brought in – a Scotsman to all intents and purposes. He was the snoop; see what he could get out of us.

Some long time passed before we knew we'd been accepted as POWs. Eventually they put us in a prison camp in Benghazi town and in due course we were put on board a ship. We were kept separate from the others. We were in the forepeak of the ship, which had taken a bomb at some time, and there were holes through the side of the forepeak with wooden plugs knocked in. We found a plug we could take out, above the water line, and we could see out where we were going. We didn't go straight to Italy, it was first to Greece and through the Corinth Canal to Patras, then to Taranto. There we were put into a shearing shed – took off all your hair, beard, etc. – and went to a prison camp at Altamura.

CHAPTER SIXTEEN

Whether by the intervention of Winston Churchill, or as the result of a feud within Middle East Headquarters between the Director of Military Operations and the Director of Combined Operations over control of raiding forces, Lady Luck was about to smile again on David Stirling.

In September, in a paper on the future of special units in the Middle East, General Alexander's Chief of Staff wrote to his superior:

'The personality of the present commander, L Detachment SAS Brigade, is such that he be given command of the whole force with appropriate rank. In view of this I make the following suggestion. That L Detachment SAS Brigade, 1 SS Regiment, Special Boat Section, should all be amalgamated under L Detachment SAS Brigade and commanded by Major D Stirling with the rank of lieutenant colonel.'

On September 28, 1942, a little over a year after David Stirling had used his crutches to scale the fence of Middle East Headquarters, Operational Instruction No. 14,521 from the very same organisation confirmed the raising of the SAS to full regiment status within the British Army, to be called 1 SAS Regiment.

The new regiment would have four combat squadrons – 'A', 'B', the Free French (later 'C' Squadron) and the Folbot Section (the SBS, later 'D' Squadron).

At the same time, David's brother Bill formed 2 SAS.

Recruitment, however, was still difficult. When Stirling visited General

Montgomery to request that he select 150 men from the 8th Army, he was turned down. The only consolation for Stirling was that he lunched in Montgomery's personal mess and ran up a massive drinks bill on the teetotaller's account. But Lady Luck was about to turn her back on Stirling.

DAVID STIRLING

My brother Bill had a unit of small-scale raiding forces, and I wrote to him, saying what about using it as a base for a second SAS, because I'd had full regimental status by then. He thought that a good wheeze and the last letter I got from him – I think it was the only two letters we wrote to each other – said that it had been confirmed that he'd got 2 SAS established.

I had to have French and Greeks, because I knew there were going to be the two main theatres, one a continuing one in the Middle East, and the Second Front in Europe, and we had to be in both.

In the eastern Mediterranean, we had to have the Greek Sacred Squadron. The Greeks had been invaluable contacts with their knowledge of the area. Remember that we always had to be able to arrive at the scene of a target area by any means open to us, and sometimes it was by sea, sometimes it was by land, or by air, by parachute. We had to be capable of using all three methods, otherwise we would have been truncated as an SAS strategic force. And therefore I hoped that in the Mediterranean base, the Greek Sacred Squadron would be of great value, and it would also require special emphasis on the SBS side of things, because in a lot of areas the most efficient means of arrival would have been the sea.

The French were important for operations in Europe. Obviously we had to get going on that as soon as we'd finished in the desert. There was a bit of ideology behind it, but it was justified on practical grounds mainly. I thought that having the French would give us substance at a later date, in terms of the Second Front, particularly as it was quite a small unit and the commander, Georges Bergé, had already won the MC, for a very gallant mission he carried out in France.

I also put it to Churchill that we could do some inviting from the soft underbelly, the southern flank of France, and penetrate through that way as well as from the north. And mainly of course operations carried out in France did take place from a base in England.

What I anticipated did happen: they provided the basis for the French SAS. And the Belgians also had Eddie Blondeel, who established a Belgian unit.

General Eisenhower, the commander-in-chief of Allied forces in Europe, sent out Anthony Head, who subsequently became a very great friend of mine, to Cairo to tell me to come back to England to discuss the Second Front. I imagine Churchill was involved in that decision. My brother's SAS was going to come out to the Middle East. I was going to leave behind some of my NCOs and they were going to be joined by other NCOs coming out from England, just to get in some experience. My brother did bring his SAS out to Philippeville.

Unfortunately, I didn't get back to England . . .

In the last three months of 1942, the new SAS regiment carried out raids in support of, and related to, the 8th Army's final offensive at Alamein. For part of this time, the strain Stirling had been under for the past year caught up with him and he was hospitalised with desert sores.

On November 8, the British-American 1st Army landed in Algeria in the Torch landings. Stirling immediately saw the advantage of the SAS being the first unit to link the two armies. On January 23, 1943, he set off, preceded by the French SAS.

Reg Seekings was supposed to accompany Stirling, Cooper and Sadler on the attempt. When the others set off, he was on his own operation, with men freshly recruited after the SAS had been awarded regimental status. The plan was for Seekings to meet up with the Stirling/Sadler/Cooper unit en route. Unfortunately, the men he was commanding were inexperienced and under-trained.

REG SEEKINGS

We were going to try to make contact with the 1st Army and also with 2 SAS. Bill was on his way out. Then David, Johnny and myself were going to England to do some more recruiting.

Before this there was a big op we'd gone on and they'd taken out the new squadron, 'B' Squadron, with Major Street. They sent me in with them, and I was in charge of that until such time as I thought fit to send them off into their areas. I took them on their first road strafe, etc., then sent them off. But they made a cock-up of it, and they all got captured. Street was lucky – the sub that was taking him back to Italy got sunk and he survived and was picked up by the British sub or destroyer that sank the sub.

Then I had my own lot, up in the Misaurata triangle. I was going to rendezvous with the colonel's lot on New Year's Day, then we were going to make the contact with the 1st Army.

I was taking the jeeps right in, blasting the hell out of the convoys. On some occasions we camped down with a battalion of Germans round us. Just kept fingers crossed that nobody got too inquisitive and come across to us. We'd then sneak off. Then we'd spend perhaps two hours laying mines on a parking lot. They might have had ideas about us mining – they knew we were around. I used to crawl out, take the mines in a sandbag, on a moonlight night too. I've even been fired at. But if you didn't move, the sentry wouldn't carry on shooting. That happened to me once or twice, but you got quite used to it. If you kept your nerve you were alright. The Ities in particular were quite trigger happy. But if you didn't move, they hadn't the guts to come across and have a look. On one occasion I got six trucks that way. At dawn, the convoys were pulling off the roads – they'd been travelling at night – into these parking lots, and by this time we'd be twenty miles away, watching the columns of smoke going up.

I had to do that sort of stuff on my own – this was the trip when some of 'B' Squadron got killed, and the men we had with us were only semi-trained: that's why the rest got captured, not up to the proper standard. Fortunately for me, Stirling had given me MacDonald, his personal driver/batman, who was one of his ghillies. Mac was first class. He wasn't really an operative, that's why I used him as a driver – he'd had no training with us but he was dependable and I could trust him.

I operated up there for weeks and weeks. Like I said, I was supposed to make the rendezvous with the colonel's lot on New Year's Day, but they never expected me back, apparently. When they didn't turn up I thought that they may have been knocked off, I don't know.

We were down to seven at that time, and we had one tin of bully beef a day left. Later, it had to last two days. At the finish we shared a tin of sardines. Tea had been rebrewed and rebrewed. I'd eaten biscuits we'd thrown away months previously, covered in engine oil – they went down very well.

Then to top it off, one morning we were laying up conserving our energy, just giving Stirling another day or two to get along, and the next thing we knew, early one morning, a gang of Jerries arrived in a big truck. I thought: what the hell's going on now? We were lying just a few yards away, with a jeep camouflaged behind us but us lying more or less in the open. I thought: I'm not going to be a prisoner. I always went to bed with my Colt .45 by my side and a couple of grenades. So I pulled the pin out of a grenade, got my Colt, and I'd have made a fight of it. I think we could have cleaned them up actually. We just prayed that nobody wandered away to have a pee.

We hung around for about two days, waiting for the opportunity to get away. They were building a defence line. We knew the 8th Army was advancing, but where it was we didn't know. We broke clear of them after about a day or two. We made a dash for it in the night, and drove off when other vehicles started up.

We ended up on top of a big plateau, terrifically high, and spotted some armoured cars. Even with glasses I couldn't see how the pennants were fixed, so I didn't know for sure if they were German or British. We were no match for armoured cars, and I wasn't going to take a chance of them being German or Italian. So we went over the side. I drove the vehicle down, attached to a chain, and we were then hanging on like mad, trying to stop it somersaulting. I don't know how, but we made it to the bottom. It was hundreds of feet down. Things looked small at the bottom. When we got down, we ran for a bit of cover, an overhang, and I watched them up top to see what they were going to do. They were only small figures, even with binoculars, that's how high it was. They milled around, then they drove off, disappeared.

We carried on and a few hours later we nearly ran into another column of armoured cars. Luckily we'd stopped. There were a lot of wash-aways, and every time we stopped we ran into the overhangs, and watched the cars go past. We couldn't tell what they were. We carried on again – I don't know how many days it took – we were getting hellishly weak. Then one day in the afternoon, all of a sudden in front and down below us, there were these thousands of transports. There was a lot of British markings, but I knew the Germans had a factory turning out spares for all the British trucks they'd captured. The colonel had told us about this. So I went down to make a recce, leaving instructions if they heard shooting they were to get the hell out of it and not bother with me. And it took me a helluva long time: all I could manage when I started walking was ten paces at a time.

By the time I got down there, it was well dark, the fires had gone out. I got to the first truck, and a chap came out to have a pee. I bent down, doing my lace up, and I thought, He'll speak. But he didn't. He went back and I heard voices, but couldn't make out if they were English or German. Eventually I leaned up against the back of one of the trucks. I had the Colt in one hand, a grenade in the other, and I'd slung the pin away. I was going to try and make a run for it –

I thought fear would give me the strength to run. I leaned there, and it seemed hours before I heard a voice, a North Country voice. I forget what he said to his mate, but I said: 'Thank Christ.' A voice said: 'Who's there?' I said: 'It's me, Sergeant Seekings.' I had a big beard, hair hanging down my back. I thought they'd shoot me out of hand. The first thing this chap said was: 'Have a fag, mate.' So I had the smoke and told them I'd got others with me. They said: 'We'd better go and pick them up.' I said: 'If you go there, they'll shoot hell out of you. MacDonald will anyway.' I felt a bit stronger then, so I went back down the wadi and I managed to shout and make them hear – they weren't far away. So they came in.

We'd found the KDG – Kings Dancing Girls, Kings Dragoon Guards – and they immediately brewed up. When my lot came up I said: 'Take it easy with the scoff.' But no, they gorged themselves. They were screaming and groaning all night. Nearly died with pain. They'd had nothing for weeks, and we'd all lost a tremendous amount of weight.

A Colonel Smales came in later that morning with the 11th Hussars. Smales was the man who'd been chasing me all the time. He was the man I saw up on the plateau. He'd been trying to catch me for a day or so. He didn't know who we were – thought we might be a German patrol. He took me to see the brigadier – this was right up in the forward line – and we'd just got down into this wadi where there were a couple of big thorn trees and in came a Messerschmitts. Jesus. I'm looking straight at one. I could see even wings – you know if you can see a bit more of one wing than the other you're alright, it's going to miss you. They were dead on. I thought: This is it, all this bloody way for this. No way would I survive that. We'd heard the strafing earlier on. But thank God they were out of ammunition, they were just ground hugging to get away. But I thought I'd had it then.

I reported to the brigadier, then I had to go back to Division, which is when I met General John Harding, the 7th Armoured Division commander. A real fire-eater. His drivers only lasted three weeks. He had a tank with the turret off and he'd drive off into battle in this. When things got hot, he'd leave the tank and get into a jeep.

I told him what had happened to us and he said: 'I can't keep you like this.' He called a major, and he said: 'Take the sergeant and see he and his men have nothing but the best. I've got General Freyberg coming tonight. We've got a conference. We want you to attend and put us in the picture. You've got the knowledge we've been trying to get for the last few weeks.' And they didn't query any of the information I gave them. We planned the attack there in that caravan. General Freyberg, a New Zealander, a VC, reminded me of my old man. It was like talking to him too. We argued about what we could and couldn't do. There was no rank held, it was just getting down to brass tacks.

In the meantime, David Stirling and Johnny were strafing other targets, airfields, etc., then at a certain time they struck off to join up with the 1st Army. But I was held up and couldn't catch them up because after I'd finished with Harding and Freyberg I had to report back to battle HQ and spend a few days there with General Intelligence. I had to do all the maps – they had whole areas they'd mapped out, with different colours for different going. So you looked at it, and black was bad going, grey was so-so, pink was good going, some was stony going, etc., and so a quick glance while travelling, and you knew what was coming up.

Then I got bolshie, with hanging around, and said I was going to clear off and try and get through to Stirling.

Whilst Seekings was still in the desert, David Stirling set off with his convoy. Johnny Cooper and Mike Sadler were with him.

MIKE SADLER

The aim of the exercise was to get right up into Tunisia, and join up with the 1st Army, doing various operations on the way, so that we would be able to sell the whole type of operation to them, and possibly operate from that end of the war for a change. It was quite a large party. We couldn't cover the journey except by sacrificing a certain number of vehicles. This meant completely loading a number of jeeps with petrol, with a view to dumping them once their petrol could be transferred on to other ones, and just leaving them in the desert. I think we left two or three of them like that on the way.

To get into Tunisia we had to go through the Gabes Gap, which was between Gabes on the Tunisian coast, and the salt lakes, which extend out to the west. It's quite a narrow gap; to get through there, you had to make a wide sweep round the south of Tripoli and the escarpment round Tripoli, then come through this gap and up into the interior of Tunisia. And we didn't have much information about that gap.

JOHNNY COOPER

Stirling's idea was to find the route round for the 7th Armoured Division so that either myself or Mike Sadler, both navigators, would be sent back to bring General Harding's boys round, if we could find a route round to get behind the

Germans, at the Mareth line. We were due to go through to join up with the 1st Army. And we were to do sabotage in the Gabes area.

Now the Gabes Gap is very narrow, because there the Chott el Djerid, which is a salt marsh, going right inland about thirty, forty miles. You've got the salt marsh almost up to the main road, and from the main road to the sea you've only got about another 500 yards. So it's a very narrow gap.

We did this wonderful approach over the Hadda Haddak, up on to the Tunisian border, for about thirty miles. Then we left the border road, which was a rough track, and headed for the Chott el Djerid, hoping to get at least five miles from the main road.

We hit the salt marsh, and the first jeep got stuck, so we had to unload it and roll it out. Obviously we were not going to be able to get across the Chott. Dawn was coming. So David said: 'Right, we're going to bluff it.' We had about six jeeps, so with us in the front we motored on to the main tarmac road, and went through the Gabes Gap.

There was a German armoured division getting out of bed on one side, an Italian division on the other, and David said: 'Just look straight ahead.' And we just motored right through. Somebody must have recognised us – I mean we had six or seven jeeps, maybe more, with all our equipment which is so different to theirs, all the colouring of the vehicles was different to theirs, and we were dressed differently. Anyway, we motored through and nobody challenged us. A sigh of relief. Nobody shot us, nobody did anything.

MIKE SADLER

Going through there, we found ourselves driving across an airfield which we didn't know existed, and in the daylight after that, we drove through German lorry camps, people getting up and so on, and straight on. As we drove out, we tried to bisect the angle between the coast and the salt lakes, going out to the west, to get as rapidly away from the coast road as we could, to put a good distance between us and the coast road before we found a lying-up point.

We were hurrying to find shelter for the day in the mountains, or hills – which lay I suppose five or ten miles ahead, across rather open country with farms and this sort of thing, which we hadn't entirely expected, but we drove on the course that we thought was best across to the hills. The one thing we did discover was that instead of getting further and further away from the coast road, we were going along parallel to another road that we didn't know existed, which came through the hills just a mile or so up.

JOHNNY COOPER

Now it was seven or eight in the morning. David said: 'We've got to get off the road.' And we went off to the left into one of these very deep ravines, and motored up until we found a very narrow wadi, and followed that in, and then broke up and put one jeep down this wadi, one jeep down that wadi, etc. and thought we were well concealed, particularly after we'd done all the camouflage and the rest of it. I was with David and we had the wireless operator, Ginger Tatton.

MIKE SADLER

We were all extremely tired, because we'd been driving for several days and indeed the whole of the previous night. And so I'm sure our judgment was not at its best. But we were mistakenly overconfident, obviously, about our security there.

JOHNNY COOPER

Mike Sadler and I were dispatched up the hill to look at the main road. We went up there about 10am with binoculars. We got on the top of this pinnacle, and we could see the main road going through the mountain. Our boys were down in the crevasse. About noon, up came a column of Germans. And perhaps Mike and I were wrong in assessing this, but you looked down and there were lots of troops getting out of vehicles, and we thought they were all getting out just to have a pee and would get back in again. By that time we'd been up for thirty-six hours, we were tired. And we stayed there for some time, and we were so damned tired, we went back and reported we had seen these chaps in blue uniforms. We said: 'Well, the Italians . . . ' We didn't think. David didn't renew the post on the hill. For no reason. We'd only gone up to observe any reactions, you see.

MIKE SADLER

After having a look round, and certainly we saw some fellows who we thought were Italians up at the top of the wadi, we went to bed, and I think probably everyone else did as well.

I was in my sleeping bag and heard some footsteps, looked up and there were two German parachutists, standing beside me. There was nothing much one could do, because our guns were all camouflaged underneath the netting and the tarpaulins and so on, and so we were really stuck. I saw Johnny looking from his bag. I imagine I must have been looking just as anxious as he was.

JOHNNY COOPER

I was lying in a sort of culvert. David was just round the corner and Mike was there. I was in my sleeping bag, and I had my battledress on and a leather jerkin, because it was cold, it was winter. And the first thing I had was a kick at my feet, and I looked up and there was a German parachutist with a Schmeisser. I started to get up, and he just said: 'Down!' So I got down and he then went round the corner, and then ran down the wadi, so he must have been on his own and suddenly found out what was happening, and started shouting. I woke David up, and got Tatton. David said: 'Codes.' And Ginger started to destroy the codes then David said: 'Every man for himself. If we go together...' So Mike Sadler, myself and Taxis ran up the wadi and went into a side wadi, and David went down the other way.

MIKE SADLER

I've never run so hard or for so long, until I just couldn't go any further, and we then got down into a little wadi, a little gully. It must have been around midday, perhaps it was early afternoon, and then we spent the longest afternoon I've certainly ever spent, waiting for the dark. We didn't really know what was going on down in the bottom of the wadi at that stage, although there were armoured cars in the entrance to the wadi.

JOHNNY COOPER

We didn't see the other jeeps because we weren't near enough, they were all in different places. We found a little crevice and then we could hear the firing all the way round. We got into this little hole and we were trying to think of the word 'kamerad', couldn't think of it. We had no arms, no water, no food. About 4pm we could hear this scraping noise, the starting up of the jeeps – the Germans had really come in strength, Parachute Battalion. We thought: This is it.

A flock of goats came round our place. The shepherd knew we were there and he put the goats all round, and then the Germans came through the area. They were left and right of the goats, all round our little hiding place, down into the wadi – that was the final sweep, then it was nightfall.

What were we going to do? We said, 'Well, to get back to the 8th Army, we've got to go past Gabes with all those soldiers. What about going to the French?' Taxis was a French officer. Tozeur was about sixty or seventy miles to march, and we had a one in million map and a compass. We knew we had to get water, so we started walking. We walked all the first night, right through the German divisions.

Next morning we were out of the German lines and saw Bedou camps. We went down and they were very, very nice to us. They gave us a little chatti of water to carry with us, and dates. We then walked again by day until it was too hot, all through the next night, and the next morning we were lying up and we split up, ten yards apart, in little clefts in the rock.

I was woken up with a twelve-bore shotgun pointing at me. A Berber. We knew that in this area, any airmen who'd been shot down, they'd been stripped of all their clothes, etc. He started to shout at me, and Freddie Taxis said: 'Give him your leather jerkin.' I threw that at him. Next thing, about ten kids came running out with rocks and started to stone me. One hit me on the head, and then the blood was in my eyes, I couldn't see. Freddie said: 'Run, run here.' So I scrambled up and just ran like hell. Freddie got one hand, Mike got the other and ran. We lost our chatti, the water.

We kept on walking all that day, all that next night. Freddie wanted a drink – we were on the side of the Chott el Djerid, and we could see the salt water. In fact, we could then see the oasis at Tozeur in the distance, but we could hear firing, and we thought: Christ, the Germans are in there as well. But Freddie had too much salt water and he went a bit delirious. Mike and I pulled him on, into the oasis at Tozeur. There was a faladj flowing with water, and these Arabs came out – they brought us dates, etc. The next thing we saw coming round the corner was an absolute apparition. It was a French Foreign Legion black sepoy, with the old First War helmet on, 1914 rifle. It was real Beau Geste. Freddie spoke to him in French and the sepoy disappeared, and came back with an equally French sergeant, big ginger beard. The firing we'd heard had been practice firing – Tozeur was occupied by the Free French.

They took us up to the fort there, and the doctor looked after me. By that time, walking on the Chott, our shoes were all torn to bits. I was bandaged all round the head, bandages on our feet, because walking on the salt marshes ripped our feet to bits, and we were all in pretty bad condition.

MIKE SADLER

We hoped we might find the Americans in Tozeur; we actually met up with the French garrison who gave us a magnificent reception – excellent food and wine and the rest of it.

We hadn't been there very long when the French commanding officer said that he would have to pass us on to the Americans, because it was their prerogative as we were in the American sector. We were then taken up somewhere near another town in the neighbourhood, whose name I've forgotten, where we were handed over to the local American commander. He didn't like the look of us, because we'd been walking then for three days and nights, and crawling over the salt lake and avoiding Arabs and so on, and we were in a very poor way. He thought we looked suspicious and he moved in a squad of soldiers to guard us, and we were kept covered at all times while we told our story.

JOHNNY COOPER

The Americans all bristled with Thompson sub-machine guns, they thought we were spies. They put us in an ambulance/personnel carrier – they had two vehicles in front, two vehicles at the back, and a chap with a Thompson on each of us – and whisked us up into the snowline, because it was winter, right up to Tebessa, to their HQ. The snow was on the ground and we wanted to have a pee; when we got out we still had the Thompson sub-machine gun shoved in our back. They just wouldn't believe we'd come from the 8th Army. I don't even think half of them knew where the 8th Army were, anyway.

Then they sent a message to Cairo, and it was flashed into Kabrit that Mike and I were there. Then we were summoned to General Mark Clark. I was then in a wheelchair because of my legs. They wheeled me in front of one of David's great friends, in 21 Army Group, and he said: 'Listen to these sergeants, they know what they're talking about.'

MIKE SADLER

Once they accepted our credentials, matters improved considerably. I was flown back to Tripoli by the American Air Force. The advance at that stage was at Tripoli, and a plan was afoot to take a left hook through the country that we had been through, through the Gabes Gap. The New Zealand division, with General Freyberg, was doing the left hook, and I gave them such advice as I could, and went with them as far as Gabes again.

JOHNNY COOPER

They put Mike in an aircraft and flew him straight back to Cairo, then he married up with 7th Armoured and navigated them round. Then Reg came through with his patrol.

REG SEEKINGS

Stirling had tried to go through Gabes Gap. I didn't attempt the Gap. I went across the big salt lakes. I thought if camels could get across the lakes, there was no reason why a vehicle couldn't. I'd picked up an Arab and his son, and they'd taken me to water. I could talk to them quite well. They warned me on the different villages – they were warlike people up there. I dropped them off where they wanted to go and they told me to watch this certain village, they'd cut our throats.

They thought I could get across the lakes with vehicles, providing I kept on the camel track. It wasn't very wide, but the old boy reckoned it would be packed down so hard, a vehicle could go on. I had to keep down to the speed of a camel – bloody awkward.

The village they'd warned us about was quite a big one, up on a rise, with a fortified castle. We saw this lot coming down, and one of our vehicles had bogged down. We started to dig it out, and saw this retinue of people coming down. Never seen anything like it – talk about Arabian nights. There was a youngish chap there, middle twenties perhaps, with a blue silken robe, very fancily dressed, and he came and greeted us. Having been warned about them, I said to the lads: 'Dig that jeep in, don't dig it out, make it look bad. Don't argue, just do it.' So we went through the usual greetings, and this chap says: 'Are you going to be here long?' I said: 'Yes, it looks as though this is going to take a lot of time, and we've other trouble too. We'll be a long time.' So he invited us up to the palace. He wanted to know who we were, so I told him we were German. I knew they hated the French, and the Italians, but had respect for the Germans. I didn't know what they thought of Englishmen.

I said I'd come up the next day if I could, and during the night the tom-toms were going, guns fired, screeching and screaming. I said: 'We're going to be attacked if we don't get out of here.' So we worked like hell and got everything ready to move. I said: 'We'll move just before first light.' They said: 'What about sentries?' I said: 'No need to bother about sentries.' I rubbed it in a bit more, the way they attacked, etc., and this young officer we had with us, he didn't go to sleep, he sat up all night. Anyway we got up, got the vehicles going, and away we went.

The sun comes up very quickly, although it's very cold, and I was worried the engines wouldn't fire well. As we were getting away, a German Fiesler Torch landed at the village. We'd got out just in time. A New Zealand patrol came along later and they lost a truck and I think somebody was killed and one or two wounded – these buggers attacked them.

Then we hit the salt lakes. It's something to see. It's just one vast area of dried salt. The camel track was easy to follow because it showed up black, and I warned the chaps: 'If you keep your eyes open, and if a vehicle pulls up, keep behind, don't turn off.' The first time I stopped, because we thought we saw aircraft, which is what we had to keep a sharp eye open for – because of the lack of cover on this brilliant white, we stuck out like sore thumbs. The vehicle behind came careering past me and turned off, and down it went. Within seconds it was practically out of sight. Black stinking mud. We couldn't afford to lose the vehicle, so we quickly unloaded the stuff, and managed to roll the vehicle out, and off we went.

By the time we reached the other side, it had just got dark. We came to a beautiful oasis, like something out of the Arabian nights, no kidding. We stopped on the edge of the gardens, under the palm trees, and built a fire and were scoffing up. Then out of the night came an Arab on a white horse, with his flying robes. He greeted us and we returned it. He was French Foreign Legion. He said: 'Where are you from?' 'Skandireer.' 'Ah,' he said, 'so you speak proper Arabic.' I said: 'I don't speak good Arabic.' He said: 'You must, to say Skandireer' – that's old Arabic for Alexandria. I'd picked this up on my travels, and if you bring out anything like that, you immediately get respect for it.

He said: 'Come up to the barracks. We have wine, chicken, bread.' We hadn't had bread for months. I said: 'Did you say bread?' 'Yes.' I said: 'What do we do, chaps?' They said: 'Christ, let's go.' So I said alright. This chap was their warrant officer; he took us along over narrow bridges over the irrigation canals – wonderful place. It was bright moonlight, but I'd loved to have gone over it all in daylight and had a good look. On the outskirts there was a lot of rock – they were doing some building there – and then there was a drawbridge, really medieval stuff, with portcullis, and the next thing we know a French officer steps out: 'Halt.' He'd got all these Arabs with him, the rough native soldiery, wearing long woollen robes, behind these rocks, got us all covered. Was I bloody mad. I felt like blasting them. We'd been taken prisoner.

They escorted us through the narrow streets – you could smell the brothels everywhere; they had a square in the centre with a fountain, real Beau Geste stuff, cobbled, the cavalry lined up on the other side. Then a colonel took us inside, and there we were cross-examined, put through the mill. I was getting fed up with this. And they never even gave us a cup of coffee. By now it was about 12.30am. They put us on the road to the next oasis where they said there was a British detachment, and another French Foreign Legion unit. So we motored along there, arrived about three or four in the morning. I went to the French Foreign Legion barracks and knocked up a sergeant, and when we looked at the place he gave us, it was crawling with bugs. So we kipped out in the street. When we woke up, we heard this lovely cultured English girl's voice: 'Good morning, whatever are you chaps doing out here?' That was the British Consul's daughter, out for a morning walk. It seemed so strange to hear an English girl's voice again.

From there we went on to Gafza. That's when we came up against the Yanks, and eventually met up with our own forces. The Yanks had got this roadblock and I pulled up, thinking: We're going to have some trouble now. This Yank was chewing away. I looked at him and he never said anything. So I said: 'What gives?' He didn't even say: 'Who are you?' Didn't indicate whether we should go through the roadblock, he just stood there, chewing. 'What gives?' No answer. In the meantime, a split double, chewing away, comes down with a carbine on his back. A real hillbilly. Bloody hilarious. My first introduction to American combat troops. And when we got into Gafza we couldn't get any sense out of anybody. We tried to get hold of American officers to find out things. They didn't know, didn't even know why they were there.

That's where I got news of Johnny & Co. Then we saw a major or colonel, and said, 'Oh bugger this,' and got on the road and off we went. Just ignored them. We were following these roads, and the next thing we knew, we were in driving snow and the Yankee snow ploughs were trying to keep the road clear. God it nearly killed us. Then we got through to Constantine and met up with Johnny.

REG SEEKINGS

Nobody wanted to know much about us until we met up with General Anderson, and he handed us over to the Americans, because they wanted knowledge of the Gabes Gap. Johnny and I went down to Philippeville, then down to Bohn, to contact the 2 SAS.

We tried to go into action twice with the Yanks, and it petered out, we couldn't get any action. Somewhere along the North African coast we met up with the leading elements of the 8th Army and went back to Constantine. Then we decided: 'To hell with it, let's get back and see what's going on.'

We didn't go to officers to get travel permits. We just went along to the nearest aerodrome and cadged a lift. I think it was a Flying Fortress, going down to Castle Benito in Libya. They shared their rations and we had some smokes, etc. We got a load of rations, because a lot of them were sick. Flying over the desert, it really gets bouncy, and all the Yanks were sick. So we did well. When we got over Castle Benito, we saw an RAF Lodestar, just about to take off: we could see it taxiing down. So we said to the captain: 'Can you get down quick – that plane's going to Cairo. If you get down quick we can get on.' He said: 'How the hell do you guys do it?' Anyway, he went down, we got out, waved goodbye to him, tore out onto the runway and flagged the Lodestar down. He pulled up – he recognised us, we'd run in to them before. So we hopped on and he took us straight into Kabrit. And we just walked across to the mess.

We didn't know what had happened to David until we got there.

CHAPTER SEVENTEEN

When Cooper, Sadler and Taxis had managed to escape from their hiding place, David Stirling had not been so fortunate. He and (his signaller) McDermott were held up by a single German holding a pistol on them; at the mouth of the wadi where they had been hiding, the Germans were company strength. That evening, they escaped and ran for it, but lost each other during the night. The next night – incredibly seeing that he was alone and on the run, Stirling saw an airfield he did not recognise and spent three hours checking it as a possible future target. It cost him time. As dawn came up, Stirling, exhausted and needing food, tried to camouflage himself in the scrub of the desert. In late afternoon, as he stood, he was confronted by an Arab who offered to take him to food and water. Instead, he took Stirling to the Italians. And the enemy at Middle East Headquarters descended.

DAVID STIRLING

In a sense the reason I was captured was the fact that the French had begun to stir things up, going through the narrow Gabes Gap, where I was going up north behind them. I said: 'I mustn't undertake any kind of operation, we must go absolutely on tiptoe quietly through.' They were meant to be two or three days in advance of me, but they found some rather juicy target and couldn't resist beating up a German unit. Then they went north and I ran into the trouble.

It was unfortunate, because had I left Cairo four days later than I did . . .

Anthony Head, who later became Minister of Defence, had come out to see Sean Hackett, who represented us in Middle East Headquarters by then – he was an admirable officer, marvellous man. Head had come out to see us both from Eisenhower, because I'd been making quite a fuss in this time, and we were going to take the main part of 1 SAS regiment back to help train for the Second Front, just leaving behind sufficient trained personnel to look after 2 SAS who were taking over from us out there, under my brother Bill. Anthony Head came out in response to the proposals that had been put up, and I gathered from what Anthony Head told me after the war, they would have gone along with them.

When I was captured, all that proposal fell by the wayside.

And they – Middle East Headquarters – decided they would put SAS on what they called a more rational basis. Which meant putting it under some commanding officer. Not Paddy, who should have been immediately made commanding officer. But a very nice bloke who didn't know a thing about the SAS.

JOHNNY COOPER

David's capture was a great blow; we all had great misgivings. They wanted to disband us, or they wanted to take, not part of our glory, but they wanted to get rid of this small band of people who were doing so much damage to their pride because they hadn't been able to do it themselves.

BOB BENNETT

It was terrible, because no one expected it whatsoever, then we came back and we thought: Well, is this the end of SAS? We were all very, very upset by it. Stirling had been such a leader, and I couldn't possibly at that time see anyone carry on in the same sort of way. Paddy was a brilliant officer, but I think Paddy always needed an eye on him, and Colonel David was the man that kept an eye on him and kept him, you know, on the ball. But that was my personal opinion, that we were going to split up.

JOHNNY COOPER

David wasn't liked in GHQ Cairo, because he proved his point every time. He changed his tactics, he proved his point again. They couldn't go along with that. This upstart of a lieutenant who . . . I mean, he was only a colonel when he was captured. My own assessment of David's loss? I thought it was the end of us.

BOB BENNETT

It was a shock when Stirling was captured. We couldn't believe it, and we wondered what was going to happen with Stirling out of it and Paddy off somewhere – in fact, I think he was in some jail. He'd been put inside for banging a colonel or something, and of course that was a killer, because he was the only man that could take over.

REG SEEKINGS

Paddy had run foul of the police. Paddy told me the story himself. His father had died and he thought, Well, crikey, when Randolph Churchill had done his jump, he immediately rang up his mother to tell her about it – which is true, he did – and the next thing we knew, he was on an aircraft back to England. And Paddy thought: What he can do, I can do. So he went up to Cairo and applied for three or four days' leave to fly home to Ireland to help settle up the estate. That was refused. I said: 'What did you do then?' He said: 'I never did anything.'

That's when I found out he'd laid out the Provo Marshall of Cairo and smashed up half a dozen restaurants – really went to town. In the process Paddy ran foul of different people, started to lose his temper and went on the rampage. You can understand it though. There was Paddy with his record, there was nothing going on, everybody was fighting for his job. His father had died and you'd have thought they'd let him pop home for a day or two – no reason why they couldn't. But no. So Paddy went on the rampage. Eventually they got him, but not till he'd laid out the provo marshall – he was a big bugger too – and half a dozen redcaps. I know a signal went out: 'Release this officer, he's more use as an officer than other rank.' He was released next morning. General HQ sent the signal. So that was that.

BOB BENNETT

We were all pushed off to Palestine and called the Special Raiding Squadron, with some major in charge. He was gonna get a grip of this lot, you know. We were browned off to hell. Then they realised that the only one who could command the regiment was Paddy, so they dropped the charges, and a couple of days later Paddy arrived to take over CO, as colonel from major, and of course great big cheers went up.

DAVID STIRLING

It's not like leaving a will – well, I hadn't written my will, so to speak, so everything was left in total disorder, because I didn't expect to be captured. That was the stage where the wretched Paddy again got into trouble in Cairo and elsewhere. Then he finally got his command and never looked back. He exercised his status of CO in a way that only he could have done. It was the scale of his performance, which is another aspect of the SAS, which made it inevitable that it had to go on.

But he didn't know how to cope with officers above him. I had to continuously protect him in that context. I don't think he could have commanded a brigade, because military politics would have come into it. He couldn't really do himself justice except with his own range of command. If he had two other regiments and HQ to cope with, and three regiments then Brigade HQ, he'd have fucked it up properly. But it was so fortunate he was able to work his destiny, in military terms, to perfection. Nobody had a more gallant record, which was well illustrated by his four DSOs, which was more or less unparalleled. He should have had a fifth one. Paddy's story as a fighting soldier is quite staggering.

REG SEEKINGS

To John and myself, in losing David we'd lost not only a commanding officer, but a great friend. We'd been through a hell of a lot together, so it was quite devastating. To the unit, the whole symbol had gone. And of course it left everybody worried what was going to happen. And the big question was whether Paddy would have enough influence to swing the day? Of course nobody ever thought of Jellicoe or anybody like that becoming commanding officer of the SAS. It was Paddy Mayne. Paddy Mayne was the man by now – Paddy was Paddy in no uncertain terms. But we wondered whether Paddy had got the right connections, and he'd certainly ruffled a lot of feathers. We wondered whether he could weather the storm and get it. But he turned out a great fighter. But it was pretty devastating on the unit.

DAVID STIRLING

They, Middle East Headquarters, regarded it as an opportunity, I think, of reeling in the troublesome SAS, and regularising it. And for a time they apparently succeeded, but they didn't appreciate the heavy metal that Paddy and his boys represented. There was no way they were going to win. And Paddy just did his own thing, once he got command. There was no way any ordinary individual in the army, any ordinary, well qualified, commanding officer could command those blokes. It was impossible for them effectively to do so and make effective use of the regiment, because they were past responding to the old type of regulations. We had very tough regulations, we had very stern discipline, but it was of a different nature, different type. So Paddy, thank God, was able to reassert himself, and he was helped to do so by people at the top level in Middle East Headquarters, who realised what a nonsense it was trying to turn this particular regimental animal into a normal one.

My brother did bring his SAS out to Philipville, but there were hiccups after I was captured. 1 SAS were obliged to undertake operations which weren't strictly SAS, though they did brilliantly on them, under Paddy Mayne eventually. But what I anticipated did happen; they provided the basis for the French SAS, then the Belgians.

REG SEEKINGS

John and I tried hard to be scrubbed off the army list and be dropped into Italy, or wherever Stirling was, and be given a free rein, whether it took weeks or months, and to get him out. We fought and fought for this, but they certainly wouldn't wear us. We were prepared to do it, and we genuinely wanted to do that. We reckoned that the two of us together – well, nothing would beat us, we'd get him out. We had that type of confidence in ourselves.

Then the plan to get Stirling out went dead. We got the impression that there were certain people who were quite happy for him to remain where he was. It hasn't changed much today – these people with desk jobs don't like new things, new people, new ideas. Dangerous. It pushes their noses out of joint. It's bad. There was more than one would have nailed Colonel David if they'd got the chance.

DAVID STIRLING

I was taken to a place in Italy. They put me in with this chap who was executed after the war, an Englishman posing as a guy who wanted to escape. So I collaborated with him. Luckily I told him the Germans had no chance of winning the war – I think I made him rather depressed – but I was delighted to collaborate with him. He'd been in some time, as far as an escape was concerned. This was when I was taken for interrogation in Rome. I was flown to Sicily and I pretended I had a very bad leg and was dragging it. I hoped they'd think I wouldn't try and escape.

From Rome I was taken up to Berlin and somehow, and I don't know why, they got me muddled up with a chap called Brigadier Philip Stirling, who had escaped from the Vatican. They thought I was the Vatican Stirling and was a brigadier. It was quite useful because I got extra perks as a brigadier rather than those for a colonel. So they were a little muddled about that. They made it very easy for me in Berlin to get the right sort of answers, because they didn't know who I was, quite. They were very careless to allow this to happen because Pip was quite an important guy. In a different way, I suppose I was, because they did a lot of swanking when they captured me: Stirling's caught. It relieved their behind-the-lines problems. Rommel was fairly emphatic about that. Then I went to the Italian prison camp at Gavi.

David Stirling's capture signalled the end of SAS activities in the deserts of North Africa. Yet something remains of those days – the L Detachment song, the song of The Originals, based on these times. It was sung at L Detachment reunions, often by Bob Bennett, with backing by The Originals, accompanied on the piano by the Very Reverend Fraser McLuskey – like Mike Sadler an 'honorary Original', who is still to enter the story. It is sung to the tune of Lili Marlene.

There is a song we always used to hear,
Out in the desert, romantic soft and clear.
Over the ether came the strain, that lilting refrain,
Each night again.
Of poor Lili Marlene, of poor Lili Marlene.

(chorus)
Then back to Cairo we would steer,
And drink our beer, with ne'er a tear.
And poor Marlene's boyfriend
Will never see Marlene.

Check your ammunition, see your guns are right.
Wait until the convoy comes creeping through the night.
Then you can have some fun, my son,
And know the war is almost won.
And poor Marlene's boyfriend
Will never see Marlene.

(chorus)

Drive on to an airfield, thirty planes ahead,
Belching ammunition and filling them with lead.
A flamer for you, a grave for Fritz,
Just like his plane, he's shot to bits.
And poor Marlene's boyfriend
Will never see Marlene.

(chorus)

Afrika Korps has sunk into the dust,
Gone are his Stukas, his tanks have turned to rust.
No more we'll hear the soft refrain
That lilting strain, it's night again.
And poor Marlene's boyfriend
Will never see Marlene.

For The Originals, however, and even for David Stirling, the battle was far from over.

BOOK THREE

Europe

Gentleman Jim Almonds behind the lines in France.

CHAPTER EIGHTEEN

After David Stirling's capture, the SAS structure was dismantled. Bill Stirling's 2 SAS continued, but 1 SAS was cut back to a squadron and renamed Special Raiding Squadron. The North Africa campaign over, the Allies turned their attention to Southern Europe and the invasion of Italy.

The Originals' operations in Sicily and Italy, 1943.

BOB BENNETT

We went off for a rest period, to the ski school in Syria, the Cedars – sort of a holiday – and entered Palestine and started as SRS there, then we trained up for the Sicilian invasion. The object of that was to destroy the gun emplacements, so the invasion fleet could get in.

PAT RILEY

When Stirling went in the bag I decided I might as well go ahead. Paddy was all for it, so I took a commission and went off to OCTU, the Officer Cadet Training Unit, then was commissioned back into the SAS. Some of the boys were up training with skis, then finally they came back and we were all collected together and we went down to Aqaba in the Red Sea. We did quite a bit of training there, and then came back up to Suez – Montgomery come along and blessed us – and then we went to Port Said, and then on to Sicily.

REG SEEKINGS

We were getting ready for the invasion of Sicily. General Dempsey was commander of 13 Corps, and he came along to give us a pep talk. I marched them along to the cinema and Dempsey was saying: 'Don't worry, you'll get your D-Day, you'll get your lion's share, do not despair.' Everybody was browned off to hell. This was talk for recruits. As I marched them out, he asked if there were any questions. Of course there weren't any, not a murmur. As we left the hall, Paddy leant over and spoke to Dempsey and Dempsey shouted: 'Sergeant! Bring these gentlemen' – stressing *gentlemen* – 'back in.' We sat down and he got up and I don't know any other man who could have done it. He said: 'My sincere apologies, gentlemen – and I mean gentlemen – I've been giving you all this

tripe about D-Days. You've had more D-Days than I'll ever have. My apologies –
those bloody fools back at HQ will one day tell me who I'm talking to, and stop
me from making a bloody fool of myself. Now I know who you are, I'm asking
permission to stay the night and join in one of your night firing exercises.' So he
did; he came round and watched us on training, took a different interest
altogether.

We'd got night firing down to a fine art – we were good at it, I must say. We
did it down on the sand dunes. There was a point where you could fire with
safety. We got together after dark, then Dempsey came along and said: 'Put me
where I won't be in the way.' I said: 'We're not doing any complicated exercises
here, just moving in on to the targets and engaging them. Purely target practice.'
He said: 'I understand that. I don't want to get in the way but I want a good view.'

Then Dempsey saw Little Titch. He was little. Dempsey said: 'Who is that
man?' I said: 'Davison, sir.' 'How old is he?' 'I don't know, fourteen or fifteen, I
suppose.' Dempsey said: 'That's what I would reckon. I'd like to talk to him.'
'Okay, Davison, the General would like to speak to you.' So the General said:
'How old are you?' 'Twenty-one, sir.' Dempsey said: 'No, your real age.' 'Twenty-
one, sir.' 'No-no-no, I'm not going to do anything to you, I just out of curiosity
want to know your proper age.' 'Twenty-one, sir, and if you don't fucking like it,
you can fucking stuff it!'

I thought: Oh Christ, we've had it now. Dempsey just laughed and said: 'This
is a bad thing to say, but I wish I had two or three divisions like him. Keep an
eye on him, sah major.'

So we went on with firing, and there was a tremendous noise, flashes of
gunfire, and I couldn't believe my ears, I could hear screams. Christ, there's
somebody there! So I ran, screaming at the top of my voice: 'Stop firing, stop,
stop!' And I ran out so they could see me, and there were about twenty officer
cadets from up the road, in a little hollow, screaming their heads off. You should
have seen their faces when they saw a general there. Dempsey said: 'What are
you doing here?' They were on a map-reading exercise. Did he go to town. One
thing about Dempsey, he's a very mild-talking man, but he could hand out a
bollocking. He said: 'You've risked the life of a first-class sergeant here who's
worth the lot of you, and you expect to be officers? You never will be if I have
something to do with it. At 6am tomorrow I shall be visiting your CO. If any
one of you are still there, tell your CO I will personally boot him off the
premises. Now get to hell out of here.' Off they went and sure enough, 6am he
was along there.

We did our training down at Maharia. There was a section of coast, right on the border – I think the village was actually in Syria – and it was virtually identical to Murro di Porco, our main landing zone. We marked it out with boulders and tape to full scale. What wasn't there originally, we marked according to the aerial photos, and we trained on that, day after day – coming in by sea on landing craft, scaling the cliffs abseiling, etc., and then mounting full attacks onto different objectives. So when you got there, in the dark, it would all be quite familiar. And on the boats you had plenty of time to study the aerial photos. We also had very good photos taken of the actual coast from our submarines. So we were able to pick good landing spots. They were better photos than some of the aerial shots.

We trained on this full-scale replica, then we went down to Suez, went on board ship and sailed through the canal. Then we received our instructions from Dempsey, got the plans, etc., then the ship was sealed, nobody allowed off. That's when we really got down to studying the actual thing. When we were training, we didn't know what it was all about. Paddy must have done, but we didn't. The object of the exercise was to knock out coastal batteries for the main army to land. The gliders, 4th Brigade, I think, were going to support us inland.

We were deciding what to wear. We plumped for these blue Indian shirts – very nice shirts – a bright blue grey. They're very smart, but they stand out, no camouflage. We had shorts and mountaineering boots and white socks turned down at the ankles. We said: 'Won't they make us conspicuous?' Paddy said: 'Sure, you tell me you're the toughest, quickest-firing people in the world. There won't be anybody to fire at you – you'll already have shot them. What are you worried about?'

We were planning how we would attack, and we reckoned there was only one way, that was straight in. None of this business of waiting around, doing feinting movements, etc. – just in. If you broke through and your mates were having a bit of trouble, then hit the enemy from the rear, bring them forward. What we wanted was sharp, fast penetration: we mustn't allow ourselves to get pinned down, or in a prolonged shoot-out. To do that it meant we'd got to identify ourselves. Otherwise we'd be shooting up each other. Camouflage was out. That's why we decided on these bright blue shirts.

We joined up with the main invasion fleet and I've never seen anything like it in my life, it was tremendous. We steamed with them for the last day or two. That afternoon we could see Etna. The sea was getting rougher and rougher. I passed the wardroom and Paddy was talking to the skipper, an Irishman: we used to call him Haile Selassie because he had a big black curly beard. He was the flotilla leader too, the *Ulster Monarch*, it was – the boats used to go from Glasgow to Arran. He was a real so-and-so. I said to the crew: 'If he's so bad, why don't you ask for a transfer?' They said: 'What, and die? With him we keep alive – he's fantastic.' They'd been on the Murmansk run, and they reckon on those sort of runs, once they left harbour, he never left the bridge. He could smell torpedoes, they said. They thought he was absolutely fantastic.

Anyway I heard the conversation between him and Paddy, and Paddy says: 'We've got to land, got to go in.' The skipper says: 'Sure and be Christ, Paddy, not only will I land you, if necessary I'll go along the cliffs and jump you off.'

The sea was so bad we thought it would be called off, but they went ahead. One landing craft broke its moorings and dropped into the sea, and that put a pitch on the boat, and it was only the skipper intervening then, nice and cool and calm and collected, that got it righted.

We went ashore in the landing craft. I'd still held on to my Vickers guns and was up in the prow for a bit. Then we saw this thing, and I thought it was a sub coming up, but it was a glider with chaps hanging on to it. They were crying out for help. There were a lot of Yanks on the towing craft, and if searchlights and a bit of flak appeared – just trigger-happy Ities and Jerries, happened often – they seemed to panic. Their hearts weren't in it, and they'd ditch the gliders. They came down in the sea and all over the damn place. Absolute shambles. They lost quite a lot of men.

BOB BENNETT

We landed at the wrong time – if we'd landed at the right time we would have been bombed by the RAF – so that worked out right. As we were going in on that one they dropped a Para brigade, most of them in the sea. The Yanks had dropped them off too quick and they were all drowning. We couldn't do anything. We went straight through them in the flat-bottomed boats.

REG SEEKINGS

We shouted to them to hang on, but we couldn't stop to pick them up, we had to go in. We were called a few names for that, but we'd got an operation. People might find it hard to understand these days, but my first objective is to get there. I've got gun batteries to destroy. I was the sah major and so I often talk as 'I', when there would be a captain or lieutenant with me. But we'd got a job to do. We couldn't stop and mess that up. There was already one thing had been messed up – you can't add to a disaster, you've got to carry on.

The bosun on our boat came from my area, Wisbech, so we got together and painted the badge of the Isle of Ely on the boat. He'd said he was going to leave his boat – to hell with the boat, he was coming ashore with us, it was going to be an Isle of Ely concern. He was going to crash his boat on to the cliffs, and take a scaling ladder, and instead of going in on our proper beach, I was going to take the shortcut, on the pretext we couldn't get on a beach – which we wouldn't have done anyway I don't think – and we were going to scale the cliffs, bringing us up by the gun emplacements. We'd made a bamboo scaling ladder for this.

As we manoeuvred into the cliff and got the ladder up, there was a figure at the bottom of the cliff, clinging on. I nearly shouted: 'Who are you?' He was garbling out bits of the operation, and I thought, Only a Brit would know this, so I hauled him in. It was the adjutant of this airborne outfit. He'd been dropped in and made it to the cliff.

The bosun had intended to go ashore with us. He'd even got hold of a Lewes gun. But when this happened with the paras, he felt he couldn't leave them on the gliders; he said he was going back to pick them up. So he went back and picked them up, took them back to the ship. Next morning, as far as that side of it was concerned, the German fighters came in and started bombing the fleet, and he got quite a high decoration for his rescue work, our bosun. He did a lot of work under heavy fire. We were pleased about it, because he was a good lad.

Anyway, we were ashore, and we hit the wire. We knew there were minefields there so we adopted minefield procedure. Me and Jack Terry did that – it was wrong, two senior men doing it, but we found if you were prepared to do those things yourself, you never had any problem with the men, you'd tell them to do something and they'd just do it.

You have to be careful going through a minefield. They had these jack-in-a-box things, with three little prongs. If you touched those, they'd fly up and explode two or three feet above the ground. Very nasty. There were heavier ones too. But we got through without any problem, to the wire.

Jack and I had cut the wire, held it open and were passing the chaps through, which is a slow business, until the Ities decided they'd heard something and opened up with a couple of machine guns. We were through that barbed wire fence in no time. The fire was heavy, so I went forward and knocked it out, then we dealt with a mortar position, and knocked that out.

I'd worked out how to attack the pillboxes when we were on board ship. We gambled that all pillboxes were the same, giving maximum field of fire. I'd seen a lot on the east coast at the beginning of the war. I worked out heights and distances and realised that these chaps would be pulling the guns round and firing at acute angles to get crossfire. That would mean on the high ones, the fire would cross at a certain point, low ones same thing. I worked out that I could run in, jump the low ones and duck the high ones, get up alongside them, and chuck the grenades in through the slit, then nip round the back and finish off any survivors with the tommy gun. That's what I was doing, with the lads covering me. Quite simple really. Anyway we took the position. I got a citation for that. Then we sent off the green rockets. Paddy said that was the record for clearing a gun position.

Our mortars got cracking and set fire to one of the barracks, which were burning. Then I got my chaps together, and it must have been one of the few bayonet charges of the war. We'd trained with Paddy and worked out how to do a bayonet charge, to go in disciplined like the guards, working the bolt and firing on the step. Very impressive. So I got them up and took them in. We took the command post. The only casualty we had was a chap named Skinner, tall blond bloke. One of the shells exploded on his leg. I had one burst between my legs, blew my pants. A sliver went through my nose and took a bit out. That was all. So we finished it. But it was an awe-inspiring sight, to see these chaps and the volley of fire, the bayonets. The lads were very good too.

After that we were running round mopping up, and moving fast, because we wanted to clear the place fast. We were ducking through these barrack buildings, and as the chaps went past – bang-bang – we could see a figure. Next thing, in one of the buildings I heard grunting and groaning. I stopped to check, and this little Scotsman on my team is going in with a bayonet. 'Take it, you bastard,' he's going. He came out. 'I got him,' he says. Next morning, I was thinking, That chap didn't seem to fall. Everybody was talking about it: 'The bastard had a charmed life. I took a couple of shots at him.' 'So did I, he didn't seem to flinch.' I thought, Well, who was it Mac killed? So I went back and do you know what we'd been shooting at? A statue of Mussolini. It was peppered. What Mac had heard had been a donkey braying, and the poor donkey got it. Our blood was up then; we could have killed anybody.

There was a big mole there, with a long tunnel leading into it, and I shouted for people to come out, and it was the local population – old people, young ones. At the end was a young girl, I suppose about thirteen, pretty kid. She came out with her head held up, looked so proud, and a grenade went off close – most of us firing had dived down then – and that broke her, she started sobbing. That sobered me up. I thought: Christ, like my kid sister.

I heard chaps shouting, 'Come on out, come on out.' I went across and said: 'Look, I told you not to bugger around, get 'em out.' Seeing the girl break down made me think of the disaster on the French coast – they threw a grenade into cordite, there was a big flash and killed the whole lot, the German post and the raiding party. I suddenly thought of this, and I shouted: 'Stop all grenades.' We were on a heavy gun emplacement where they had bags of cordite. So I'm shouting 'Hold your grenades' and these chaps were shouting down this hole for them to come out. I bawled them out for not getting on with the job. They said: 'But there's some British down there.' I said: 'Well, they shouldn't be down there.' So I shouted down, and there were three of them. I said: 'Right, well, come out then.' 'Well, don't shoot us, be careful.' 'Oh for God's sake, come out.' The buggers wouldn't come out, they were scared. So I said: 'I'm counting three, if you don't come out; British or not British, I'm throwing a grenade down.' They still didn't come out, so I put a grenade down. It was the only thing to do. They came out then.

At dawn next day, we'd sent the signals off that we'd blown the guns, then we had to get organised. We had a hell of a crowd of prisoners. We had to take them with us. Just on the outskirts of this gun emplacement there was a farm building. The Ities were running around, getting milk and stuff, so I stopped that, because there wasn't enough for us. We'd also got the British Airborne brigade commander. They'd been captured. They were straight out from UK, green, and they didn't like the way we were going about things, particularly when I put a burst of tommy gun fire at an Itie's feet to drive him back from the farm.

We came to a farm building, which had big red crosses on, but by this time we were coming up against German troops who were defending this farm. So we mortared it, and there again the brigadier and his lot were kicking up hell because they said there were Brits in there. But you can't stop wars for that sort of thing. I don't know whether we actually killed any of our own, probably some wounded, but we took the place, and they did agree afterwards it was the only thing to do.

We had an instance there, the only one I came across – this is when the Germans were on the scene – where they collected up Italian women and drove them in front. My chaps stopped firing; I wondered what the hell was going wrong. They said: 'There's women there. We can't fire at women.' I said: 'If you don't, the bloody Germans will kill us. Fire.' And the women were shouting for us to fire. We opened up again and the women went down and we nailed the

Germans that were driving them along. Fortunately no women were killed. Three or four of them were hit in the leg. But the women were full of praise for us. These British officers took a dim view of it, at the time.

There was another emplacement down on the far side of the peninsula. I broke off and went down to knock over five or six pillboxes. That's where I lost two of my best men, under this white flag. I dealt with that. By this time the mortars had engaged the other main batteries further along, and another troop had captured the HQ, so we'd cleared up all the artillery.

We got the Italian brigadier, the lot. I later met him doing point duty. They came over on the British side later, and although he was a brigadier, some wag put him on point duty. It was quite funny. I took him up to say goodbye to his wife – I think she was glad to see the back of him. He was a supercilious type.

The next morning SRS and The Originals left on the Ulster Monarch; *that afternoon they received orders to take the port of Augusta.*

BOB BENNETT

They said: 'Don't bother about too much ammunition: they've surrendered. It's just a matter of making a landing.' We sailed into the harbour on the *Monarch*

An SRS mortar team in action.

and as she came to a halt, the Germans opened up. They thought we were a decoy, and we didn't know they were there. Their shells were going right over the top of the *Monarch*, but we went ashore and had quite a lot of casualties.

REG SEEKINGS

The way we fought then, I had one troop up, one in reserve and the other troop guarding the prisoners. They far outnumbered us – there were only about a hundred of us. As we took prisoners, the attacking troop came back round, took over the prisoners, shoved the ones they'd taken in with the main lot, the reserve troop moved up, and then the original prisoner guards moved into reserve. This is how we fought through all the day. We moved fast that way. We slaughtered a lot. Lord knows how many prisoners got away; we couldn't hold them all.

In one of the reports it said Paddy gave permission to loot – that's all baloney. He never ever did. I admit he would turn a blind eye – he wasn't too much of a spoilsport. But Paddy was a lawyer, no way would he give that order. We did take a lot of stuff though. It had all been abandoned. It was quite funny when the order came for us to go down to the harbour; there was a Greek destroyer that was going to take us off. Chaps were taking prams and God knows what on board, and we took a beautiful big radiogram to give to the skipper, Haile Selassie.

Already some of the chaps were flogging ladies' hats to the Greek soldiers. The Greeks thought they'd do well with the women in Alexandria with these hats. I was just thinking what would happen if we were attacked, when in came some Fokker Wolfs, and straddled us with bombs. Those Greeks really moved. And those boats, after British Navy boats, they were bloody filthy. But the guns worked alright.

When we got to the boat the old captain said: 'It's good to have you aboard, gentlemen.' But he said: 'I'll have no drunken men aboard my boats.' In the meantime they'd slung a hook down and we're hauling up this radiogram for him. We said: 'A present for you, you black-bearded bastard. Keep quiet.' He said, 'Take over, Jimmy,' and off he went. We took the 'gram along to his cabin – he didn't turn it down. It was a lovely bit of work.

Over the next days, SRS were briefed on a number of operations, all of which were cancelled. Then they were landed by the navy at Bagnara in Calabria, on the Italian mainland.

REG SEEKINGS

We had a lot of messing around. There was a big scare on with the navy, about magnetic bombs, radio-controlled bombs, all this sort of nonsense. We transferred from one boat to another. Some said they daren't start up the engines, there were aircraft overhead – so much nonsense it wasn't true.

The moon had come up bright, we were in this beautiful bay. We went in eventually; it was damned near dawn. I was in the leading boat, and you could see some emplacements had been pushed up in the sand, and at one stage it looked like a glint of helmets. The naval people were getting jumpy and wanted to turn back. I stuck my tommy gun in the officer's back and said: 'Land us.' So we went in.

There were gun crews in there, but they pulled out. It was just before dawn. We got ashore OK, no problem. My job was to get through the village, climb up the cliffs, get into the mountains and hold a bridge for the army. So we weren't going to play around, clearing any of the villages, we were going to drive straight through. If any action started in the village, we would avoid it.

PAT RILEY

We were on the beach and I was supposed to go to the top of the beach, but Paddy suddenly said: 'Go through the town and hold that bridge, so the 8th Army can get up.' So I went along with my boys and finally got into the village, and one of my chaps ran to me and said: 'Look, sir. There's lots of Germans down there.' I looked down and of course there they were, facing the wrong way as far as I was concerned, facing toward the 8th Army.

I had the good fortune to catch the first twenty German prisoners. They were a tough little mob, I must say. They'd been on the Russian front. But there was a rather interesting thing. Jerry give us a bit of a reception, shall we say, and during that thing one of my chaps was hit, and this Jerry jumped up – I thought he was going to make a run for it, but he wasn't. He ran to the side of this chap of mine and attended to him. And that was a hardened man – you know, you hear stories, but I thought it was rather interesting.

REG SEEKINGS

By this time it was daylight. We stopped and I said: 'I'm going to have a recce.' I spotted a German mortar team coming down the mountainside and went to move back and they must have spotted me. I wasn't too worried about cover because the angle was so steep; I didn't think they could fire at me. But they were better than I thought. They got the right range on me and really hammered it. I came round the corner all dust and muck, and there was Johnny Wiseman and Major Fraser, saying: 'Sergeant Seekings' had it.'

There was a very steep cliff face and we decided that was the only place where we could get up without being spotted. Much to their disgust, I'd got hold of a Vickers gun. They're ideal, you can fire all day and all night. They're water cooled. I got every man to carry extra belts of ammunition, so each one had at least an extra 250 rounds. I had belts with 300 rounds, and I had four of these, so we were very heavily laden. The one thing that was bothering me was how we'd climb this cliff, but we went up that cliff as though it wasn't there, forgot about the weight.

We took up a position in some vineyards, overlooking the bridge, 600 yards away and down below us, so we were in an ideal spot to cover it and keep everything back, bar tanks – we'd be no good against them.

From our position it was 1,000 yards across to the other peak, where the road came down. It came through a little narrow village road, so you could cover that. Jerry tried to push through and we pushed him back. They had a Tiger tank at the top and that started to give us a bit of trouble. Dempsey had given us permission to call up anything we wanted, so during the day we called up a naval destroyer. The navy came in but they didn't read our signals right and started firing at the bridge. We wanted the bridge intact. They also started the mortars, which put smoke down. But the Tiger scored two hits on the destroyer, he beetled out, came round again, and the Tiger caught him again. The navy beat a retreat. The Tiger won that one. We got the mortars on eventually, and had a very lucky hit – one of the mortars dropped through the open turret and the Tiger tank was knocked out.

Then the Germans sent a demolition squad down, but we spotted them coming. Tom Rennie was one of my snipers – he had a proper sniper's rifle – and I said: 'Right Rennie, that's 600 yards.' We'd previously tested it out for range, and I said: 'You take the left hand one, I'll take the right'. I had an ordinary rifle. I made the finest shot of my life there – 600 yards, a little man, got him right in the thigh. Rennie got his smack in the stomach, but mine died first. They were the only two we got, but it broke the others up and they crawled away in the ditches. It saved the bridge.

Their small arms fire was very accurate, then they brought in mortars and gave us a rough time with those, but we dug in and used the retaining walls of the vineyard as cover. It brought on Rennie's sinus trouble – one of the shells buried him. Their gunners were so accurate, even at that range. I reached up to get a lovely bunch of grapes, and I was spotted. Grape juice squirted all over me – they shot it practically out of my hand.

We'd run out of water, because we'd been there all day and night and it was hot. It was dangerous to try and collect dates and things, so we moved back and I took a party down to bring up some more supplies. We'd also started to have radio trouble, and I wanted to find out what the trouble was. Rennie came with me – I wanted to get him out of it. He said it was the most terrifying trip he'd ever done, because he couldn't hear a thing, he'd gone completely deaf. He had to keep watching me, and dive for cover when I did. And there was a lot of firing going on. It must have been terrifying.

When we got down to the mountain road below the vineyard, a thing that upset me more than anything during the war, horrifying – there was a house built onto the side of the mountain, and you could see where a stick of bombs, probably from a Yankee Flying Fortress, had pinpointed along the road and hit the house. The last bomb had hit what was obviously a donkey cart, with a load of belongings. There were bits and pieces scattered around, and there lying in the gutter was an old woman's arm, with a wedding ring on. I think it affected the whole party more than anything we'd ever seen. That was all that was left – this old hand, with a wedding ring on.

We held that road for two or three days, something like that. We got highly commended on that job. My men came down to the town and then we marched back to Reggio Calabria, picked up our mail, which we hadn't had for a hell of a long time, and then we went on up to Termoli.

Termoli was terrible.

CHAPTER NINETEEN

The object of the Termoli landings was to take the town to help Allied forces trying to break through the so-called Termoli line north of Bari. The overall mission was assigned to the Special Service Brigade. The task of SRS was to land with 2 Commando and take two bridges. Members of 2 SAS were also present, having driven in with jeeps and intending to use Termoli as a base for behind-the-line operations.

REG SEEKINGS

Termoli was one of the worst times of the unit. Really we were just shock troops. The navy had cocked it up and we were late getting ashore. We worked in conjunction with the Marine Commando. They were going down into the harbour there. There were some bridges they wanted us to take, to stop the Germans from blowing them up. We were trying to speed up the advances. Anyway, it was late, just on dawn, when we landed. We made our way across country, and it was getting so light then that we had to take to the ditches and wade waist-high – it was the only way we could get across, because it was all so open. We were making our way to the main road, and there was a big farmhouse there.

We'd just about reached the main road when we heard vehicles starting up in the farm.

We could hear Germans shouting. Firing had started down in the harbour, and it was obvious that the troops in the farm were going down to support them. So we poured out of our ditches, where they were defending the road. There was a three-wheel track motorcycle pulling a recoilless gun – one of the first we saw – and we realised then this was Airborne, because they were the only troops that had them then. There were twenty-odd piled onto this bike and trailer, all laughing and chatting. So we ran – got over the ditch we were wading through, to keep under cover a bit, stop ourselves from being skylined. I've never experienced fire like it. Those lads of mine were bloody magnificent. They opened up and the air was thick with lead. Practically cut chunks of it out. And in seconds they'd gone. It pinned the driver, he was killed immediately, and all of 'em, in seconds. Two could have survived. They survived the initial blast and ran. We got one, and the other one stopped, turned round, brought his gun up and I got him. They could have got away, those two, but they turned to have a go – good fighters.

Then the action started. And then we found out that it was the German 1st Parachute Division, the people from Crete – they had Cretan armbands – and we had all morning fighting them. It was one of their company command posts at this farmhouse. We had quite a battle there with them until Alec Muirhead, a mortar man, managed to make contact with them and he could see me, and so I said: 'Can you see me?' He said: 'Yes.' I said: 'Well, aim on me plus twenty-five, and you'll be spot on.' And he was spot on. I had that confidence in this man. He was fantastic with the mortar. So he aimed on me plus twenty-five and we wiped 'em out.

These people were either dead or wounded before they surrendered. Their major was a huge chap. Everyone was wounded, even he had got wounds. When they came in, one, a lieutenant, was being carried on a stretcher, and that was his young brother, and this major said: 'Please shoot him, he's beyond it.' And he was; his stomach was all blown out. So Chalky White finished him off, and this major just blinked and he said: 'The trouble is with you people, you are too hard.' I said: 'Well, that's good, coming from people like you.' They'd been in Crete and all over; they were prouder of their Cretan armbands than of their Iron Crosses.

But when he saw us he said: 'Ah! SAS. I said to my men, "This is strange, I've never known men to fight this hard." If I had known we would never have fought like this.' I said: 'Why not?' He said: 'What? Good men kill good men? Our job is to kill the ordinary troops. You kill the panzer people, the tank people, the infantry. But you don't kill each other.'

That was their attitude. I can't understand it; it was amazing. We come across it in different periods. That was their attitude throughout the war with the German crack units: why should good men kill each other? You just go and kill the minions. I suppose there's something to be said for it, you've got to admit that. It's safer to kill somebody from the pioneers than it is a crack unit.

We were given the order to withdraw, but the Germans didn't know that, and so I quickly knocked out some more machine gun nests. The only way we could pull out was through a sewer, where all the pig filth was. It went under the road, in a culvert, and you had to clean your weapon when you got to the other side – all this slime and crap. I was helping to get chaps through, and I had a pack on my back and being big too, I ducked down, and I had to get down so low, my face went under. Jesus!

One of the funniest things I've seen was this physical training instructor who'd come with us, and he'd got a mortar, and we were in wet ploughed fields, it was greasy, and I said: 'Gus, get across to the machine gunner over there.' Titch, the little kid who'd given a false age to get in, was doing wonders over there. I said to Gus: 'You'd better run, Gus, they've got a good gunner there.' And to see Gus running, and he was marking time, he was skidding. I'm sure the German gunner had a sense of humour. He wasn't trying to hit Gus, he was just laughing because he looked so funny. Looked like one of those comedy acts.

Fraser, Wiseman and the rest joined us and went quite a distance to this bridge. It had already been blown the day before, the locals told us. Whilst we were waiting there, having a rest and a brew-up, the ordinary infantry were coming across and moving up a ridge taking up positions. They'd been having an easy ride up to that time. I ran into the colonel and I told him he wanted to get a grip on his men or they'd be wiped out – the way they were moving, you see. I got a blast from him, told to mind my own bloody business; I was just a bloody sergeant and he'd take no advice from a sergeant. A few seconds later he'd lost the biggest part of his men, hundreds of them. Oh God, you've never seen casualties like it in your life. They wouldn't believe me that they were walking right into the 88 area, where all the batteries were. They were really slaughtered, mown down by all sorts of fire.

PAT RILEY

We took Termoli and we went back and billeted ourselves in a big place inside the town. There was a billiard table there and we were sort of putting ourselves comfortable – Paddy and Bill Fraser and Bill Gunn the doctor. After some time Paddy said: 'Let's have a game of billiards.' So we all said alright, and the four of us got around the table and started playing, and at that moment Jerry put in a counter attack – there were really shells dropping all round the place, and it was a bit of a shambles. Paddy never ever showed any emotion whatsoever. He just carried on with the game. I thought to myself: Well, if you can do it, chum, I'll do it with you. And we did. We finished that game, and then we went out to get things sorted.

There's a lighthouse in Termoli, and Jerry was up there, and as far as we know, directing artillery fire. Unfortunately I lost most of my chaps there. I was lucky. When I say lucky, Harry Milne, my batman, came up to me and said that Paddy wanted to speak to me, and I went back with him, and that's when the shells landed and the next thing I knew I was halfway down the street, lying on my back, laughing like hell. It must have been shock or whatever you like to say.

We picked ourselves up and got back and it was terrible. Jockie Henderson, my sergeant, I picked him up and his arm had gone. I'd got him onto a stretcher, and his arm fell down, and he reached across and pulled his arm over his body, and then just stuck his thumb up. He died later on. But just shows the type of chap we had.

REG SEEKINGS

We moved back and took up quarters in a monastery in the middle of Termoli, and the rest of the troops came in waiting for the next move. I was in a cafe with two or three men and the brigadier was in there with some of his senior officers, and a despatch rider came in with a despatch. I heard the brigadier say: 'We'd better get the SRS on this.' Immediately I rushed out and told Paddy that something was coming along, we were being moved, so we were all more or less prepared when the instructions came. Then this chap arrived, and we'd got to take up positions: the Germans were attacking hard, reckoned they were going to capture the place.

The Germans had been ranging directions from someone in the town for days. But these new troops from Britain laughed at us, said we didn't know what we were talking about. We were getting bracketing fire – a shell would come in and the next one would be way back there, the next one a bit more, the next one, bomp, then they'd change to somewhere else. It was obvious to experienced men that there was an OP, an observation post, somewhere, and he was ranging all the different spots in the town.

We got up on captured German trucks, outside the monastery. We were carrying 78 grenades – about a foot long, four or five inches wide, carrying a couple of pounds of explosive and a long red detonator that went in the centre. You could throw them at a tank and they'd explode on contact, or just drop them off and they were enough to blow the tracks off a tank. Under no circumstances were you supposed to carry these armed because the det was a bit sensitive. So I carried the dets, and we all had a grenade in our pack, because we were expecting to come up against tanks.

My truck was being driven by Sergeant McInch. He was sick but said he could drive a truck. They'd said they wanted every man possible for this – things were serious. We got on the truck, then fresh orders and more orders –

off the truck, on the truck, off the truck. We were browned off. Next minute we'd get blown to hell, because we knew Jerry had the range. After messing around the first salvoes started to come over, and I was all: 'Come on, let's get moving.' We'd just had the order to get off, and I was just kicking the fastening loose on the back of the tailboard, and the next thing, Christ, a God Almighty crash and explosion, and one landed right smack in the truck.

I was carrying all the dets, plus a bomb, but mine never went off, and practically everybody else's exploded. And some of these mines exploded on the chaps' backs. The funny thing was, the shell landed nearer to me than anybody, and all I got was just a bit hit, didn't even break the skin, or perhaps jumping out of the blast I scraped my finger against something – I had a minute fracture in my fingernail and was blown off the truck, along with two others that survived. Mac, a little Scot, a roughneck, complained of a sore foot later on. He took his boot off and the sole was cut in half – a piece of shrapnel had sliced his stocking like a razor blade, and hadn't touched the skin. Amazing. But we were smothered in bits of flesh; it was hanging on the phone wires, on the roof, a hell of a mess.

I went to the cab of the truck and saw McInch still sitting there. I said: 'Christ, Mac, what the hell's wrong with you? Come on, get out and give us a hand. Don't sit there grinning like a bloody Cheshire cat.' I thought his nerves had gone. He didn't move; he was still grinning. I was mad by this time and I yanked the door open. Dead as a doornail. There wasn't a mark on him, just sitting there with a big smile on his face. Piece of shrapnel had gone right through and killed him instantly, with a grin on his face. The ones that were still alive were taken away. This chap Gilmour with his eye blown out, came up and saluted and asked permission to go to hospital.

I had two men throw their arms away that day. One, Sergeant Patterson, was hanging upside down with all his chest blown open – I could see his lungs and heart beating – and his tommy gun was on his chest. He said: 'Reg, take that gun off, it's hurting me.' Seemed calm and collected. I got him down, and he got his arm and pulled it off and said: 'It's a bad one this time.' I said: 'You'll be alright, we'll get you to hospital.' I knew we wouldn't. He wanted some water. I stepped across a mass of pulp and a voice, calm as hell, said: 'Sergeant, can you get me a drink please, I'm thirsty.' It was Corporal Grant. His face was pulp – I couldn't recognise him, only his voice. He was the other one that took his arm and dropped it to one side. Again the heart and lungs were visible. One lived an hour and a quarter, the other an hour and a half. They were good lads.

There was a whole family that had been doing a bit of washing for us – they were standing there, waving us off. They were dead, lying in a heap. The women must have been split open. The man was blown apart, disembowelled, and a young boy about twelve years old. One of my men was burning, it was the first time I'd seen a body burning, and I didn't realise how fast a body can burn. That was Skinner. He was dead, but it was a bit horrible to see him burning away. And I don't know, it was just one of those things, all the other carnage around you, but the sight of your friends, burning, I thought, Hell, the first thing that came to mind: I've got to put it out. There was a big jug of water in this house, and I was stepping over bodies to get the water to pour on Skinner, and this young lad was lying on the top and his guts were blown out like a huge balloon. Suddenly he got up and ran around screaming. Terrible sight. I had to shoot him. There was absolutely no hope for him, and you couldn't let anybody suffer like that. So I caught him and I shot him – there was nothing you could do. As I was stepping over to pour the water over Skinner, put him out, I stepped over a body that was just pulp – face, no – just pulp, you couldn't possibly recognise it.

Another man, Davison, Little Titch, he'd given the false age to Dempsey – I should imagine when he got killed he was no more than fifteen – and I did recognise him, but his face from his nose, his jaw and everything had been blown away, and he was laying on his back, and so I got hold of his equipment to lift him out of the way, so I could see what else was going on, and the body just dropped away from the equipment, he was so shattered.

There were only two alive, Gilmour and one other lad. And myself. This other chap later went round the bend, never spoke again. Two nights later we caught him smashing his head against a brick wall. We had to tie him down and send him off – I don't know what happened to him.

It's shattering, because these were the first men I'd actually commanded. When I say 'commanded', I had always been working with John and Stirling in small parties, and I'd never had any men really of my own. And this time I'd had men which I'd trained, new men, and moulded them together. And so you had a real rapport with them, and they were good, they were more than . . . And it'd been a long campaign too, and they'd become more than just your men; they were your friends, your pals.

I don't know why the delay occurred. This is the typical sort of thing that you get. It's the old story very often – you're highly trained, specialised training, and you come under the command of a man that hasn't done one iota of specialised training. But the mere fact that he's an officer, and particularly a senior officer – he knows a damned sight more than you do, and he's allowed to direct you. And this is where the whole thing breaks down. This brigadier, he was hopeless. Shocking. Indecision, no decisions. All that on/off was all him, nothing to do with Paddy. Brigade kept sending messages.

I knew where Paddy was, so I thought: Well, the best thing I can do is go and report this all to Paddy, and they said that they would bury the mess. And so I stayed with Paddy, and told him what had happened. I was smothered from head to foot in flesh and blood – it was terrible for the next two or three days, because of the smell and the flies. Then news came through to us that Corporal Kit Kennedy's troop – part of SRS – was cut off a little bit further along the coast. Kennedy was an ex-Scots Greys man. He found an old horse in a farmyard, and rode it through the German lines, and reported that his unit was cut off and were needing help.

Paddy said to me: 'How about it?' My reaction was: 'They got into trouble, let them get out.' I was going to leave it to them themselves to get out of it. Then Doc Gunn said: 'Where's Little Seekings?' That was my kid brother. And I realised: 'Oh good God, he's with them.' So I went off, as the only reinforcement.

The only way I could find them was to more or less join in the German attack on them. The Germans were firing at these farm buildings, across a couple of hundred yards of ploughed fields. I thought the only way I could get across was to just walk across, not do any firing, and just hope they think it's somebody gone mad. I kept on walking, and actually the firing stopped. The only bullets fired at me were fired by Pat Riley, who was in the farmhouse and didn't recognise me. My brother recognised me and stopped him. I think the reason the Germans didn't shoot me down was because they didn't know what was going on.

And it paid off. I knew if I could make a few yards, I could perhaps dive between furrows and crawl over that way. But I made it across, and got them organised. When I was moving up, I could see that on the beach was some dead ground, and no German troops there. As I was moving towards the farm I was also looking for an escape route. So I sent them off in little groups of four or five to rendezvous at a railway bridge, with a stream going out into the sea. There was a great big culvert there. That would be their rendezvous – it was under cover from fire. The last batch out was the officers and they came out with me. Naturally I'd come with Pat Riley, because he was an old mate.

When we got back I reported to Paddy. In the meantime, Paddy had anticipated that they'd be short of food, etc., and he and Bob Bennett collected up quite a bit of food. Bob and I put all the stuff in a tin bath and carried it down to them. We had to carry it over this railway line. I'd been over it two or three times. There was a German mortar team, and they had these multiple mortars, which fired about half a dozen rounds. They'd fired on me every time, so I said to Bob: 'We've got to run like hell across this line, otherwise they'll blow us to hell. We can't stop, we've just got to go, and pray.' Sure enough, they came down, and I'm not kidding, one bomb went between Bennett and I, under the bath, and dived into the deck just a yard or two in front of us. Fortunately for us it was a dud.

Another funny thing I saw there – I wandered off into the middle of town. Things had quietened down a lot there but there was a hell of a mess, absolute shambles. By this time the army had come through, tanks, etc., and a Bofors team had set up by the crossroads. I came along and they said: 'Watch it, sir, there's a sniper up there.' 'Well, why don't you have a go at him?' But they didn't know where he was.

There was only one building that could really have had a sniper in, a tall one: by some miracle the windows were still intact. Well, you can't fire through a window without breaking glass, and there was one window open, so it was obvious this was where the chap was.

Whilst we were walking, an old boy came out, crawling along on his walking stick, bent double, and this German must have had a sense of humour – he took the old chap's hat off, clean as a whistle. This old chap was away down the road with his walking stick – oh, it was hilarious. I said: 'We'll fix him.' I went across the street to have a go, but this German obviously realised when he spotted me and there was no more fire. He knew we'd got his number and he got the hell out of it.

There was a shortage of ammunition. The 25-pounder batteries were rationed in the number of shells they could use in a day. But I found this battery of 4.5 mortars, which I'd never heard of before. They'd got a stack of ammunition there. So I said they should join in and take an extra 150. They did, and I believe they did a good job. They were so green, they were wondering what sort of bees were buzzing through the orchard. They were bullets.

That had been a terrible day. It didn't seem possible anybody could survive, because shells were landing hail after hail. We had German Tiger tanks, Mark 4s, the lot, against us. One of our sections were actually fighting a Tiger tank with bare hands. My young brother in the churchyard even got singed by the muzzle blast of the tanks. We were using other people's anti-tank guns, where the crews had deserted. We used anything we could get to try and stem the attack. We lost good young officers there.

Dempsey came up in the middle of all this and talked to one or two of us, then he went back through a hail of fire and got back to this river that was holding everything up. The Royal Engineers were getting heavy fire and taking cover, and getting a Bailey bridge across. Dempsey himself got on the bridge and got it across. Montgomery came up, saw what was going on, and joined Dempsey on the bridge, and they got it across, and got the tanks rolling. But the people who actually saved our bacon was a squadron or maybe more of Canadian tanks. They came from the central sector of Italy, tore across country and joined us. They quickly disposed of one or two Tigers and several Mark 4s, and broke up the attack. So we really owed everything to them. They were very good indeed.

I'd been promised that someone would clean up all my boys and bury them. When I got back they were still there, been there for three days – what a mess. Doc Gunn found me there. One torso we found fifty or sixty yards away in D Squadron's office on the second floor, blown right through the window. We only recognised the body by the torso. He was a man that had a very sensitive skin – the only one I'd come across who had permission to wear linen shirts, army shirts brought him out in a rash – and he couldn't take sun in any way. That's all we found of him.

We buried the pieces we could find in the monastery gardens. I was picking up the identity tags when Doc came along and kicked up hell because I was doing the job. It wasn't a job for me to do, they were all my mates, but nobody else had done it. So he kicked up and made a hell of a fuss. It would have been bad enough anyway, but with the stench . . .

I was wondering where Jock Finlay was – he was another sergeant, absolutely first class. Very clever man, studying to be an auctioneer, he'd practically passed all his exams, engaged to be married. There were big bushes of mock orange in this garden, and as I hacked that away, there was Jock. His face was unmarked, a grin on it – it had been so sudden, all of this, you see – a perfect bust. But that was all we could find of him, just his head. Not a mark on it. That was one of the worst experiences of the lot really.

It was very bad. It was a shame that people with those qualities were used in that manner. We were the hack-on outfit. But in my opinion, we got into these fixes because we were directed by people who didn't know what they were doing. This was the brigadiers, they were the trouble. Certainly wasn't Dempsey's fault.

The initial decision was to go in and hold the bridge. Fair enough, it's important to hold bridges open – a job that's worth it. But there was bad information – the bridge had been blown, and they should have known about that. They were boasting about their up-to-date information. And they were late in putting us in. You may be small parties but if you're determined and you've got the supplies and use a bit of guile, it doesn't take much to hold up an army. As long as you've got men with guts and the physical ability. But it's no good sending those men on a lost cause.

Paddy Mayne was fantastic. The first infantry into Termoli were the London Irish. Paddy said: 'Sure, you'll see some fighting now.' Oh Christ! When he went to his billet, the London Irish had looted all his kit. He didn't mention London Irish after that!

PAT RILEY

That was the end of the activities, as far as it comes. We went down to Bari, further down the coast, and we were drinking there one night with Paddy – I was anyway – and he suddenly turned to me and says: 'I'd like you to go back to England, I think there's something happening back there.' So I said: 'Yeah, OK.' I liked the idea quite truthfully. And a little later on that night, we were still having a drink and he said: 'I thought I said to you to get back to England.' I said: 'Yeah, just give me time to drink this and then I'll go.'

REG SEEKINGS

You hear people speculating why Paddy didn't get the VC, etc., but the simple reason was you couldn't get the VC in our crowd. There was never a buckshee officer there to witness the deed. Only once were VCs offered, and that was the crossing at Casino.

They couldn't get across. The Guards had been beaten back, they'd suffered tremendous casualties trying to cross this flooded river. Paddy had called me down and told me my Military Medal had come through, and then he told about the crossing. I forget which squadron he said was going to do it, and I blew my top. He said: 'No.1 troop has been in the thick of everything, you've done the whole lot, I thought it was time you had a rest.' I said: 'On a thing like this, there's only one troop that can do it, and that's No.1. We've done all the crap, we've got to do this.'

Paddy said: 'I'm going.' I said: 'Well, we can get across together.' As I was going out the door, he called me back: 'By the way, I've been told there's two VCs on this if we can do it. I've put my name on one, I'll put your name on the other.' I said: 'Right.' So we planned how to get across. He said: 'What sort of swimmer are you?' 'Quite good, what about you?' 'Not so hot,' he said, 'but I won't drown.' So I said: 'We'll strip and take a light line over – our chaps can give us covering fire, and if we can get two heavy ropes across the lads will go across like greased lightning.' That was our plan. But then the army didn't want to use us, they said we were far too valuable for a thing like that – said they were giving it another go with the Guards. They made it, and our chance of a VC went out the window. We weren't really so worried about that, but we would have liked to have done that. It was a challenge.

Paddy was always in control of himself. He wasn't an excitable man. You'd think so if you read some of the reports about him. But he wasn't, he was a very intelligent man, he was a very quiet man, and he was hard, ruthless. When things got rough, Paddy got more and more determined and I think he became more clear cut in what he wanted and what he was going to do. He didn't go ranting and raving mad. Paddy was much like myself on that. He just became colder and colder and colder.

CHAPTER TWENTY

After his capture, and good fortune of having his identity mistaken in Berlin, David Stirling spent time in a variety of prison camps. Together with the remarkable Jack Pringle, whom he had met before the war, he attempted a number of escapes. In typical Stirling fashion, he is fairly offhand about describing his exploits.

DAVID STIRLING

In the camps I met Jack Pringle. He was very important to me at that time. We set up various escapes together. I was out two or three times.

At one camp I had an escape op, which resulted, I think, in fifty-eight prisoners getting out. I was moved on from there to Marisch Trubau about three weeks before the escape took place. Pringle wasn't in that camp. The prisoners had to qualify before they could be put on the escape list. It was a fairly large camp, about 1,800 or so, and there were lots to consider. We took about two hundred into consideration, and they had to make a certain time round the perimeter, and under their coats they had to carry a very large amount of weight. They had to pass exams in respect of their escape routes. They had to know everything. They had to make their own clothes to the highest standard. The whole thing was run in a highly disciplined way, thoroughly rationalised, and it did come off. Two or three guys got away. That was a pure escape proposition.

When we were moved from Italy, Jack and I escaped off the Innsbruck station. We had quite a time then we were recaptured. About four days after our recapture we were taken into a camp where there were Russians next door to us. We were in a small enclave; it was a very nasty place to be in; they were really after us. We got out of there in the early morning, there was a fog down and we had to swim a river. It was a very fast current and we both came up swimming back in the direction in which we'd come. But then the current took over, and we were washed up on the opposite bank, the one we wanted to get to. Our footprints showed as we raced across the fields. We got into the woods and they sent the dogs after us. I was immensely sick and that delayed the dogs, while they lapped up our breakfast. We made a bit of time then. We got away from the dogs, but we were captured about three days later. Fitzroy Maclean, who had been with me in the desert, was in Yugoslavia. I was going down there to join him.

The important one was in Bohemia, in Czechoslovakia, which we planned as a major undertaking. It wasn't an escape. The purpose of that for us was to create hell within Czechoslovakia and make effective the partisans there. They were outraged at the Sudetenland being taken away. They were very anti-German – their President was Benes, I think, and he was very opposed to the German occupation. It could have had quite an effect: the Germans weren't very strong on the ground there.

It took an awful lot of laying on. There were two thousand prisoners in this camp, and I had to get the Senior British Officer to agree. The first one was no good, I had him sacked, then there was another one who gave consent. I had a marvellous time planning the whole thing. If we'd been caught, I think we would have been done in.

We had to plan the escape very carefully. We had sixty-five going out. We were going to use a third of the escapees to help strengthen the partisans in Bohemia and Czechoslovakia. Of the other two-thirds, one lot was going to try and make it back northwards, or to Switzerland; the others were going south. We therefore had to have three parties out to do reconnaissance in all those areas, so we had to have three escapes, in addition to the main one. The chaps had to get out, then get themselves recaptured.

Jack Pringle was able to persuade the Germans that he required special medical treatment, and so he used to go out of the camp, accompanied by someone who put him in touch with various authentic intelligence experts who let him know what was going on, particularly within Czechoslovakia as a whole, and how we could best implement that part of the plan. So we were fairly well fixed for that escape to be a success.

We got the first echelon out OK. One of us was to go down to Bratislava and get himself recaptured so he came back to us. Another one went to Prague, and so on. They were deliberately letting themselves be recaptured so they could bring back the information; they weren't allowed to escape, they were reconnaissance. The first echelon was very successful; we had all the information necessary. I think two were caught and executed, and two we met later in Colditz.

The mass escape was by a platform constructed out of Red Cross boxes, which broke down into twelve fairly strong sections to make a bridge. The escape involved breaking up the platform, making it into the bridge, and putting the bridge across the wire perimeter from the windows, which were quite close to the side of the camp. Then there was the outside wire, where we had the guard bribed.

The bridge was based on the proposition of a highland platform for the enthusiasts who liked to keep fit and go in for their dancing – the Highland method. And it was really rather cruel to see these wretched English having to learn Highland customs and techniques in dancing, but they had to, to make it creditable. There weren't enough Highlanders in the entire camp to provide a supply.

In order to bring this escape to success, it was necessary to do two things. First of all we had to make it clear to the Germans that they had a reliable individual in the camp who was prepared to keep them informed about what escapes were going on. In order to keep credibility behind that individual, who would write letters to the German camp commandant, it was necessary to betray two tunnels, one of which was already below the wire, but which I knew wasn't necessarily going to succeed – there were a lot of technical difficulties with it. By telling the Germans, this 'traitor' – who was actually Jack Pringle, who was my No. 1 assistant on the escape side, writing with his left hand – enabled the Germans to catch these blokes underground. They were all put into jug for a month, but it meant that we had an intelligence direct to the Germans, and they thought they had an inside chap whom they trusted.

It was a rather ferocious step to have to take, but it paid off, because they really believed this guy. Because when we did have the over-the-wire escape, it was vital that they were looking confidently at another point in the camp, where the informer would have told them that there was going to be an escape that night. We had to establish a trusty situation. This was after we'd got back the reports we needed from the reconnaissance. It was quite elaborately planned. And that worked admirably, and there were various – to the Germans – movements made which, to them, carried authenticity. My security intelligence officer for this later became Deputy Director General of MI5.

But they rumbled us. I think they discovered something. Jack and I could never decide what caused it: someone may have figured out what we were up to and reported back to the Germans. I think it was due to that. We did have a particular guy who might have been a double agent, who was giving us various stuff but he might also have been giving stuff to the Germans. Ten days before the actual break took place, we were moved in chains to Brunswick, much further west.

I think they moved us there partly because they wanted prisoners next door to the Goering works, which were in a huge 4,000-acre wood, camouflaged. It was turning out very important stuff, and they thought it would never be attacked if it was so close to a prison camp. I think the Germans were beginning to be very apprehensive about the very accurate night bombing of the RAF, and also the Americans in daytime.

They thought that if the camp was next door to them, it would protect them from being bombed. That was their theory anyway. We sent information back about what they were producing in there. Codes back to London made it clear that the works were there and that everyone in the camp were expecting near misses, while they did their utmost to eliminate the Hermann Goering works.

There was a particular fellow called Black, quite a famous racing correspondent. He hated being bombed. He went into a sort of tin cupboard that was shared between ten or so prisoners, and he got into this tin and closed the door. This was a preliminary false alarm air raid and – this is the sort of thing one remembers – we made all the noises of bombers coming down and exploding, with the whistles, etc. We turned his box over every which way, with him still inside it. He thought it was an appalling raid. Finally we said the raid was over, and he emerged from his tin box, absolutely white and whackeroo. He was properly teased.

There were several major bombing raids on the works. I was there for the first one or two but missed the final raid, where there were quite a few casualties in the camp. We were also organising an escape there. Then they moved me and Jack Pringle to Colditz.

Colditz was very different – it was a marvellous camp. It was made up of all nationalities, and I met up with three of my former French colleagues. But they were not only all countries, but all services, and it was quite small, and the atmosphere was really exceptionally good – it was a very enjoyable camp. They were fairly well practised at chemin de fer as well, so I polished up my techniques while I was there. I also drew up my plans for the Chunking project, to take SAS and American Special Forces to the Far East, while I was there. I presented these to Churchill when I came back.

As has been said, Stirling was characteristically dismissive of his escape attempts.

At his first camp, Gavi (a fortress sitting on an outcrop of rock) he managed to join a group already planning an escape, but was spotted by guards during the attempt and fought off three before being dragged down. When Gavi was closed and the prisoners moved to Austria, several concealed themselves in prearranged hideouts; Pringle and Stirling spent two very cramped days in a cavity under a toilet before they were discovered. En route to their new camp, in a rail convoy of cattle trucks, the two escaped but were caught two days later. (Stirling does describe the escape from the camp for Russian POWs at Markt Pongau.) At Marisch Trubau, when a large group were moved to Brunswick shortly before the mass breakout, Stirling hid in another hiding place, but was eventually found.

In all of these escapes, of course, Stirling had one great disadvantage – his height. At six feet four inches tall, it was difficult not to stand out.

But what of Colditz?

During the interview, Stirling did not go into details of his period there – the suggestion being that all he did was polish up his chemin de fer. As well as developing his Chunking project, however, what he actually did in Colditz was remarkable, and possibly more important than his plans for a guerrilla army to break out from Marisch Trubau.

And what of the other Original, 'Gentleman' Jim Almonds, captured during the big Benghazi raid?

JIM ALMONDS

I ended up in the POW camp at Altamura, in Puglia. I used to walk round the prison camp and I was sure, if I placed my feet right, I could go right over that barbed wire fence. I never put it to the test. It wasn't that high, but it was wide. It was a matter of getting your feet on the right strand, the tension being right, and you could maintain your balance. If you'd stood on one that was too loose, you'd miss your distance to the next one.

I eventually got myself a job through cultivating the warrant officer in charge of the camp – it was an Other Ranks camp, from the British point of view – and he was set aside in a hut on his own. He got me a job helping with the Red Cross parcels. The parcels were stored in what was once probably a coach-house. We would go across there when parcels were available, all stood behind a long table, and you opened each parcel, took a tin out and punctured it, so no food would keep. This was to prevent it being stored away by potential escapees.

There were a number of other POWs working there – a New Zealander, Merlyn Craw, from the Long Range Desert Group; an Australian serving in the British Navy, he got sunk on a destroyer outside of Tobruk; the third was a red-haired South African, taken prisoner at Tobruk, and myself.

After a bit I noticed one of the guards had a lot of weaknesses. One of them was coffee, which was in the Red Cross parcels.

It was getting near dusk, when our locking-up time came along. The South African, Jan, took Tinenti, the Italian officer in charge, outside to look at the Red Cross parcel boxes. That got rid of No.1. There was only the corporal and the sentry left. We sent the sentry, Dragonetti, to get some water to brew the coffee, which left the corporal. He stood looking out the door, instead of looking in at us, and I went behind him, round his neck, and shut his wind off. We pulled him down, tied him up, and put him in a corner. Then Dragonetti came back with the water, and he went the same way. When Jan brought the officer back, he came in the door and suddenly stopped short. He saw there was no sentry on the door. We all made a dive for him. He had a pistol on his belt. We got him down, and were struggling in the darkness to stop him from calling out. We were gagging each other in the dark. Anyway we got him down, shoved one sock inside his mouth, tied it with another, and tied his hands and feet. Then we grabbed bags and took everything we could, raisins, etc., stuffed them in, and crept outside. Over a wall, and we decided to do a detour. We thought the first thing they'd think was we'd gone one way, so we went out, right round the camp, then back and headed south.

The first night we covered about eighteen miles, which got us to the foothills. As dawn was breaking we split up. There were bushes scattered about and each one went into a bush – they weren't big enough to take two – and crouched down in the middle of the bush. There was a man grazing cattle round the bushes all day, with a dog. The dog would come along and stare fixedly at you, then he'd go away and go and stare at somebody else. He never gave us away.

Nightfall we set off again and we went on until we came to the Bay of Taranto and we got right down near the beach and we were walking along it and came to a stream which ran into the bay and as we got over near the side, there was a sentry box there. The bloke shouted out and we didn't say a word; we all scarpered. He fired a shot but we carried on.

We got down as far as Rocco in Reggio Calabria. I was quite fit myself, the South African was fit and the New Zealander was fit, but Tom, the Australian, was in rather a bad way. He couldn't go any further and we didn't know what to do. It was a question then, do we leave him and carry on without him, or what do we do? So we decided we'd stay with him.

The Allies hadn't landed, so we decided to pack it in. I don't know how many days we'd been on the go. It's like all these escape stories. At night time you go along the road, and find all the beans planted for the spring. We ate dried nettles. Most of the stuff in our bags was by this time just a huge mass. You didn't know whether you had soup or raisins or what.

It was winter time, and cold, and climbing up these hills . . . that's what upset the Aussie. Anyway, we went into a farmhouse and said: 'We're escaped POWs.' The carabinieri arrived and took us to the town and the local inhabitants were kindness itself. They made us omelettes, etc., they were very hospitable. The carabinieri took us back by train. On the train were some German troops and they were all laughing and cheering – they thought we were fliers that had been shot down. The Italians were really annoyed about this.

When we got back to this camp, the first bloke I saw, waiting on the platform, was Tinenti, the Italian officer we'd duffed up and tied and gagged and so on. He was terribly agitated. He was wild, he couldn't keep still – he was in a terrible state. Incidentally, the corporal was stripped of his rank. I don't know what happened to the lieutenant, but he was obviously in great disgrace. They told us we'd be court-martialled. An advocate had been arranged for our defence, from Rome, and we were in close confinement from then on. They let it be known that the penalty for striking an Italian officer, for a POW, was the same as the penalty for an Italian private soldier – which was death. So the thing began to take on a serious look.

Then the camp was closed down and they moved us up to PG71, at Fermor, near Ancona. While we were at Ancona the Italian government collapsed and it looked as though the Germans were going to take over the country. The Italians were also frightened about what the Germans were going to do, now that the Italian government had given up the war. The camp commandant came to see me and said: 'Would you do a reconnaissance and report back on the German troop positions in the area?' Why he didn't send his own people I can't think, but anyway I went out for him and I rang him up from villages round the camp and told him what the German positions were – there was only one real bad concentration and that was at San Giorgio. I worked round until I was at the most southerly part of my circuit, then I rang him up and told him: 'That's the lot, I've been right round.' He said: 'Well, you can come back into camp.' I said: 'No, I'm going south, I'm going to join up with my own people.' And I set off to walk down from Ancona – I think it was about 600km.

There were three of us. We set off down south and then split. It wasn't my old party and I couldn't get on with them. Every one was a leader and wanted to do their own thing. I felt I had more chance on my own. One day I did fifty miles in twenty-four hours.

On the way there were one or two interesting little episodes, one of them where I entered the village of Civitella Casanovo, just having passed the Gran Sasso d'Italia, and turned round the corner into the bottom of the main village street, and on the other side of the road there was a German truck loading up. I daren't retrace my steps, because it'd look suspicious, because they'd seen me. I was too tall really for an Italian; I had to walk in a silly crouched fashion anyway. I opened the first door I came to and went into an Italian house, then through into a passage and through another door on the left-hand side. There was a family sitting down having a meal. I walked past them and put my fingers up to my lips as a sign for them to keep quiet and opened the window at the back of the house and went out down the garden. Then I went round the village and got back on my trek southwards.

Another occasion, I had to cross a main road which was heavily picketed by the Germans, and the only feasible way of getting across after dark was to float down a stream under a bridge. There were sentries on the bridge, and I had a bunch of nettles you put over my face to stop the glint of the white of a face. You just lay and you eased yourself along with your fingers over the pebbles, down in this water.

Another time, I was crossing a road with lots of traffic on it. Across the road was a potato patch and a man hoeing it. As the German trucks came past, I laid down between two rows of potatoes. This man who was hoeing looked at me. I looked at him.

I came out the other end and there was a party of partisans who wanted me to join them. I was just walking along the river and they were there fishing. I had a meal of trout with them. They said they were forming a resistance movement and asked me to join them. I said: 'I've got some important business further down the line.' We parted good friends and off I went.

I picked up an American pilot, a Captain Nielson of the American Air Force. He'd been shot down in the area and I got in touch with him. The Italians told me about him; we got together by passing notes. We holed up in a village and I went into a little place, right on its own, where there was a man called Paolo. He had one donkey and a few sheep. He lived in one half of the place and the stable was the other half, with a little hayloft above. He agreed for me to go up there. There was a German 88mm battery in the back of the paddock behind this house, and the German officers used to come in, and barter with the farmer for chickens and things. By looking through the cracks in the floorboards I could see the Germans down below, bartering for goods. They used to give the owner a little ticket. I don't think the Italian would ever get any money back on those tickets.

We decided to make a break on a certain day and carry on down. Crossing one main road was very difficult. We tried several times, but there was always somebody to see you. We passed at night, floating under a bridge. The bridge was guarded, all ready for demolition probably. But by floating down in the dark, we got away with it. This was September – better time to escape really. One night walk, we passed a hidden encampment and walked through it very carefully, hairs standing up on the back of your neck. There were all sorts of things strewn around – cooking pots, etc. Then the next night, we billeted up in a place where an Italian was very friendly.

I knew we were at the front. We hadn't seen signs of Germans for a day or so and we'd noticed the positions on the ground where mines had been laid and so on. Finally we met up with a patrol of the American Rangers, and they led us back into their camp. We were able to help them a bit by telling them where the mines were laid. The American pilot went back with his own people, and I eventually found my way down to a place just outside of Naples, and in due course I got repatriated, went back to North Africa. The SAS were just leaving for home then and I came home to England with them.

Arriving in England . . . Down to Croydon, a rehabilitation place, trick cyclists – psychiatrists – questioned me, checked my well-being. I said I was alright and all I wanted to do was go back and rejoin my regiment. My old regiment – not the SAS – had been posted to Chequers as a guard and I was sent there.

I felt it was a great waste being at Chequers, because there's so many people who can guard the Prime Minister there, who probably weren't as capable as I was. And also, I longed for the companionship I'd experienced before, and so thought I'd probably be doing a better job if I could get back with my own people. There's a certain sense, too, of patriotism, I suppose you'd call it.

While I was at Chequers I got in touch with Ian Collins, a Lieutenant Colonel then doing something in the War Office, and I wrote to him and asked if he could pull strings to get me out of it. They did that, and I got a posting straight back to SAS.

CHAPTER TWENTY-ONE

The Originals and the rest of SRS left to return to the UK on Christmas Eve, 1943, to prepare for D-Day. SRS was given back its old status of 1 SAS and along with 2 SAS and the French and Belgians was expanded, with a large intake of new recruits, and incorporated into a brigade under the Airborne Corps.

Included amongst the new recruits were members of the so-called Auxiliary Units, the British Resistance, which had been in place with a full operational capacity since the summer of 1940.

Within the new structure, however, The Originals and the SAS were required to give up their sand-coloured beret for the red beret of the Airborne. Paddy Mayne refused.

But there were other issues.

One was locating the SAS within the overall battleplan for D-Day; another was its role. Initial plans were for the SAS to be used tactically, to be dropped close to the D-Day beaches to hold up German reinforcements. This was clearly against the First Principles established by David Stirling, which saw SAS's role as strategic.

In Sicily and Italy, the SRS had been used as frontal assault troops; Bill Stirling's 2 SAS, however, had been able to launch a number of classic SAS operations behind the lines in keeping with David's original notion.

In the spring of 1944, when Bill Stirling heard of the intended D-Day role for the SAS, he objected in the strongest possible terms. A meeting was held in mid-May, *after which the SAS role reverted back to a more strategic nature, with drops deep in France. In return Bill Stirling was forced to relinquish his command. The man who took over, however, Brian Franks, not only proved himself an outstanding replacement, but he also played a key role in the post-war story of the SAS.*

The Originals, meanwhile, carried on in their usual manner. And even in his POW camp, David Stirling was still guiding the regiment.

DAVID STIRLING

We heard the SAS was still going on; we got rather intermittent information, depending on newly arrived prisoners in the camps.

It seemed to me a danger that the Airborne Division would try and put SAS under their command, which would have ruined the strategic concept, and I wasn't sure Bill would have the arguments. So I got a letter back to him from my prisoner-of-war camp to urge him to refuse absolutely to ever allow 2 SAS regiment to be used in semi-tactical roles, that he must keep to the effective function of the regiment. Which meant collaborating with the French, deep behind the lines, and dealing with strategic target areas, rather than ones which belonged more to the Commandos and the Parachute Regiment.

Whereas the Airborne and the Commandos would be dealing with situations which were close to the front line, dealing with obstructions to their progressing satisfactorily, we went, for instance, to a major communication or railway junction, perhaps 200 miles away from the front, working with the local French Maquis, operating at night, right in the depths of France.

If Bill hadn't taken his stand, I think that they would have merged the SAS into, in effect, an airborne command. Airborne was very anxious to get hold of us at that time, and it was absolutely essential for us to retain our independence from them, because of the difference in roles.

It was difficult after I got captured, because Bill hadn't had, at that time, any operational experience. Paddy, who eventually got control of 1 SAS, had spent a lot of time operating not on the true classic SAS role in Sicily and Italy, but gradually moving towards regaining it. But Paddy didn't know his way round the headquarters, where the decision-taking all occurred, and therefore if Bill hadn't made a stand on this issue, I think it would probably have put Paddy's regiment in jeopardy as well. And, of course, the French SAS which had been formed by that time.

It was a fairly ferocious showdown, and went up to the Army Council for decision, and they never took one. I think it's probably the only unresolved case still in front of the Army Council. I don't know the technicalities of it, but in any event he had to resign and he never really got a proper function after that, which was very frustrating for him. But in resigning, he saved the regiment. He lost his battle, but the regiment won theirs.

Luckily he knew Brian Franks, who would take over command, and who would be equally true to the proper function of the regiment. Brian had the special advantage of having been in the desert with Layforce. And indeed, I'd wanted very much to recruit him into the L Detachment before 1 SAS regiment came into being, but unfortunately he'd caught some kind of bug and I could only see him in hospital and he was invalided back. Nevertheless I had a lot of discussions with him about the principles which determined the SAS operational formulas, and therefore he had a grasp of them, perhaps more so than my brother Bill.

JOHNNY COOPER

I came back first with Mike Sadler and we set up the new HQ. Pat Riley was the advance party and we were then up at Mauchline in Scotland. We then made the move to Darvel, then the squadrons were formed, 'A', 'B', 'C', 'D', and we trained for the drop. I was made air liaison officer at Ayr, because we had been jumping out of doors and now we had to jump out of apertures. I moved to the aerodrome at Ayr, and troop by troop came down, because the Albemarle bomber would only accept about nine. It had a bathtub aperture – it wasn't a circular hole. Before we went to jump in Halifaxes and Stirlings we did an Albemarle. At that stage I did plenty of jumps because I could go up every day if I needed. I stayed down there for about a month, in 'A' Squadron.

PAT RILEY

We were up in the north of England training. I jumped a wall and didn't realise one side of the wall was about three feet but the other side was about a twelve-feet drop, and I broke my thigh, so I ended up in hospital, with plaster all up the legs, all the body, right up to the chest. While I was in there, there was an officer in the next bed to me. He was getting discharged. He turned to me and he says: 'Here you are. Pat. I'm going to give you the finest gift you've ever had.'

And he handed me a knitting needle. I didn't realise what he was talking about then, but I did after a while, when I started itching, you know, and sticking a needle down to get the scratch up.

I don't know how long I was there. The boys had been awarded their various decorations down in Buckingham Palace, which I couldn't attend. That disappointed them, I think. But then they came back: it was Johnny Cooper and Reg Seekings, and Johnny Rose and another character, I can't remember who. I'm in bed in the ward and suddenly this clomping of boots comes along the corridor of the hospital. They wanted to take me out, and I said: 'Look at me, I can't go anywhere like this, I'm trapped.' And they said: 'Yeah.' Then they spotted a sort of long pram thing. 'We'll take you out in that.' And I said: 'Alright.'

The nurse agreed to let me lie in it, for half an hour, to see that I couldn't go out in it – it would be too painful. Anyway, I got into it and oh to hell. So off we went, these four characters and me. They were full of beans. We went along the road, and then they decided to find a public house so we could all go and have a drink. So they found this pub but they couldn't get me in because the door wasn't big enough. And finally there was a pub down a hill, and they found that there was a nice big double door that they could get me through. So they decided to take me down the hill. That was alright, to a certain extent, but they had great ideas. They'd let the pram go, and then they'd run after it and catch it. I visualised me ending up in a heap of plaster of Paris down the bottom of the hill, and the more I told them, the more they did it.

Anyway, I ended up in the pub eventually, and that was very convenient – I could just put my arm up and get it on the bar. Have you ever tried drinking a pint of beer with a plaster round the middle of you, where you can't expand or anything? But we carried on drinking. They got rather jolly and there was quite a bit of fun in the place, but eventually, of course, I wanted to go somewhere, and there's two old ladies sitting alongside the pram. I said: 'Excuse me, ladies, but do you mind going away for a second?' 'Aye, lad, we've been wondering how you'd manage.' I had a bottle with me, and Johnny was relief man from there on. Every time I wanted to go somewhere, he attended to it.

Anyway, we stopped there, and then they loaded the whole pram up with beer, and finally we came out the place. We ended up back in the hospital and of course you can just imagine, there was clink-clink-clink of these bottles in my pram, and of course, they all got lit up. And around were these poor chaps who were wounded fellas, and they would hand them a bottle of beer and of course all that night they called: 'Bottle, nurse.' I wasn't very popular next morning.

JIM ALMONDS

After I got in touch with Ian Collins at the War Office, he pulled some strings to get me back to SAS, and I went up to Scotland. On arrival I saw the CO, and he said: 'You're just in time for a refresher parachute course.' Then I was posted to 'D' Squadron, a new squadron that had been formed, chiefly of new lads. The officers were new too. I think I was the only L Detachment person in the unit. I became sergeant major, because of my experience.

REG SEEKINGS

Everything was being planned and Paddy called me down to the hotel where all the officers were and told me what was happening. We had regimental status, so now we'd have sah major rank, warrant ranks, etc. They'd done a bit of fiddling – the staff ranks were called troop sah majors. Also they were going to commission officers from the lads. He showed me a list and said: 'What do you think?' My name was first on the list, and I crossed it off. I said: 'No, I won't, and that's that, finish.' There was trouble over that, because they just scrapped everybody then and brought in a lot of new young officers from all over the place. I don't think any of us were commissioned at that stage. Paddy said: 'Will you take warrant rank?' I said: 'That's all I want, I'm happy with that.' So I became a fully fledged sah major. I took 'A' Squadron. Then we trained, and that was hard training too.

We recruited up quite fast. Paddy and the old senior officers were very busy interviewing, etc. The sah majors just got on with the training. We trained over the Scottish moors, then we moved down to Fairford before France.

Fairford was like a concentration camp, surrounded by barbed wire, watch towers, machine guns, searchlights. It took three security checks to go and have a shower and that was under armed guard. That's how strict it was. It was hell down there for a couple of weeks. But we had access to everything. We had big marquees put up, marked off into big cubicles, with a phone in each. We'd already been split up into little sections of half a dozen men, and given our areas. We had all the maps and the phones available, and we had a reconnaissance Spitfire and squadron attached to us. Anyone in command of an area, be it a sergeant, a warrant officer or a lieutenant, could ask for a sortie to be flown, to bring back photos of any area we picked out.

We had no actual role in D-Day apart from a party of volunteers. Everybody was upset because they didn't get picked for that. Three were picked but weren't briefed, and then the job was off, then they were told what it was. It was really a suicide job. They were going to drop just before the invasion with masses of dummy parachutists, with charges attached – their job was to attract attention. The three would have real mortars dropped with them, and they were supposed to keep the battle going on the ground, to make sure the armour came in. De Gaulle said he'd give them the Legion of Honour and they thought no wonder when they found out. They all breathed a sigh of relief when they were stood down. Then the next thing, it was laid on again. They weren't happy about it. One bloke survived, but was a bit of a nutcase afterwards. Terrible job to do.

The punch-up with Bill Stirling and 2 SAS was high politics. David's brother felt they weren't being used in the proper manner and he was kicking up about it. How they were being used, I don't know. I know very little about that – Paddy never talked about it. I think Bill resigned in protest or something. If Paddy didn't speak to someone like me about it, he wouldn't mention it to anyone else. He just passed it off: 'They're having these disagreements.' Bill packed up and Franks took over.

It was at this time, very quietly, that another SAS legend was born. So quietly, in fact, that later in a very distinguished life, the man concerned never even saw fit to talk about it. After the war in the desert, The Originals had voted that Mike Sadler, the Long Range Desert Group navigator poached by David Stirling, be made an honorary Original. Later, a second man received the same vote. In Scotland, as SAS prepared to drop into France for D-Day, he was still unknown.

JOHNNY COOPER

In Darvel, we'd set up on the hill, above the town where all the factories were. The officers' mess was in this lovely mansion house. Paddy, being the colonel he was, had all new officers who arrived in to be indoctrinated. In other words, they had to go through a drinking session with him to see what they were like.

I was the only one of the old tribe at this particular party, and one by one he dismissed these new officers, who talked and he asked them questions in his very quiet way. With Paddy, he'd got very good hearing. You had to lean forward to listen to Paddy – very quiet, gentle voice. And he'd turn round and say: 'Lieutenant Grace, go to bed. Captain So-and-so, go to bed.' I suppose there were about eight subalterns who joined and he talked to each one, and as his voice grew quieter and quieter you knew Paddy was meaning what he said. A chap wouldn't get the message and someone would say: 'Better go to bed.'

This went on until I was alone with Paddy. We had a beer cask on the table and he said: 'Take down the blackouts.' 'But sir . . .' He said: 'Don't be stupid, it's light outside.' I hadn't realised.

As I was struggling to get the blackouts down, there was a bang on the front door. 'Go and see who it is.' None of the mess staff were on duty; I mean, everybody was still in bed. So I opened the door, and there was a military figure, collar the wrong way round.

'Captain McLuskey, reporting Padre to 1 SAS regiment.'

REVD FRASER McLUSKEY

My first impression was somewhat chaotic. The commanding officer and some of his best friends had been . . . celebrating . . . the night before, and indeed into the morning. So the appearance of the mess was pleasantly confused, and I hadn't expected that situation.

JOHNNY COOPER

I stood looking at him and Paddy yelled: 'Who's that?' 'The new padre's arrived, sir.' 'Bring him in.'

Revd Fraser McLuskey

REVD FRASER McLUSKEY

I suppose I entered the church mainly because I was brought up in a Christian home, in which the church was very important. My mother always wanted me to be a minister. She didn't actually put me in at gunpoint, but she prayed I would go in, and I think prayer is significant. And as a youngster I had a remarkable minister, whom I greatly admired. I suppose a combination of circumstances.

In 1938 I had just finished studies and I was given a travel fellowship to live in Germany for a few months, to learn German and mainly to find out what was happening to the church under Hitler. In Germany, Hitler encountered almost no opposition from the main bodies in the community. The one exception was the Christian church, in which there was a very strong resistance movement, which came to be called the Confessing – the church which stood by the classic confessions of Christian faith, and refused to let Hitler corrupt the church. And I saw with my own eyes what was happening in Germany, what was happening to anyone who objected to Hitler's policies. The Jews, of course, mainly, but really it was like living in a large prison camp, in which the lights of freedom have almost entirely been extinguished. I lived there with members of the Confessing or Confessional church.

I suppose the man best known in this country would be Pastor Neimπller, who was a U-boat commander in the First Great War, and then Dietrich Bonhoeffer, who was remarkable in that not only did he stand up for the freedom of the church to run its own life, but that he also saw that he must challenge Hitler on political grounds, as a Christian citizen.

Once in the church, I volunteered for active service because I felt very much that I must take some share in the burdens which my contemporaries were carrying so patiently and bravely, and of course I wasn't in for as long as most people were, but I'm very thankful that at least for a period I was able to stand by their side.

I joined up as an ordinary chaplain, and I'd been in for I suppose six months or so when I noticed an appeal being sent round the existing padres, that if you were young enough and fit enough, you might volunteer for a parachute service. Well, I was young, and fit, so I thought that was the obvious thing to do, and I trained and got my wings, and then oddly enough, no sooner had I qualified than the SAS needed a padre. At this time they were back in this country, in Scotland actually, and they'd had a chap who, for some reason or other, had had to move away and they didn't have a padre, and I was suggested to them and went up to offer my services.

JOHNNY COOPER

So in came McLuskey. Paddy said: 'What are you drinking?' And McLuskey said: 'Same as you.' 'Give him a pint of beer.' So I poured him a pint. Paddy shook hands with him: 'Oh, you're a Scot. Well, it's breakfast time, pick up your beers.' So we picked them up and walked through to the dining room to have our breakfast with beer. The padre with his pint of beer, and Paddy and myself with our pints of beer, and that was Fraser's introduction into the SAS.

He parachuted in to France with me. He was upside down in a bloody tree – forgot to cut his lines.

He was fantastic. I wouldn't say everyone loved him, but liked him, and a lot of them did love him. He was first class. OK, he was Church of Scotland, but nobody cared a damn about their own personal religions. When he came into France, it was just the same everywhere he went – he smoothed the feathers of fear. He did a terrific amount of good. Just his presence. That's the sort of person he is.

REG SEEKINGS

When he joined us at Darvel, he was a very prim and proper parson. The padre more or less admitted it afterwards. He was with the medical officer, and this medical officer – I don't care if he hears me say it, he knows what I think of him – he was useless as far as I was concerned. We were moving in to Fairford, into this concentration area. We were put in a concentration camp; we weren't allowed access to anybody. We'd got a lot of briefing, a lot of training to do – familiarising ourselves with maps and all that sort of stuff. I wanted to get moving, I'd got a lot of work to do, but all my NCOs and everybody was up for their jabs, everybody had to have their jabs.

I kept chasing one of my sergeants: 'What the hell's happening up there?' He said: 'Would you believe it? This so-and-so doctor, he's changing the needle every time.' I said: 'You're kidding?' He said: 'He's changing the needle, he's using a new needle on everybody.' So I went up there in the end and I called the doc everything under the ruddy sun, and I made everybody strip their shirts off, put their arms on the hip, the old army way, and parade in front – and just jab-jab-jab. And I was using some choice language, I think, and the padre was down there and I couldn't give a so-and-so. Parsons didn't particularly interest me. I always reckoned it was hypocrisy to go and pray for forgiveness when it was too late to forgive anything. So I could see him looking very disapproving at me.

The padre had plans to go with another squadron, and next thing I knew – because we was the first people in France – the padre was landed with us. That's the best thing that ever happened to me, because he saved my life.

CHAPTER TWENTY-TWO

The first SAS drops into France were originally planned to take place before D-Day, but this was later changed. Compared with the numbers of L Detachment in the desert, SAS Brigade now numbered 2,500 men, of whom 2,000 were operational. Both 1 and 2 SAS operated in France.

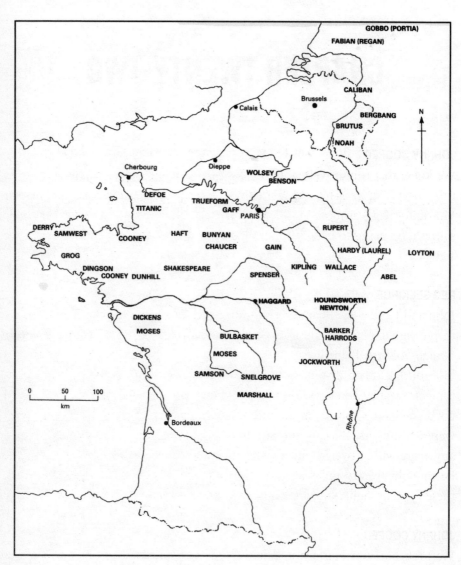

SAS operations in France, 1944.

JOHNNY COOPER

We knew that things were going to happen. Reg and I were singled out to do this special drop. They were talking in terms of us jumping out of this Mosquito. Reg was more in the planning stage of that; I wasn't there. Then they said no, it's going to be a Stirling, with some Phantom people, the intelligence signallers.

REG SEEKINGS

John and I and a few Phantom chaps dropped into France on the original recce, to put lights, etc., for the next drops. Everything had been held up for days because of bad flying weather, and John and I volunteered to drop from a Mosquito. Paddy didn't like it. Eventually they said: 'If the weather doesn't clear tonight, we'll let you go ahead.' We got down to the airport at night, and they'd got a crack crew there. The skipper was Johnny McNamara, a little chap. They were Pathfinders, but new aircraft, Stirlings. We were prepared to be dropped anywhere within twenty miles of the target. McNamara wasn't too keen on this; he thought twenty miles an awful lot. But the brigadier said: 'No, we insist, these men are right, anywhere in twenty miles is OK.'

JOHNNY COOPER

We took off from Fairford and joined up with a bomber stream, which was going to cross Orleans, up into Germany. We had a brand new Stirling, Australian pilot – absolutely incredible, threw it all over the place. We split off, left the bomber stream, then hit terrible weather. Across the channel we were shot up by the navy, because we were under 8,000 feet.

REG SEEKINGS

At Caen we really got hammered. We got caught in the big blue master searchlights and had to take evasive action, put the nose down and dive like hell. Got out of that, with a lot of flak – it was funny to see these chaps who'd never been in flak before. Up to then we'd taken our chutes off, because it was a three or four hour journey, but we put them back on quick when the flak appeared. I was on the intercom, which was very interesting, keeping in touch with the pilot.

After we took evasive action, McNamara yelled out: 'Christ, she handles well for a new kite.' The navigator yelled: 'Bugger you, Johnny, I've got a course to keep!' All these arguments going on – it was quite funny, quite an experience. Then all of a sudden there was a shudder in the back – I'd never experienced that before. The rear gunner was shouting: 'Fighters! One o'clock!' He was hammering away at them, and again we took some evasive action, rolling out of the way. We had two or three goes with fighters, but our luck was in, we got through alright.

JOHNNY COOPER

The pilot said: 'Cloud is over the mountains. I cannot meet your reception committee. We'll fly back to Fairford.' I said: 'How near can you put us?' He said: 'Within twenty miles.' I'd seen them go out on different missions, SOE, and come back and go out again in bad weather like that, so I said we'd drop blind.

REG SEEKINGS

When we were getting near the target area, he put the red light on, to warn us, and we got everything together. We had these hampers, which were a bloody nuisance, with the wireless gear in. The normal procedure for dropping is they go into a slight glide and they cut the inboard motors – particularly with the Stirling, because they've got a tremendous slipstream – but there was no cutting of motors this time, we went into a diving run. We could feel this and I thought: Christ, what's he doing? He had no experience of dropping paras. Then came the green light and we had to jump.

JOHNNY COOPER

Before we baled through the aperture in the Stirling, which is huge – it's not like the circular Wellington one – it's a great big box, I could occasionally see lakes, etc. Anyway, we baled out, in cloud. We all jumped out, and the only one to hit the ground was yours truly.

REG SEEKINGS

I would never wear a helmet, a stupid thing of mine, and the slipstream slipped round my ears, skinned them, nearly took them off. Before that thing opened we were tossed around like feathers, in a whirlpool. Then the chutes opened. It was pouring with rain. I let my kitbag go – it was a new idea then to have a kitbag on a twelve- to fifteen-feet rope. You dropped that off and it dangled behind you, and later when you landed you got a more gentle landing. Also you had your weapons and stuff with you.

There wasn't supposed to be anything over sixty pounds. But as we were leaving, the chap doing quartermaster, a captain, hell of a good chap, came rushing across and said: 'I've got some news for you, soap's at a premium out there.' We used to take stuff for the bribery and corruption business, you see – coffee etc. I said: 'Okay, get me as much soap as you can.' He came back from the canteen, he'd bought up the complete supply – all Lifebuoy. So I stuffed this into my kitbag.

McNamara, the pilot, couldn't lift it – over a hundredweight. So I baled out and let this go, and of course we hit the deck with a bang, and the bloody lot split. With it raining, you could smell Lifebuoy for miles!

JOHNNY COOPER

I hit a wall of a farmhouse and went into a ditch; everybody else went into the trees in the forest. I can't remember much, but I buried my parachute – with the trenching tool – and I came to after I'd buried it.

REG SEEKINGS

With McNamara going in at such speed, we were scattered over a hell of a distance. Some of the chaps were strung up in trees and you've never heard such a collection of owls in your life as there was in France that night. Owls calling all over the place.

JOHNNY COOPER

We had a circular glass fluorescent ball, and a pea whistle which you blew. Reg was my sah major further down the line. I'd jumped No. 1, so I started walking down the line, blowing the pea whistle, holding this bloody fluorescent ball.

You know the line to take, because the pilot says, 'We're steering so-and-so, and the wind is in this direction, so your stick should be on the line. What you should do is all stay firm and No. 1 picks everybody up on the stick. Every man had a compass and is taught navigation. Anyway, blowing whistles, shouting like hell, and suddenly, there's Reg up in a tree.

REG SEEKINGS

Eventually we all collected together, buried our chutes, found a little hollow and tried to get our heads down. It was pouring with rain. Dawn broke, and we were wet and miserable. John and I left the chaps, told them not to move, and climbed a hill, quite a steep one, to see if we could pinpoint our position. We got up the top, here's these lakes. We thought: Oh, right on target. No, not quite right. We eventually worked out where we were. In the area we were dropping into, there were some little lakes. But there was another area, twenty-one miles away, which was identical, and we got dropped on the wrong lot.

JOHNNY COOPER

By morning we'd got everybody down, then we said: 'Where the hell are we?' Beautiful mountains, lakes but no villages, bugger all but a few farmhouses. Vaculik was with us; he was Yugoslav and also spoke Russian. And we had this special Phantom troop. So we set up a radio and got through to the UK, and said: 'We've arrived. Sabu 9 in situ.'

Every man had a receiver which could contact the BBC. It was about eighteen inches long with a pack on the end, which strapped in, and a battery that would last thirty-six hours. It was purely to receive the BBC giving messages to us in code. Our end, we had the one time pad, and the silk map which gave us the code. Tojo was the code name for 1 SAS – I was Sabu 9. When the BBC came on, you had this Lili Marlene signature tune, then you'd have the messages for the following: Sabu 1, 5, 16, 24; Tojo, 23, 26 – whatever it was. You waited for your call, then took it down as they said it. To transmit, I had a hand generator and a Phantom SAS signaller with the morse.

Anyway, I got through, said we'd arrived. Don't know where we are. I had two pigeons I'd jumped with, so I made out the thing for the pigeon, put it on his foot and fed it with corn, and released it on the edge of this ploughed field. There's Reg and I, tearing round this field, trying to get this bloody pigeon airborne. The second one we ate. We told the pigeon fanciers that afterwards – they went bloody wild.

But then the messages got through, so in the end I said to Vaculik: 'Come on.' Then he and Reg and I went down to this farmhouse.

REG SEEKINGS

There were two big houses and John said: 'Which one?' 'Eeny meeny – that one.' Our luck was in. The chap who opened the door had a big handlebar moustache – could only belong to a military man. He quickly whipped us inside, because the man on the other side was a collaborator, a big favourite of the Germans. This chap confirmed where we were and said: 'You'll have to stay here now for a bit. I can't risk this other chap seeing you.' His daughter was a courier for the Maquis. We couldn't have been luckier.

A little later that day a youngster came to the house – our silly chaps, being all wet, had lit a fire, and there was smoke coming from the wood. Our chap was worried about this – he thought it would bring the police down on them. I'd been talking to the old chap, and he and my old man had probably been on the booze together – their two units were stationed together for quite a time in the first war. I'd often heard Dad talk about this French unit. So I was well in then with the old boy.

The daughter arrived, and we immediately stood up. And the youngster said: 'Ah, now I know you're English. You must remember not to do that'. He shook his sleeve and out came a mallet. I said: 'What do you think you're going to do?' He said: 'I would have attacked you.' I said: 'Where do you think this gun's pointing?' He hadn't spotted that. There'd been a tommy gun pointing at his guts all the time, never left him. Later on we found out he was a collaborator, and he was hung by the French. Whether he'd gone over to them at that time, I don't know.

JOHNNY COOPER

Vaculik talked to them and me in my schoolboy French: 'We're looking for the Maquis Jean.' So next day, Reg and I were told: 'You and your sah major must be at a point at the crossroads, down in the valley, and they'll come and pick you up. Take your men down, put them well away from the road, but you two have got to be in the ditch at this T-junction.' This was roughly between Auxerre and Chateau Chinon and Dijon. A very minor road.

So we go down there, then suddenly through the night we see these lights coming over the top, and a thirty-five-seater bus arrives, gasogen bus with the wooden burner at the back, that they'd just commandeered from Dijon to pick us up. On the top, two French with Bren guns. Anyway, we were grabbed, and had to produce this thing from General Leclerc. All the SAS boys had an individual letter, English on one side, French on the other, which we had to produce. Then we were taken in and off we went up into the mountains again to the Maquis Jean.

REG SEEKINGS

We were there for several days. The planes kept coming over and they couldn't see our lights or fires. The weather was so bad they had to turn back. Night after night this went on.

The chaps got browned off; a gang of NCOs got together and they all got on the same plane. It was the only plane that was lost. That was a big blow to my squadron. The plane just disappeared, no report of a crash, going into the sea. Simply disappeared.

Then came the night the rest did land and we got them in. We had one chap who landed on a roof and broke an arm, and Chalky White broke something too. We took them to a little chateau the French had turned into a hospital.

JIM ALMONDS

The time came for the Second Front to open, and we trained down to Swindon. There we were briefed, and after that moved to another part of the compound where we had no contact with those who were not briefed. Then the time came when we were put on the plane. We'd seen beforehand where we were going to go – to the south and east of Paris. The zone allotted to our party formed a triangle running from Orléans to Montargis, with a base at Fontainebleau.

We knew by that stage of Hitler's commando order that if we were caught we should be shot. I thought it was inevitable, because I had doubts before, when I was in Italy, because it was a long while before they recognised me as a POW. I don't know that it took any effect on anyone. Most people probably forgot the same day as they heard the story. I never heard of anyone refusing to go. And everybody was told. So presumably maybe some were frightened to back out on account of what other people think of them – I don't know. That's what Colonel David says: the moral fear of letting down your mates. It's a very definite thing. In a plane, if you were doing a parachute jump, a lot of people go out because they won't let their mates down, they just go. It's not one of the best of motives, I suppose, but that's what I believe happens. I mean, it's a fate worse than death, isn't it? When you get so close, to let somebody down, it's a terrible thing.

We arrived over the dropping zone and away we went. I made a bad landing. It was a dark night, raining and blowing. One leg went down in a dyke, and I sprained the knee very badly. I saw this figure approaching and ascertained that it was the farmer, and we all got back together. We went down to the farmhouse and he sent somebody on a bicycle to fetch a local masseur. He did a bit of manipulating and put a bandage on – they used eau de vie as an anesthetic. A M. Blanchard from the village arrived with a big baker's delivery van, and took us into the forest of Orléans to the point that had been selected as our HQ.

We got esconced there, then I took my section down to another part, within easy reach of HQ. There were two parties – Major Fenwick and his party of three; there was myself with a party of four; and then some HQ staff, signallers, etc. We got dug in, then went out to have a look round the countryside. The first night they asked me to go and blow the railway line between Montargis and Orléans. My party went down, found a suitable spot, and blew the line, getting back under forest cover before broad daylight. In the meantime Fenwick had been out in the countryside, talking to the Resistance people, and scouting the possibilities. He made some very useful contacts, both in Orléans and in a lovely little village, Chambon-la-Forât.

The French Resistance unloading weapons and supplies after an SAS-organised delivery.

JOHNNY COOPER

Then the first armoured jeeps were dropped. I took the first one into France. We operated with the Maquis in ambushes, etc., but our main role was to watch and report back on the railway line from Lyons. Dijon is the main terminal, and the tanks would be going this way on flat cars. We were doing an LRDG job in Europe. Troops going east, west, either reinforcing, withdrawing or maintaining. That's what we had to ascertain. I had a direct line into Dijon. When any Germans came out on patrols to get us in the forest, we'd know, through the Maquis, when they'd leave.

JIM ALMONDS

Then they dropped us jeeps – they came down on trays, partly dismantled, steering wheel off, tanks off, etc. They were designed to have four petrol tanks, give you a range of about a thousand miles with one fill-up. This jeep duly came down, but instead of landing where it should have done, it landed in an oak tree beside the main road. As the Germans used the road in the daytime, what were we to do? Eventually we shinned up and cut a branch off and let it fall. It broke the front engine mountings. One of the useful local contacts was a garage owner, a general motor mechanic – a White Russian from the First World War who'd settled there. He worked wonders on that jeep. We got it put together, towed it to his place and he fixed it up. Then it was serviceable. Then we got a second jeep, which landed alright, and having got the guns out of the containers, we were then in a position to take some serious action.

We went on the road with the intention of ambushing convoys or parties of Germans, and we shot up one laager where some Germans were stationed. We went through the village first, noted where they were, then came back ready to fire. Then we went back to the bridge, and had a go at the railway line between Fontainebleau and Montargis.

There was one place we had to cross the line, by the main road, and there was a German who kept the level crossing. He knew who we were, because whenever we went to that level crossing and brought him out to open the gates, he'd avert his gaze – he daren't look at you. I suppose he'd be able to tell people he never saw us. He never refused to open them and he never interfered. He was an elderly chap. I suppose he was what you call one of the fifth-line troops.

There was one place where the road ran from Montargis beside the railway, which was ideal for waylaying trains. We found out when the trains were running, waited for the train to come along, put the charges on the track then we swept up and down with machine guns on the train. What the casualties were I've no idea. Having done that, we set off back, and the chap at the roadblock obligingly opened the gates for us again. That happened on two or three occasions. On one occasion a Sergeant Dunkley got stopped at the same roadblock, and they'd made some alterations there, and Dunkley was shot up and killed.

CHAPTER TWENTY-THREE

One of the first to parachute into Occupied France was the Reverend McLuskey; he was also one of the last to leave. Much of that time was spent with The Originals.

REVD FRASER McLUSKEY

There was never a conflict between my role as a man of God and my role as a member of the SAS. I had no doubt that the war was necessary. I was quite sure that we were there, quite literally to liberate an enslaved people, and to keep the torch of freedom burning throughout the world as far as we could.

The SAS were a group of the most highly trained, highly specialised soldiers you could find. Their work was rather unusual in that it was needed behind enemy lines, involving first of all sabotage work and then ambush work. But the work they were doing was necessary, they did it with great skill, and I didn't see any ethical problems under the circumstances.

Of course war is a great tragedy and an evil, but so often it's the lesser of two evils, and I had no doubt at all that those who were conducting the war were doing so for good and sufficient reasons, and I was – well, I was privileged at least to have a small part with them.

REG SEEKINGS

The padre had been dropped in another area, then he came across and joined us. We got settled in and he was holding a church service, on a Sunday afternoon. All of a sudden, bullets started whistling through the tree tops, gunfire, etc., and some Frenchmen came tearing into camp – they'd been attacked. We quickly finished off the service and went off to give the French a hand. They led us right into the Germans.

I spotted the enemy transport on the other side of the valley. I called down that I would go and attack it. In my section, apart from Jack Terry, everybody was new. I spotted the gunner protecting the trucks. I told the chaps the transport was over there, but I didn't tell them about the guard, because they'd never been in action before, and we'd got quite a bit of dead ground to travel. When I say quite a distance, most probably seven or eight hundred yards. And I thought, Well, I won't tell the chaps that until I get them over. I knew we were safe. Jack knew, but it's a bit of a job to convince green troops of that. So we went across, but we came out closer to the gunner than I'd expected, face to face a few yards away.

. He reacted fast and dropped down behind the transport. I turned to shout and luckily I did turn my head, because he got a shot off and that caught me in the head, and – you know your skull has a recess, into which the spine fits – this bullet went through my skull and was coming out through the back, and lodged between my spine and skull, in that gap. Fortunately for me his gun jammed. Then he slung two grenades. One landed on one side, and the other on the other side of me. I never got a scratch off those – just a tremendous bang and a flash. I went to fire back at him, because I didn't feel any pain at all, and I couldn't move my bloody arm. I'm left-handed for firing, and I couldn't lift my gun up. The arm flopped down, and with the creases in the battle dress, it looked as though my arm was blown off. It was all a mass of blood. I thought: Oh good God, my bloody arm's gone.'

I felt as if I was in an underground river, no pain, going like the clappers in this river, a raging torrent, but silent, going like the hammers of hell. All my life went past me: when I was kid, girlfriends, etc., like watching a film. I was falling deeper and deeper and deeper into this. Somehow I pulled myself out of it, and this is when I tried to fire the gun. I gave instructions for the others to get round to the left. They didn't know what had happened, because I hadn't told them about this bloody man. Jack Terry was on my heels, and he grabbed me and was buggering around with my head.

I said: 'Leave my head, get a tourniquet on my arm, it's my arm, you stupid bastard, not my head.' I was convinced it was the arm. I got up and made a run for a tree that had been knocked down, and running across I dropped my pipe, and like a bloody idiot I went back and picked it up, then hit the deck behind this tree. The others put in the attack, and wiped this chap out. Jack took my carbine – which the bugger had always wanted – and we called one chap, Elliott, whose nerves were a bit dicey, to help me back to camp.

Suddenly there was a tremendous thunderstorm – never seen thunder and lightning like it, terrific. That cleared my head a lot. I'd memorised all the area and Elliott supported me along the track. We got to a branch in the track, and I said: 'We can't afford to go wrong here – go up there and within a hundred yards you should see a little white hut. If that's there, we take this fork and go over the bridge.'

We made our way two or three miles through the mountains back to our base, where the doctor and the padre were. By this time it'd got dark and they started to try and operate on me, try to get this bullet out. In the end, after all the probing and whatnot, no anaesthetic or nothing, this doc decided there was a bit of dirt or something perhaps in there. I don't know how he came to that conclusion at all, because there was a gaping hole.

The engagement was still going on all round, and I was left there, on my own, stark naked, everybody cleared off, rain coming down, bullets flying around, and I thought: This is a nice way to go, be captured stark naked – wounded and stark naked. Fortunately Jack Terry came back to see how I was. He'd hidden my spare uniform away, and he got that out and got me dressed and I got him to go and find Major Fraser and break off the engagement. So we broke off and we managed to organise ourselves and take the biggest part of the supplies, and get the hell out of it.

Then we marched for some time and hid up again whilst the Germans – well, German forces I should say, they were what we call the White Russians – chaps who'd come over to the German side, and also some of 'em who'd been living in exile I think in Paris and places – they went around and slaughtered every living thing. It was terrible to see the cattle, beautiful animals – they just shot them for the sake of shooting.

And this is where the padre, I maintain, saved my life, because by this time I'd seized up. If I wanted to look behind me, the whole body had to turn round, you see. I was feeling lousy. Our kits were heavy. But the padre carried my kit as well.

We marched all night, wading through swamps and Lord knows what, until we reached a clearing and this is where we stopped for the next week or two, because by this time I was just about delirious. We couldn't get any food; no aircraft coming in. And the chaps went back to the camp and salvaged stuff there, and they brought the padre's panier back with his little altar and all that.

McLuskey nursed me, really looked after me. After a few days I came round a bit, and the padre come to me and said: 'Can I give you a shave, Reggie? You'll feel better with a shave.' So I said: 'Yes, be an idea.' He said: 'How do you like it – a heavy shave, a close shave, or a light shave? I'm very good at this, you know.' I said: 'Any shave you like.' He gave me a shave and this is where we started to get to know each other. And he said: 'You know, I told a little fib then – I've never shaved anybody in my life before.' I said: 'I suspected that.'

Then we got talking and he said: 'God willing, when I get back to Scotland, I can preach real religion. Not the stuff I've been preaching. This last few days, I've seen religion lived. Men helping one another. No thought of reward or anything, they just go and they help and do all they can to help. Seeing men without thought for themselves, sacrificing themselves, helping each other.'

And then he asked me about books. He'd brought in things like the Soldier's Handbook, the New Testament etc. We'd rescued some of it for him. He said: 'The boys don't seem to be too interested in that sort of thing.' He was talking about the language used – he'd decided it wasn't blasphemy, just army dialect. Which is true. He wanted to know what reading matter the lads would like. What came to my mind was things like Lemmy Caution, cowboy stuff with blood and thunder. He said: 'I'd have thought they already had enough of that.' 'Yes, but it's nice to read how it should be done.' He got this stuff across to us eventually and he started reading Lemmy Caution and became rather a fan. He'd come up and say: 'I'm just gumshoeing around.'

REVD FRASER McLUSKEY

I certainly couldn't have done my job if I hadn't been where the men were, and I was very fortunate in that, in the type of work they were doing, it was possible for a padre to be there without being a nuisance to them. There were jobs to be done. We had drops from the air, where another pair of hands were useful. I could help the doctor sometimes. And of course I could wander round and see the scattered groups and carry out my own ministerial duties, take services and even at one point, take a small confirmation class, celebrate communion, and really do my own job, which one would have done anywhere. But the circumstances were such that I could be around with people without being a nuisance to them.

REG SEEKINGS

When we got organised, we started requisitioning cars, and the padre took a fancy to a little Fiat. I had delegated big Wilson to bodyguard him – he used a Bren gun like other men use a pistol, and it was cruelty to cars to see these big so-and-so's sitting in this tiny Fiat. Wilson was powerful enough to lift it out of any trouble.

REVD FRASER McLUSKEY

I can't honestly say that I ever asked, 'What am I doing here?' Our time was very fully occupied in one way or another. Perhaps it was simply a matter of trying to keep as dry as possible in pouring rain when you were living without any cover, as we were for a fair part of the time. We were sleeping and living out of doors. Trying to get a brew up, get a little tea or something. We were always busy. And I didn't ask any particularly philosophical questions at the time. I always had plenty to do.

REG SEEKINGS

The padre asked me about carrying weapons. I didn't think it was a good idea; neither did the boys. People admired him for that, and there was enough of us to protect him. We'd had one parson for a little short period of time, and he was more interested in target practice after an action than in burying our own dead. So that didn't encourage us and enhance the reputation of padres with us. And we were all unanimous that we would look after the padre.

But any rate, he came and he asked my opinion, and I told him, then he said: 'But how would you feel if I was on your vehicle, and the mere fact that I could use a weapon would get you to safety? Say something happened – you'd been wounded or something like that – and there's only me that could do it. By me firing a shot, am I justified in saving your crew?' I said: 'I think so, Padre, I'd go along with that.' He said: 'Well, teach me the weapons.' And so this is what I did.

REVD FRASER McLUSKEY

Padres, by the Geneva Convention, are unarmed, and I never carried arms, and I think the men were glad to see the padre as a kind of symbol of the will of God for peace for all men. But I had no doubt that the carriage of arms was necessary, and I suppose you might have said I wasn't altogether unprotected, because I had a large and burly batman, who came with me in the jeep or car or whatever I had, and who was possibly armed to excess.

REG SEEKINGS

I tell you. This man, you know what he used to do – unarmed – when there was action, when we were under fire or attacked or anything, he had quickly got to know the ones that were a little bit on the nervy side, and although he was unarmed he would crawl away to them and pass such remarks as: 'It's alright, don't worry, it's just Lemmy Caution, check it out.' And he would stop and have a little chat with them and see they were nicely cooled down, and off he'd go to the next man he thought might be a little bit on the nervy side. Sometimes they weren't. Some people look nervous but they're not nervous. The chaps really appreciated it – that really calmed them down. This is the way the padre operated. He was exceptional; he was really wonderful.

REVD FRASER McLUSKEY

I didn't ever see anything which tested my beliefs. I was well aware of what was going on, of the cruelty of the Gestapo and the cruelty of the French police and others.

Fortunately, I wasn't myself captured at any point, or didn't have to face what so many of my fellow men had to face, and I didn't actually witness any atrocities, except that I did see from time to time the villages, one in particular suspected of harbouring the Maquis, which the Germans burnt down.

I owe a great debt – I mean a much greater debt than I can evaluate or express – to my friends in the SAS. One of the things they taught me was to try to speak to other people about the Christian faith in a direct and simple and personal way. You can't read a sermon to a group of men in the middle of nowhere, in the middle of a forest; you've either got to talk to them direct about what you believe, or say nothing. They taught me many things, but one was the somewhat obvious fact that if you're going to get anywhere in sharing your faith with other people, you've got to be simple, direct, and as honest as you possibly can.

REG SEEKINGS

Later on, as I became more fit, he'd sometimes come round with me as my driver. Though I'd got the padre with me, it didn't stop me engaging the enemy in action. As he wasn't taking up arms, it was logical that he be driver. He took part in shooting up staff cars. When we heard the German division was moving out, we'd go along and knock off the first half-dozen trucks and then get out of it.

REVD FRASER McLUSKEY

I went on operations, whenever that was convenient. Very often, you know, an odd driver was needed, or as I said, the medical officer was glad to have someone to give him a hand. I drove sometimes for Reg Seekings. I wasn't trained to bear arms, so I would have been more of a danger to my own men than the enemy if I'd had them, I'm quite sure. But that wasn't my job. But anything that I could do to help my flock I did gladly.

REG SEEKINGS

The only thing he didn't realise was that guns made such a big noise as they did. But he was with me on two or three occasions when I did some ambushing. I had to shout at him on one occasion, but he soon got used to it. The first time was a shock. I told him he was in the wrong position, and this one he had twin Vickers firing over his head – you know, just devastating.

REVD FRASER McLUSKEY

When you're up against it, as people found in the Blitz in London, it's easier to feel religious. When things are going well and you haven't a care in the world as it seems, God is rather apt to recede into the background. When you are made uncomfortably aware of the fact that you're very fallible, finite, mortal, and want some help, and when you pray and worship God and when you find, in spite of your own weakness, that help comes, that's a powerful fortifying of your faith, and I thank God for what that experience during the war taught me, as I'm sure it taught many other people.

REG SEEKINGS

The padre denied it, but he spoke quite good French. He would get along with anybody. He was very, very handy for liaison work. Having him with us made it so much easier because we could get better information, easier obtained, from the public, because the French trusted a padre. On one occasion when we were out with him, we passed a place, in new territory, and we were being greeted as the liberators – all the girls in the village with bouquets of flowers. We used to be loaded with flowers. He and Paddy got on really well together.

REVD FRASER McLUSKEY

Paddy Mayne was larger than life – physically and every other way. I conceived not only an enormous admiration for him, but a very great affection. We became great friends. Perhaps because I was a padre and a little older than the others and had a special position therefore in the regiment, it was maybe easier for the two of us to get together than if I'd been under his command in a different way.

We met frequently after the war. In fact I had the sad privilege of conducting his funeral in Ireland when he met his death as the result of a tragic road accident. He was, of course, a very clever man. He wasn't secretary of the Law Society in the North of Ireland for nothing. I considered him a brilliant soldier.

He was quite unique, I think, in his ability to win the confidence of his men, who felt, quite rightly, that if he said go somewhere, whatever the dangers, it was a sensible risk, and he would not have allowed any of his men to be subjected to some crazy escapade, or death-and-glory mission, so to speak. He was one of the most remarkable men I have ever known, and I shall remember him with equal vividness till the end of my life.

REG SEEKINGS

One time, we passed an isolated house near the main road, and they must have recognised us as we passed, this woman and her husband. Later on they heard the firing, then heard the vehicles come back, and when they saw it was us they stopped us, took us into their house and insisted we have tea. The woman got an old bag of tea from a vase on the mantelpiece – two or three spoonfuls of it. It was the last of the tea from the time of France's capitulation. They'd saved it with the idea that the first liberating soldier they saw would have a cup of tea. And so we sat down with them, the padre and I, and had this old tea.

CHAPTER TWENTY-FOUR

Total SAS casualties in France are given as 330 killed, wounded or missing. One hundred of these were British, most of them executed after being captured. SAS Brigade reports, which include actions in conjunction with the French Resistance, indicate 7,733 enemy dead and 4,784 taken prisoner.

But the SAS had more than a fighting role.

JOHNNY COOPER

We weren't there so much to disrupt but to give information. If we could tell the high commands whether the German army or their air force was being reinforced, withdrawn, or just maintained in any one area after D-Day, it gave them a terrific fillip. We had on tap three squadrons, one of Lightnings and two of Mustangs. So say, for instance, we were watching the railway line just south of Dijon and we saw a train going north, we'd say: 'Three hundred tanks, troop train so-and-so and so-and-so.' And we transmitted this from Area D, and the aircraft would pick them up in Area A. The intelligence work I think was far more value to our side than the ambushing of the roads and the destruction of certain parts. We also had to be very careful of the civilian population, and the threat of reprisals.

REG SEEKINGS

Our main job was to work with the Maquis, who were really political parties who'd run away into the woods. The one I ended up with was a good one, a military one, Maquis Jean. 'A' Squadron were the backbone of that; we were the most successful by far. Alec Muirhead was our main senior officer there; he was the mortar man in the other operations and did a wonderful job with those too. He took the main area, and Johnny Wiseman went further over to the outskirts of Dijon. I used to run around between different groups – that was after we'd got vehicles, and I'd recovered from the neck wound.

JOHNNY COOPER

There was always the risk of betrayal. You've got to realise there were different types of Maquis. You had the military Maquis, escaped prisoners of war, who wanted to fight. You had the political Maquis, who would not operate in their own area, because they wanted to become the local governor or mayor in that area, but they'd go into somebody else's. Then you had the people who were just escaping. And I was with the three different types. The military Maquis were the best Maquis. The political ones were quite capable of stopping you doing any act of sabotage in their area, because the reprisals in their area would affect their political significance after the war. The military Maquis were escaped POWs, and they were first class. But the others were a load of bloody rubbish, and we were supplying them with arms.

REG SEEKINGS

The biggest Maquis group in our area were Communists, led by a long-haired individual of about nineteen, a self-appointed colonel. We had two Russian officers and a Czech officer called Alex who escaped and joined up with us. They were nice fellows, Georgians I think, blond-haired, stumpy. Both captains, captured at Stalingrad, the other being a Czech who escaped with them. We'd speak to the Czech in French, then he'd speak to them in – I can't remember, but it went all the way round, one spoke a bit of German, a great mix-up. Alex was a lovely little chap, all smiles, and he'd stand there grinning, waiting for the translation to come round. Really funny. He had a girlfriend some distance away, and when it was a bit quiet, he'd asked if he could go and see her. He'd go off on his bicycle. He was coming back from a weekend with her, came to a Resistance roadblock, and for some unknown reason they tried to get shirty with him. They reckoned he went for his pistol. They'd said: 'Name?' He'd said: 'Nama.' That was their excuse. So the guards shot him. Then this self-appointed colonel came along and put a couple of shots in the back of his head.

I had to go over to identify the body, do everything properly. London had been informed. When I got down to my Ford V-8, which I'd requisitioned, you never saw anything like it – it was like an arsenal. There were machine guns, grenades all laid out. The two Russians were absolutely foaming; they were going to shoot every Frenchman they could find. Eventually I went unarmed: it was the only thing I could do. I couldn't drive a vehicle and protect myself against them. One of the Russians was like a young animal in the back of the car.

We got there and they'd put Alex in a stable, poor bugger, lying there with half his head blown out. And I was mad too. Jesus. When this officer appeared, if I had had a gun, I'd have shot him. But the Russian jumped him, nearly managed to pull his skull open. I managed to pull him off. Others in their group were very concerned by this time, and also there was a lot of them that supported Alex. They agreed to arrest this chap and he was passed through the underground back to London, and put on trial for murder. I believe he was executed.

JOHNNY COOPER

We went down to Autun and set fire to a synthetic petrol plant. We had to be very careful, because of the French people working underground in the factory. The shift changed between 3am and 4am. We took two jeeps, and Reg and I went down with Alec Muirhead – he was an expert with a mortar. We set up in the field and got the mortar all lined up and ready, all the bombs out, the fuses, etc. As soon as the whistle went, and the shift came out – there was an hour when nobody was underground, before the next lot came in – we popped off fifty bombs, bang-bang-bang. The only mark in the field was where the base plate had gone right in deep through firing so many rounds. The plant burned for four days.

REG SEEKINGS

We mined railways. We gave the French better arms, we had planeloads of stuff delivered. We got everything better organised, and generally boosted up the morale of the local population.

We were in Vichy France. The one thing I didn't like about it, in these hamlets and small towns, anybody they didn't like was labelled a collaborator and bumped off. Some were lucky to get away, like some women, with just their heads shaved. I saved one of our agents that way. A beautiful young woman. She had run a cafe on the Pas de Calais where all the rockets were going from, and she put out the signal lights for the RAF, showing them where to bomb. She got it out of the German officers. I was sitting in a cafe in this town I'd taken over, I had the padre with me, and she came running in, with a horde behind her, screaming out to me to save her. They were going to shave her head, and she had beautiful hair – what a beautiful girl! I threatened to shoot these people, and I would have shot them too – if they step over the line, you just shoot the buggers. They were after her because she spoke German, but how can you get information from them if you don't speak their language? Then she was moved up through our agents, out of the way.

One day some Germans came in to a cafe before we realised who they were, sat down, ordered a bottle of cognac and saluted, Heil Hitler, out the door, into the car and away. And we're sitting there watching them. We wore slacks and jerseys, khaki sometimes, but you looked like a civvy. The business of uniforms didn't matter. As long as you didn't have weapons on show you were alright. We never wore our insignia; that would have been asking for trouble.

I was known for miles around as le Anglais Maquis. I'd been wounded in the head and had a great big bandage on it. I saw a pretty little place one day and decided to drop in for a glass of wine – this was before people got to know me – and I went in, asked for cognac, got a very abrupt answer: no bloody cognac, no this, no that, everybody surly. And two or three old ex-soldiers muttering away about the bloody Bosche. So I said: 'I'm not German, I'm English.' A couple of little kids came in and I said: 'Chocolat?' They didn't know what it was. I was talking to the kids and I heard: 'The Germans never do this, he must be English.' The next thing, a very pretty young girl came along and she spoke English – well she was half English and she had a twin. Christ, they were beautiful. Their father was one of the bigwigs in the French Resistance in Paris, and he'd moved his family to their country home. I often called in there after that, had tea with them.

JOHNNY COOPER

We clobbered this Russian unit who were fighting for the Germans. They'd laid an ambush for us, but we watched them lay it, and then we laid one outside the village when they came out. Round the corner we had the wire across, because the motorcycles came first. Myself and Reg, and I think Alec Muirhead, were on one side, with Bren guns. The Maquis had a pile of logs, waiting for the first lorry to get alongside. There were motorcycles up front, then three lorry loads of Russians and behind that cars with French hostages in, and behind that more motorcycles. So the cycles went round the corner – they took the heads off with the wire across. Then we opened fire and the French Maquis threw the bombs from behind the log pile onto the vehicles, then we went across to the killing ground and killed them from that side

We captured this Russian lieutenant there. He'd been terribly shot up in the ambush. He wasn't going to live, but the Maquis were going to torture him. We took him into the woods and he told us that he'd been taken prisoner at Stalingrad. He said: 'My prisoner of war cage was barbed wire and snow. But they said if I volunteer for lines of communication troops in France, I would be spared.' They had German sergeants and German officers. Vaculik was there with us; he was Yugoslavian who spoke Russian. This Russian officer said:

'What would you do? And now the Maquis want to kill me. If I go back to Russia, I'll be shot. If I go back to my German masters, I'll be shot. And now these Frenchmen want to shoot me too for what I've done here.' Because they went into Montsauche, killed the mayor, raped four or five girls of about eleven, put them all in the church and set fire to it. Anyway, this Russian was going to be tortured; he was absolutely on his last legs. Reg stopped them and shot him through the back of the head. After that, the Gestapo came down and they burnt the whole town.

REG SEEKINGS

The Germans and Milice, the French special police, were terrorising the population, led by one man in particular. Just a few days after we landed – and this took the heat off us for a bit – some Frenchmen, keen-eyed countrymen, dug up some of our jumping smocks, the overalls, and the silly buggers were wearing them, and of course they were picked up and hung on the spot. The Germans and Milice went round with loudhailers, telling people this was what happened to traitors of the Reich. They thought they'd hung English agents. Then we started to do things and then it started to hot up. This chap we're talking about, he never moved without about three hundred men.

JOHNNY COOPER

The Milice were the bastards. The French thought they were worse than the Gestapo. The Germans released these all from the jails. They had a black beret, with a white bugle as their badge. They came to attack us one day, but we knew they were coming. We had about thirty Bren guns brought in. We were training the French all night on the Bren guns. The village was below, there was an open field, trees all the way down, into the valley. We put about eight of them all the way round, and the Milice came up, got out of their car – they had all the Citroën cars, etc., with badges on the side – and they had mostly captured British weapons, and they came up into this trap. The French commander said: 'Fire.' We couldn't stop the buggers firing. The Milice were all killed, but they went on and on and on; magazine after magazine was going off.

JIM ALMONDS

We made a trip to a factory in Montargis with the intention of sabotage. We were in a wood beside the factory, camouflaged up with branches, and we were horrified to find the following morning that the Germans were advancing through the wood and we had to get out quick. We started up and set off on the track to come out of the wood, and as we were leaving the wood we passed trestle tables set up and there were some of the general staff there, planning something.

There were a couple of staff cars, and they waved to us to stop, and we sort of waved back and said: 'No, sorry, we can't.' As we went on out onto the main road, we noticed that some troops had piled into one of these staff cars and started to follow us. Major Fenwick was in the leading jeep, and he'd seen this and he speeded up, and so we kept pace with him, and the staff car kept pace with us. Then we came to a road fork; we took the left fork and the staff car went down the right. So we stopped and had a confab, and decided we were panicking, and we turned round and followed the staff car, to see where it went.

It went down into a village where there was a school – they seemed to use schools as storehouses. The staff car was parked outside. The sentry on the gate saluted as we went past, and shouted something, then he turned and looked up the passageway and shouted something, and they came out and they got in the car again and started to follow. They were obviously interested in us but they didn't know what to make of us.

We carried on and we suddenly realised – I don't know if Fenwick knew it or not – we were approaching the town itself. You couldn't get off the road with the jeep, and in front was the railway crossing. Fortunately the gates were open and we went over the railway crossing and round a left-hand bend, and there was a knife rest in the road – one of these wooden frameworks with barbed wire stretched across it, but it's mobile, you can pull it aside. And beyond that there was a glimpse of tank turrets and all sorts of things, and there was no possible way of retreat, because this car was coming up behind.

So we entered the town, and weaved through the marketplace, and down the main street with all the German troops wandering around, and the tanks and armoured cars. And we just weaved in and out amongst them until we came to the other end of the town, where another knife rest was removed. And we again got a salute and we carried on back to base.

JOHNNY COOPER

We picked up this Lightning pilot, Bill, who had been strafing the railway. This chap came over, was very low, and a flat car on the back of the train caught him, 40mm. He managed to bale out. We picked him up and got out of it quickly, because the Germans were soon on to the crashed aircraft. Bill stayed with us and the Maquis. He was from Minnesota. He said: 'I wanna get outa here.' 'Well, Bill, we'll see what we can do.' He said: 'I'll bicycle.' So we went down into Dijon and grabbed some new bicycles from a shop, through the Maquis. So we got him a bicycle. I'd just had a parachute drop of stuff, and my mother had knitted me a polo neck jumper, and he had those light-coloured flying pants on, my jumper, an old deerstalker hat on and he pedalled off. He got through the lines, and got home.

JIM ALMONDS

We got back to our place, and then our radio transmitter was detected by the Germans. They had a spotter plane up, obviously in contact with a ground force, and Fenwick saw the ground force and thought it would be a good thing to strafe them. He was following behind to get a good shot at them and he got hit. Some were waiting in a field beside the road and got him. He was killed, the very first shot.

Simon Duffy was thrown out of the vehicle and suffered some injuries, among which was a broken jaw. He was taken to hospital by the Germans, where they patched him up, presumably prior to interrogation. While he was in hospital, he got the French nurse to bring him in a uniform in a pail, which she did while the German soldiers in the ward were sleeping, afternoon siesta. He managed to get dressed while still in bed and walked out. He had a pair of shoes, two sizes too small, and was having a job to get along in them. He got a salute from the sentry at the hospital entrance; off up the road, he threw his shoes away and took off cross-country, and eventually got back.

After this, this ground force attacked our camp in the forest of Orléans. I was across at HQ with Mike Riding, another officer who'd come down with a second officer, Jimmy Watson, from the area of Fontainebleau which had become too hot for them. My party was established some way away – I'd built a log cabin there, with parachute green as camouflage over the top, built bunks into the side. I always carried an axe and saw with me.

The next thing that happened, we lost two of our signallers. They went out in a jeep to relieve a watch we kept on the main road, and on the way out they ran into a German armoured car in the wood, were captured, taken to a chateau on the outskirts of the forest, and there they were interrogated and executed. Their bodies were left by the road, by the side of the moat. We didn't know what had happened to them, except they'd gone missing.

JOHNNY COOPER

Nobody has worked out who of our lot was killed during this period. I heard the total was over a hundred, mostly wounded and taken prisoner, tortured and shot. I was told Rommel tried to stop this.

REG SEEKINGS

What happened with some of the other squadrons when they came in, they didn't take time to get themselves established. They hadn't got the experience, but were all eager to make their mark. The difference with people like Johnny and Jim and I, we settled in, and that was important – we got to know the people, got our own agents set up, with information coming in. We picked school teachers and parsons – they mixed a lot and were more intelligent. We had about a dozen of those. So we were able to keep one jump ahead all the time, where the others didn't. Some of the others seemed to ignore the local population, and you can't operate without them. They got cracking before they were really organised, and didn't stand a chance.

JOHNNY COOPER

I don't think 'A' Squadron lost anybody captured. We had people killed. The fat man that came with us last time, he ended up a sah major and he got caught in a convoy that went through the village. They didn't realise it was a whole convoy, they thought it was a single vehicle. They let rip and went around the corner, and there was about fifty German trucks, so they had to go all the way down, firing, and the last truck poked a gun out the back and fired at them, and hit the chap in the back. The jeep went into the ditch. Chalky White, that was his name. DCM/MM. His medals are in the sergeants' mess. He wore them to France.

REG SEEKINGS

One of the drops was betrayed and the Germans were waiting. I only know what Ginger Jones told me. A couple of men managed to escape, but some were taken by the Gestapo to Paris. One of them was Vaculik, who'd dropped with John and me. Then they were made to dress in civilian clothes, their identity stuff taken off them, then they were taken out to these woods, and machine guns were set up. Vaculik asked one of the guards if they were to be shot and was told yes. He said: 'They're going to shoot us – when I shout all make a run for it, and perhaps some of us will survive.' This is what they did. As they were about to fire, he shouted 'Go!' and they turned to run. As Ginger turned, he tripped on a root and went down, and there he stayed. They opened up and the Germans chased the others into the woods, shooting them down. Ginger didn't have a scratch. He got away to the French. Vaculik also got away. Ginger got back to us, and when I got back to base, he was already installed as storeman. Ginger gave me stuff from the stores to make our wedding cake. Not many people had a wedding cake like ours.

JOHNNY COOPER

We had to witness executions. The military Maquis were very, very strict. In one case, a chap was in the black market, dropping off flour, eggs, sugar, etc., and he was court martialled. I had to go and watch all these executions. This one guy, up against the tree, just sings the Marseillaise until he's shot. The blood feud between the Maquis was terrible.

We had a parachute drop one night, and the Germans were bloody cunning. They put the lights on the railway station, and all the supplies were dropped there. And this Frenchman was compelled to help collect that stuff. After the war he went back to the Haute Savoie and two chaps came to his door – his wife tells the story: 'Is Jacques in?' 'Yes.' He went to the door. 'You come with us, Jacques.' Never seen again. So much of that went on, after the war. They would do an act of sabotage in somebody else's area, because the reprisals from the Gestapo would be in that area, but they didn't want a reprisal in their own area. The other side of that coin were people like the telephone operator, who was tipping us off. She was not in the Resistance, but she was helping us. She was running a pub, she'd tip us off if any Germans were in the village. We'd go down, and certain washing on the line meant, Don't come in the village, Gestapo, so you'd turn round and go back out. Hers was the last house at the edge of the village, and depending on the clothes on the line, we could always turn round and go back up.

One day, I was with Reg, and this didn't happen. We had a bit too much wine, and we came out and we were motoring our jeep up the hill and there at the corner were all these bloody Germans. Reg just let rip, and we pissed off into the hills. She didn't know the Germans had come in at the other end of the village.

MIKE SADLER

At that time I was the assistant intelligence officer in the regiment, and was involved in the planning of the initial parties going in and their launching. I went on a number of the flights to drop people in different parts of France after D-Day. Eventually, when one of the parties had gone off the air – that was Ian Fenwick's squadron in the forest of Orléans – Paddy decided to go in himself to see what had happened, and he decided to take me along with him. So four of us went in.

We were going in with a load of stores and various other things. Our aircraft crashed on take-off, but it luckily didn't go on fire, so we were able to get out, and although we lost our despatcher, who was carried off to hospital, they wheeled up another aircraft after a delay and we went up in that instead, but minus most of our stores.

We were dropped to a reception party down in the Morvan mountains. Johnny Wiseman's patrol was there. We were subsequently dropped two jeeps, which we used to travel up to the forest of Orléans, through minor roads, up beside the Loire. We made contact with Jim Almonds and the survivors of Ian Fenwick's squadron there, and spent some time finding out what had happened and making contact with the Resistance and so on.

JIM ALMONDS

Paddy arrived, with Mike Sadler. They stood on the side of the road, watching the columns of Germans going by. Paddy said to me: 'Go round the back of that farm building and see what you can see.' So I went round and had a look and came back and told him it looked like a retreat.

MIKE SADLER

Then Paddy and I drove back. The break-out from the Normandy bridgehead had taken place by that time and we had no tremendous difficulty driving back up to the French coast, north of Le Mans. Paddy and a few of us had a lunch in Le Mans, and it became a slightly inebriated lunch in celebration. I recall that at one stage Roy Farran from 2 SAS said: 'The trouble with you chaps in the 1st SAS is that you look down on us in the 2nd SAS.' And Paddy said: 'Oh no, we never think of you at all.' After that the proceedings got heartier, and we eventually set off for a drive through the town, and gave a blast de joie on our Vickers Ks up between the buildings as we drove along through the town, which I think upset some of the locals, because we were then in the American zone.

JIM ALMONDS

I went to a Resistance meeting to discuss the progress of the war, what was to happen next, etc., and on the way back, there was a shout from the ditch: 'Put those goddam lights out.' An American section came out of the ditch. They said: 'What are you doing with an American jeep?' 'It was parachuted in to us.' 'What are you doing driving with lights on?' 'Well, it's the custom to drive with sidelights on.' They took us down to their HQ, where the captain in charge said: 'If you're English, I guess it's alright. Have you any proof?' We said: 'Oh, we're English alright, but we've no proof, we don't carry anything with us.' Then he started to bargain for the MI carbines – he didn't have any and wanted some. The next morning we had to go down to their HQ, where we were met by a general. I like to think it was Patton, but maybe it wasn't. He stood in front of the jeep and he said: 'If you're British, I guess you're alright. If you're not, you'll be shot, I'll do it myself.' Very boastful sort.

MIKE SADLER

We drove out of the town and were eventually stopped by what seemed to be something like an American ambush, and Paddy said: 'Talk French.' So we all put on our best French accents – 'Qu'est-ce que c'est' and all this – and the unfortunate American lieutenant who came to address us kept patting our guns and saying: 'No bon, no bon.' Eventually the American sergeant who was with him said: 'Don't you fool yourself, sir, these men speak English better than you do.' So we were then obliged to go along with him to see the local area commander, and we were wheeled in front of him, and Paddy with great presence of mind, after saluting – he was a brigadier – said: 'I hope we didn't frighten your men, sir.' Whereupon the brigadier was obliged to confess that of course they hadn't been frightened at all. So he said: 'Well, that's no problem then.' And after getting a bit of a reprimand we were allowed to go on our way.

JIM ALMONDS

When I got back to the hut, my section had all gone. With the firing, etc., they must have decided to disperse. I never did find any of them again. I was on my own by this time. After dark I went in search of the HQ party who'd moved their position, and by sheer luck I found it and joined up with them.

After the American army started to arrive, we decided our job there was finished and we set off down towards Chartres. There we bargained with the officer in charge of the American base for a flight back to the UK. We left the jeeps with him, we couldn't fly them back. And so we arrived back in the UK.

MIKE SADLER

Paddy was enjoying himself. Although to some extent there was an anxious kind of time, because one was hiding in forests, and making contact with people, and you weren't quite sure whose side they were on a great deal of the time. There was a great rivalry between different types of Maquis in these areas; they were getting ready for post-war takeovers. There were communist Maquis and there were anti-communist Maquis, and you could never be quite sure who you were talking to. So there was a great anxiety about that, but apart from that, I think Paddy treated it as rather a holiday, a break you know, driving around and having a sort of exciting but not unpleasant time.

The French, on the whole, were doing a lot of good work. One of the things that the SAS were doing was helping with resupply and training, and supplying them with explosives and so on. It was just that there was this political problem, that there was always the chance that they would – what's the word – give you away in fact to the local Germans. It certainly happened in some areas, but it didn't happen to us.

We had a great celebration in Paris. We were among the early arrivals there. Paddy made a point of getting us there and we had a very amusing and enjoyable week. On one occasion Paddy gave an illustration of the sort of chap he was. He had a slightly warped sense of humour in some ways, and after a splendid lunch that we had in a black market restaurant, we were all sitting round drinking our coffee and so on, and he suddenly produced a hand grenade and pulled the pin out and stood it in the middle of the table, with the smoke coming out of it. We didn't quite know what to do. We all sat, wondering whether to dive under the table – some people did – and others thought: Well, he can't be intending to blow himself to pieces and us, so we just sat there, and of course he'd kept the detonator off, so it was alright.

JOHNNY COOPER

We all had cars by the end, we came out by car. We motored back through the lines, in a little red Peugeot. Then we flogged them to the Americans at Orléans for a flight back in the Liberators.

REG SEEKINGS

I think it was 'D' Squadron that came and relieved us. They filtered through the lines. This became the practice later with 1 and 2 SAS, through with their jeeps, after the main front had been cracked up. When they took over, we got a convoy together of civvy cars we'd requisitioned – we'd handed over the jeeps – and the other squadron gave us an escort, about three jeeps, and took us through to Orléans. It took us two days to get there.

The Yanks were in occupation in Orléans and the air force was coming in, flying in flour, with Liberators. We thought we'd as usual just climb into aircraft and get home. But the Yanks had had strict instructions that under no circumstances were they to fly anybody out of France. We talked and talked to this Yankee colonel, from Texas. We were kipping down in a hangar there, and I noticed he kept eyeing up our Bren guns. 'Are you interested?' He had a big ranch in Texas, and he reckoned the Brens would be ideal – just what he wanted, he could really have some fun. We said: 'One Bren gun, and give us the first Liberators out in the morning.' Eventually we talked him into it – we gave him three or four guns – and the first Liberators in, we piled in and flew out of France.

We upset the crew by sitting in the hatchways – like you sit in a window, watching the ground below. They were frightened we were going to fall out. It's actually quite hard to fall out of an aircraft. We were diverted to Middle Wallop and we looked below and there were Liberators who'd been in front of us, dotted all over the drome. The Yanks couldn't pick out the right runway – it was all grass. 'Goddamn, it's a goddamn grass field.' It was funny to see, all these Liberators touching down just anywhere on the ground. They'd never landed on grass in their life. How they didn't prang up, I don't know. That's how we came home.

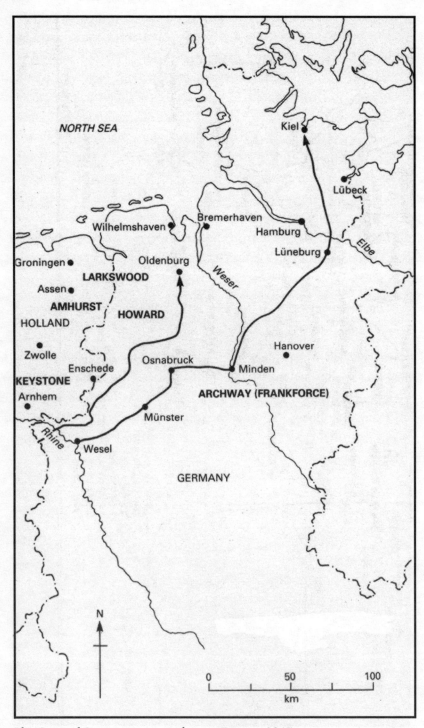

The Originals' campaign in north-west Europe, 1945

CHAPTER TWENTY-FIVE

After France, the SAS returned to Britain to regroup, and to look for a role in the rest of the war. From early 1945, units of 2 SAS were employed in classic SAS roles in Italy. In north-west Europe, 1 SAS went first into Belgium, then into Germany. In France, they had been able to count on at least a certain level of support from the local population; in Germany this would not be the case. As in France, the SAS knew they were under threat from Hitler's commando order – that if captured, they were to be executed. The Originals, as usual, were at the forefront.

JIM ALMONDS

The first move was to go to Belgium. In the interim period, Paddy got me promoted to lieutenant and I was put in charge of the preparations for the coming op – armour plating the jeeps, making the gun mountings, putting on the petrol tanks, etc. We set off by road for Dover, went to Ostend and into Belgium. There was nothing particularly of note there. From there we moved to Holland, then into Germany.

PAT RILEY

I rejoined for the Rhine crossing. We went over in Buffalos. The 101st American Parachute Division were ahead of us. We set off across the river, and unfortunately, the engine on one of the Buffalos alongside us failed and away it went sailing down the Rhine. I don't know if it was the last we saw of 'em, but everyone was very nice and waved to them. Finally we landed and got in the wood there. The Germans took a hell of a tanning, from artillery, bombing, everything.

JOHNNY COOPER

We crossed the Rhine and did an advance recce for the Airborne Division. Myself with 'A' Squadron were advance reconnaissance for 8th Battalion Parachute Regiment. We were out in front, skirmishing, etc. By that time the Germans were very, very negative, they were running like hell.

REG SEEKINGS

Hitler had given the order that we SAS were to be shot on sight, so they gave us a new identity, classified us as tank corps, gave us new pay books, and we wore black berets.

Johnny Cooper's jeep, in Germany.

Our first real action was with some Canadian paratroopers who had been held up in a little copse. They sent us in and we blasted hell out of the German paratroopers, knocked them for six, and the Canadians couldn't make this out – 'They can't be tank men to fight like that.' It upset them, because they were red berets. When they found out we were red berets too, they were happy. In that first action, Fraser was the first one to get hit – they turned his jeep over. He was the only casualty we had.

We took the position and were mopping up – we'd inflicted quite heavy casualties on them – and I saw an arm waving, and I shouted for them to come out and I ran across, and there was a German paratroop sergeant. I looked at him, and I'd hit him with a .5, in the thigh. You can imagine what a mess he was in – bone everywhere. I got him out, but he died about half an hour later; there was no hope for him. This was how we were being used at the time.

There was a young German paratrooper who nearly got me. I faced him out. He was only about fourteen or fifteen, with a couple of spud mashers in his hand, a belt of ammunition round his neck. I shouted to him in German – I was right in the open – to throw his grenades down. He was making out he was going to throw them. I had a feeling we were being watched. All firing had ceased. I was just about to blast this kid, when he dropped his grenades.

Then we took a German command post, and the colonel of this German para regiment congratulated me on my bravery, as he said, watching me catch this youngster. He said: 'If you'd shot him, you were dead, and your men. But when we saw your action, we thought, these are fair men, they've beaten us, we'll surrender. But if you'd shot him, we would have fought to the death.'

JIM ALMONDS

We were attached to the Canadian armoured division, doing forward reconnaissance. They had great difficulty in spotting people hiding in ditches, etc. This was the time when the German home guard were brought in. They were using Panzerfaust rockets for attacking armoured vehicles. We had jeeps with a couple of bars in front and a spreader across with mine detectors on it; the hope was that you detected a mine before you hit it. Whether you'd be able to pull up in time was another matter.

REG SEEKINGS

I had the wireless on my jeep. This was lovely. I received all the messages, and they didn't know it at the time, but I made all the decisions – Fraser had been invalided out of course. We went into a number of attacks, which if I'd passed the message properly to any of the officers, they wouldn't have done it. I'd turn round and say: 'Right, we've got to take so-and-so, direct order from General Dempsey.' As a matter of fact, Dempsey had spoken to me a couple of times privately – personally rather – on the phone, because he knew me. These young officers weren't prepared to argue the toss with me. I found out afterwards they were shit scared of me.

We used to attach ourselves to the forward elements which often, in 1st Army, were the 11th Hussars. These were the ones I'd met in the desert and I knew them. We loved working with them: they were different, not like ordinary British. They were old campaigners and treated you right. Their code call was the Cherries, because they had the cherrypickers. It was my uncle's regiment. They used to wear bright cherry pants. They used to call us Little Cherries:

'Would the Little Cherries like to have a go?' We knew then they'd got something up ahead that was holding them up and we used to race up there and have a go at whatever it was. Sometimes machine gun nests, which they couldn't really deal with, and we'd go and blast it out for them.

A few days after we'd crossed the Rhine, our objective was a railway embankment. We had to cross quite a wide plain, three or four miles perhaps, and along one side was a nice high ridge, well wooded. The village at the start of the plain had been well fortified and we had those tanks with a bulldozer blade to demolish pillboxes. But every time they stuck their heads out of the village, the 88s on the ridge were knocking hell out of them, so they called up rocket-firing Typhoons.

The German 88s were keeping pretty quiet, only firing when they saw something to fire at. The tank men didn't fancy sticking their noses out any more, so they asked us to go – the brass neck of these people. Perhaps we had better communications than them, I don't know. I set off. The Typhoons were Red and Blue Hunter, two squadrons; we were called the Little Boys. We motored out to see if we could draw fire. We'd gone about half a mile or so, well out into the plain. Still no fire. We carried on further onto the plain, and you could just faintly hear these planes, at a hell of an altitude. 'Red Hunter to Little Boys, doesn't look like they're going to bite. Get out and have a little wee-wee in a group. Please draw fire, please old boy, be a sport. We guarantee they'll only fire one salvo and we'll get them.' 'Will do, Red Hunter, but make sure you get the bastards.'

So we got out, collected into a bunch – I didn't like that, because it was against all our training. And sure enough, the bloody hillside erupted, their shells went screaming over. 'Red Hunter, Blue Hunter, tally ho, tally ho.' I've never seen anything like it in my life. I could see these Typhies screaming down. They came down full belt in formation, and they fired, and it looked as though they'd gone backwards. We could see these puffs of smoke, and the whole ridge erupted. Not another shell fired. I never saw anything so devastating in my life. They reckoned they used a salvo equivalent to a broadside from a six-inch gun cruiser and I believe it. It was fantastic. 'Red Hunter/Blue Hunter, back to base.' Red Hunter dived down over us. 'Thank you, Little Boys, hope we can have a beer some time in the mess.' Off they went, bacon and eggs. Really fantastic.

PAT RILEY

We went to a town which the SS were holding. I got as far as the crossroads with my chaps, and there were some slit trenches there which the Jerries had very kindly dug for us, and we carried on the battle from there. My batman said: 'You'll never take this place. There's a pub behind us.' We fought on, of course; took the thing and held on.

REG SEEKINGS

Our job there was to speed up the attack. Wherever anybody was held up, our job was to hit hard, drive through the German lines, turn back and shoot them up the rear, and make a gap for the ordinary army to come through. About the only time I really was frightened was one time we ran out of ammunition. I was down to my Colt .45 and I realised what a little popgun it was.

JOHNNY COOPER

We came to these crossroads, an all forest area, and as we came round the corner, I think it was a Panzerfaust came across the road. I was driving, and turned my jeep right into the side. Reg's jeep was on the other side of the road – we only had three jeeps – and we started to fire back. They were well camouflaged, well in situ. They started peppering away at us, and a couple of blokes were wounded. We got them back into the jeep, then Reg and I went forward on foot to try and find out where they were. But you couldn't see. All you could see was the gun flashes in the wood. They'd got us pretty well surrounded.

REG SEEKINGS

This is when I ran out of ammunition. I dived into a ditch for cover, and hit this little hollow near an old tree stump. I was practically in tears with just this popgun. Next thing, thump, a body landed on top of me – that was Johnny Cooper. The same thing with him, tears of frustration.

I thought: We've got to get out of this or we'll just be cut to ribbons. Fortunately, and I don't know why I did it, but I'd come across this two-inch mortar, and I'd slung it with a few shells on the back of my jeep. I thought if I can bash through there, I can mortar the sides of the road, I'll do it before I go, then drive through and mortar the other side to get the remnants out.

JOHNNY COOPER

I said: 'Reg, we break.' So we rushed back and I started the jeep, my hand on the accelerator and said: 'All pile in.'

REG SEEKINGS

I shouted orders for half the men, numbered them off, to load up the wounded and prepare to fight themselves out with me. I could have cried – everybody was carrying a wounded man. I took that half through, and put half a dozen mortar shells down one side of the road, hopped in the jeep and we drove through, turned round, and mortared the other side of the road. John brought out the other half.

JOHNNY COOPER

We belted out of there like shit off a shovel. I don't think we saw a single German.

REG SEEKINGS

I forget how many we had killed there, but it was a lot for us – six or seven – and a big number wounded.

JOHNNY COOPER

Then there was the time that pillock wouldn't open fire. This chap was in the top of the turret, doing nothing. Ask Reg about that one. I can't remember all the details.

REG SEEKINGS

This message came through that Inns of Court regiment had some problems, could I go and sort it out. They gave me a map reference, but it was the wrong one, so I went past this place then had to come back. They themselves hadn't got to the point where they wanted to meet me. They started to come back with us.

On the way back we ran right into an SS ambush, a great big one. As we turned back, one of the vehicles in front of me spotted a Panzer tank – the gunner fired immediately and hit the thing just as it was about to fire, and that blew up. His driver got a dumdum straight in the head. I've never seen anything like it. His head just exploded and it was like a red fountain – like some of the horror stuff you see now.

Then we ran into the armoured cars in a hollow in the middle of some woods. All hell broke loose, we fired back, but the armoured cars that we had with us were doing nothing. Major Pote had come up to see what was going on. He was our second in command. Four big German armoured carriers came out of the woods, and they were actually running over my chaps and killing them. I was begging for our armoured cars to fire, and they reckoned they were their own tanks. I said: 'I don't give a bugger whether they're our tanks or not, they're killing my men. For Christ sake, knock 'em out. I don't care whether they're British.' 'We can't do that.' I said to Pote: 'Give them an order.' He said: 'I can't, that's not my unit.' I said: 'You're the senior man, give the order.' And I went so bloody mad, so he said to the captain of the armoured cars: 'Open fire.' To give them credit, they knocked three out straight away and scored two or three hits as the fourth one tried to get away. But in the meantime they'd made a mess of some of my chaps.

We got back to the next village down the road – it was getting dusk. I think it was Benny's squadron that came across. They'd heard that we'd been wiped out and that I'd been killed. I was in tatters, but I hadn't got a mark on me. I picked my bedroll up and it all fell to bits; my heavy raincoat had holes all over it. The jeep was riddled. But I never got a scratch. You know the Spitfire armoured windscreen – what the hell they were using I don't know, but they knocked a hole right through that.

John and I went back next day. There were seven graves of ours, and twenty-six of theirs. We had an idea who was dead, but the real reason we went back was

Twin Vickers and armour windshield on an SAS jeep in Germany.

that there were two we couldn't account for. We went to two or three towns for the next couple of days, trying to trace them, and we got to the final place, traced them to the hospital, and the Gestapo had come along and taken them away.

At that place, a trainload of concentration camp inmates had been caught by the RAF and strafed. They'd tried to escape and had been shot down by German guards as well, and there were hundreds and hundreds of them killed. They put them in big communal trenches. John and I spent bloody hours going through these bodies, trying to find our own chaps. To this day we don't know what happened to them – never been any sign of them. Obviously bumped off by the Gestapo. We may have missed them, among all these bodies, they may have put them into a uniform we didn't recognise, but we couldn't find them.

That's when I went and got the red berets. That made a lot of difference. Like I said, Hitler had given the order that we were to be shot on sight, so they gave us new identity, classified us as tank corps. But that's when I disobeyed orders. I went back, against orders, and got the red berets. That made a lot of difference. If the British troops knew they were up against German paratroopers, they were half beaten already. It's the psychological effect you have on ordinary troops. They can't stand up to specialist troops. We never had any more hard fighting after that.

BOB BENNETT

We were given information that there were SS in a certain village. We surrounded the village at night and at dawn we took the jeeps right in. There wasn't a man in there, wasn't a single soldier. The only people that we found were women and kids, that were very hungry. And all my squadron, the Irish boys, were all getting their rations off, bully beef and everything, and actually giving it to these women and kids, that really needed it. And I thought then: Well, I don't know, they've all got this name of tough SAS, but they're quite – you know, quite good at heart.

REG SEEKINGS

This is when the atrocities started with the SS. We were in Germany by now. They were using any cover they could to fire on British troops, which is to be expected. Dempsey warned them that any more of this and he would flatten these places. If the SS took advantage of this, he would flatten everything. We sat there for one day, and all day long and all night they pounded this town. I've never seen so many guns – you couldn't hear each other, the noise was deafening. All manner of guns, in line after line. It actually held us up for three days, because we couldn't get through the town. When we got there, there was just chimney stacks. There'd been so much tonnage of bombs and shells rained on that place that the rubble was dust, pulverised. That was his example of what he would do.

They were still trying to force German people to put the white flag out whilst they took over their positions to fire on us. At this place I'm talking about, they wiped out an entire farmer's family, the farm buildings. This SS crowd we were fighting killed their own people, because young kids wouldn't take rifles and fire. So they killed them, shot them. The woman objected to the flags and took them in, and they flattened the bloody lot, her and her daughters, all the family. Their own people. These nine- and ten-year-old kids weren't even big enough to hold a rifle, and this bastard shot quite a number of them. They were getting so desperate then.

BOB BENNETT

In Germany, Paddy was going round the different squadrons and we had the info he was coming up to 'D' Squadron. We were in a little village, and Tonkin said: 'Paddy's coming up with the padre, Fraser.' So we tipped all the Germans out of this place upstairs and took the bar over, and we filled a great big galvanised bath with the hooch – it was all colours of the rainbow, schnapps, green, blue, pink. We brought a piano in. Fraser is a beautiful pianist. So they arrived and we had a terrific evening. Fraser was sitting there playing that piano, and all these Irish chaps of mine were sitting there, getting drunker and drunker and hitting him on the back, saying: 'Don't effing play that.' 'Okay Paddy,' he'd say. The padre was a terrific man.

REG SEEKINGS

When we got to Luneburg Heath, we were moving in with the tanks and jeeps – one jeep, one tank, one jeep, one tank. The Germans were getting boys, everybody, and sticking them down on the roadsides and blasting away at the tanks. With our firepower lower down, we were more effective than the tanks against this sort of thing. When we came up against some resistance like that, we'd rush ahead and blast hell out of them. But they had tremendous firepower.

We were driving a wedge through on the main road, and leaving everything behind us. We weren't clearing the country, cleaning up. The units coming behind had to fan out and do that. We were just driving a wedge all the time; that's why we were advancing so fast.

At one stage the convoy halted in a little valley, and we were taking a bit of a rest and had dropped back with the troop transporters, because the troops were all in lorries.

I got out of my vehicle. Jack Terry was at the rear. I saw him get out, and we strolled towards each other. He said: 'Are you feeling like I do? My hair's standing on end. I can't believe it. How could they leave a place like this?' There was a ridge there, a beautiful place. I said: 'I don't like it.' And Jack said: 'I'm bloody sure somebody's watching us.' I said: 'Go back, tell the chaps to get out and have a pee, be very casual, and we'll gradually stroll up to the ridge . . .'

So we strolled up, chatting away. We went up to the top of the ridge. There were all these young cadets, from a military academy up the road. Most of them were about eleven years old. They looked surprised, didn't know what to do, all scared. So we said to them: 'What are you doing here? Why didn't you fire?' One of them said: 'We were trying to make up our minds what to do.' I said: 'Who's in charge?' They said: 'Our sergeant – he's gone up the road to see what's happening up there.' So there was no one in command. They could have knocked hell out of us. The only ones that had a go were right out on the front, alongside the trucks.

PAT RILEY

We pushed on through various places, with a scrap here and a scrap there, and eventually we got on to Luneburg. Paddy said to me that they had an officer shot in 'C' Squadron, would I mind joining it. I said: 'I will, providing I can come back to 'A' Squadron after we get this business over.' Which was agreed to. And I asked my two chaps that were with me regular whether they was willing to come with me, and they said the same thing as I did: providing they could get back to 'A' Squadron. So we went over and joined 'C' Squadron, where we got into several scraps and things that side of the place. We were going up towards Oldenburg. That's where Paddy won his fourth DSO.

JIM ALMONDS

Why he never got the VC, I don't know. He earned it more than once. I can't understand why he never got it. Probably his character went against him. He certainly deserved it. One of the most decorated men in the army: DSO, four bars, Legion of Honour. His face didn't fit, but his actions did.

REG SEEKINGS

We motored further on. I don't know how the hell it got there, but there was an airborne light tank. The next thing I know a fire-fight started, then all hell broke loose. So we opened up, firing away, and the slaughter was terrible. A lot of them were German Home Guard. One of my boys shouted: 'Behind you, Sah Major.' I was busy firing the jeep gun. So I grabbed the Bren gun we carried and swung round, and there was a whole section of these. What the hell they thought they were doing I don't know. I backed under a culvert and they were coming along this ditch. Whether they thought we were Germans, or whether they thought they could capture us I just don't know. Eleven of them, all in single file. I opened up with a whole magazine, chopped them down. It was only a few yards range.

There was an 88 there, but we knocked that out before it got mobile, knocked the crew out. Then my gunner Mac said: 'I've been hit.' He was a former first-class medical orderly. He got kicked out of the medical corps for taking up arms against the Germans at Sidi Roseg, way back in the desert. So he joined us. Rough little Scots lad. I was the only one who'd have him. Everybody else was a bit scared of him. But he helped a lot of our lads with wounds.

Back in the UK, before D-Day, when we were getting our crews ready to go to France and Germany, we'd all pick our crew, and we got all these men together, and they said: 'Of course sah major's picked the best already.' Fraser said: 'The sah major hasn't picked anybody.' I said: 'I'll tell you what I'll do. I'll write down the names of my crew, I'll put them in an envelope, give it to the major, and I guarantee that none of you will select either of them.' So they all picked their crews, and the major read out the names I'd picked and couldn't believe it. They said: 'You taking MacKenzie?' I forget the name of the other chap. Two of the roughest bloody rogues in creation. I don't really know how they were kept in the unit. They had a rotten name.

Once in Italy, Mac threatened to get me with a bayonet; he reckoned he'd kill me while I was sleeping. There was a Sicilian woman who looked after our gear, did our washing, who had a young daughter, fourteen or fifteen, lovely little kid, Maria, and he was trying to knock her off. I'd told her that he was a married man and so she wouldn't have anything to do with him. They were brought up very strict. So Mac was going to murder me, and people were frightened of him. They said: 'How do you dare go to sleep?' I said: 'Don't worry about him, he needs me to lead him into action, so he'll keep me alive.'

So Mac then said: 'I'm hit,' I got him out and tried to find it, and said: 'I can't find anything. Get back behind that gun.' He had a name as a coward amongst certain people, you see. 'No, I'm hit.' My gunner/wireless operator said: 'I've been hit also, sir.' Christ almighty. So I pulled Mac out and he said: 'I know I'm bleeding to death, I can feel it.' And I couldn't find anything. Then when I went to pick him up to put him in the seat again I saw a big pool of blood. I ripped open his sleeve, and a bullet had gone through and exploded and blew out his armpit. The hole was so big, I stuffed in two big shell dressings, and got him to hold down on it.

The other one was stitched all the way down, at inch and a half intervals, all down his arm. I knew Airborne was not far away; I'd seen their advanced dressing station when we'd left to go across the valley. So I shouted out to the lads to carry on, that I was getting my two wounded men back. I'll give the pair of them their due – Mac had started to come round a bit and was firing away with one hand: 'You bastards . . .' Mind you, it would only have hit aircraft. And that started the rear gunner off too. He had a go with his one hand. I drove on. The Airborne tried to stop me, bloody stupid major, and I just bashed past. I got to the medical tent, got the doctor, got Mac straight out and the doctor said: 'A few seconds more and he'd have been gone, I wouldn't have been able to help him.'

They both lost their arm.

I never saw either of them after the war. Mac got very bitter. I was away when he came back to camp and picked his gear up. The only man he wanted to speak to was me, but I wasn't there. I don't know what happened to him. He was a rough little so-and-so, he'd done two stretches in prison for arson – £5 a time for setting fire to a factory, before the war. But he was good.

The reason I shot my way through to get him to the doctor was I suddenly became a little bit frightened. A night or two before when we were sitting waiting for this big barrage, we were being sniped at, and old Mac, he was a great scrounger, and he'd found a jar of rum, he'd pinched it from some store. He suddenly disclosed this when we were under the jeep with the bullets flying around, so we had a sip. He said to me: 'I hear you're getting married.' I said: 'Yes, if we get through this.' He said: 'I know it's a lot to ask, but could I come to your wedding?' 'Yes, mate, you would have been invited anyway.' He'd just got married in Scotland, on the leave we'd just had. He said: 'I want you to promise me something. I'm going to cop it.' I said: 'Don't be bloody stupid.' 'No,' he said, 'I'm going to cop it.' I was a bit concerned because I'd had this happen before. It does happen, people have a premonition and pretty often it's bloody true. He said: 'I want you to promise to write to the wife and tell her I went down shooting your guns.'

Poor old Mac.

But he survived.

CHAPTER TWENTY-SIX

In mid-April 1945, The Originals were pushing hard through Germany, at the front – even ahead of – the Allied advance. Though they would not say it in so many words, they might have believed they had seen it all. They had not.

REG SEEKINGS

We'd been coming up through the forest, and for a day or so we'd had this horrible stink.

BOB BENNETT

We were proceeding north in Germany with the Inns of Courts regiment, and we were ordered back to a map reference.

JOHNNY COOPER

'A' Squadron had to motor in with the doctors. We were there to escort them in and protect them while they could do something. We were armed. We had to have injections before we went in.

BOB BENNETT

It was Belsen.

REG SEEKINGS

We were going around the outside, and an SS armoured division came the other way. Their commander said: 'If we engage and fight here, the people inside will escape, and they are full of typhoid, etc. This will spread all over Germany.' He said: 'You may say that's a good thing, but remember the cream of the British army is here too.' So they asked permission to withdraw to a certain line and that's what happened. A three-day truce was made. It was peculiar, sitting there watching the tanks go past. We were chatting to German soldiers, yelling out as they went past.

BOB BENNETT

They'd surrounded Belsen with small anti-tank guns, and I met a chap I went to school with who was with the Oxford & Bucks, a chap named Jim Steele, and I said: 'Of all places to meet an old school friend.'

JOHNNY COOPER

You go down the road to it, with high fir trees on both sides – you'd never think it was a concentration camp. The gateway looks like going into any normal military camp. Beautiful trees. You'd got to go at least a quarter of a mile inside before you saw the concentration camp. We motored to the gate, and there was the Beast of Belsen, the lieutenant who took all the rap. Then you turn and go in.

The thing is about eight square miles – a fantastic sight. I didn't know I was going to see what I saw. I didn't know I would see dead bodies in thousands. In action, I'd never seen women and kids, all lying there, absolutely stark naked, absolutely emaciated as they were. My reaction was nothing but horror, never seen anything like it. There were 300 SS left behind, plus 700 or 800 Hungarian guards.

BOB BENNETT

The camp was absolute chaos; there were all these starving people. No one expected anything – anything – like this. We walked right up to the pit where they were making them crawl, when they were in their dying minutes, and saw all that. There was still a lot of shooting going on, because it was a very, very vast camp. The SS, I think, were killing political prisoners in there, but we couldn't do anything about it at all in that respect: we were under a treaty not to shoot.

JOHNNY COOPER

We stayed the whole day there. They made these big tureens of soup. The only thing we could give them was soup – giving them solid food would have killed them. So we were feeding them soup. Nobody else could go in. We had tanks circulating to stop them breaking out. If they'd broken out, the whole of the area and our own forces would have been exposed to typhoid.

We'd seen the bodies on the railway line. They'd slaughtered 2,000 and the bodies were still on the platform. As soldiers, we knew what the Germans were doing in the concentration camps. But when you saw this bloody great big pit, and it had been lined and lined and lined – how many bodies were under there . . . That pit was 150 yards long and thirty yards wide, full of human flesh.

I only went into one block, and there were about six rows of stalls, and the people who'd died at the top, they had no energy to take them out. Dead people were lying there, with living people lying alongside them. They were coming into that camp at the rate of about 20,000 a day, by train, even then. They reckoned 60,000 a day were dying.

JOHNNY COOPER

This little woman put a hand through the wire to the old mangel-wurzels, and this Rumanian shot her dead. The padre, Fraser, was standing very close to that, and he tried to grab – I think it was Reg's revolver . . .

McLuskey would have shot the first German he could have got his hands on that day. But nobody shot anybody, we had a treaty. When the Rumanian shot that woman who put her hand underneath the wire, the Rumanians were all taken into custody and the SAS motored out.

In Germany the SAS were also hunting war criminals, particularly an SS general who was responsible for the murder of SAS men.

REG SEEKINGS

The trouble was, once you got into Germany, you couldn't find any Nazis. The older people, those who'd fought in the First War, they'd say: 'You've come two or three years too late to save Germany.' I don't suppose for a minute they felt like that at the beginning of the war. But they could see Germany was getting hammered and they felt it should stop and not let Germany get ruined as it was being. But the kids, that was the big trouble. They were fanatical, no two ways about it.

We were told to hang on for a bit, something was happening further along the line, and so I pulled in at this farmhouse, a chance for something to eat. I went in this little hamlet, and said to the old girl could we brew up, etc. She said: 'Yes certainly.' We were talking to her; she was quite pleasant. The old man was there. Then in came the daughter, ten or twelve years old. God, she screamed. She struck her mother and father, she kicked and spat, screamed her bloody head off. The mother and old man belted her. We said: 'What's all this?' 'It's because you're British soldiers coming into our home. We daren't do a thing, because she would have reported us, and we'd have finished up in a concentration camp.' This happened all over Germany. Hitler had the kids with them, and the older folks just had to knuckle down. It was definitely so, they were terrified of the kids.

JOHNNY COOPER

Before going into Luneberg, we met the fourteen-year-old German boys in the cave. They were going to defend Luneburg Heath, with a Panzerfaust. They were dedicated little boys, but they didn't know how to fire their weapons and they got trampled on by everybody. They must have lost thousands of them. We shot a lot that came up with the Panzerfaust. I think that was too heavy for them to hold; the Panzerfaust was quite a heavy anti-tank rocket, with a great bulbous front to it. Then we went into Lubeck and Luneburg, after Gestapo and war criminals, etc. We did house-to-house searches. We had the Special Intelligence Corps team with us, and we had the addresses to go to. We picked up a hell of a lot there.

REG SEEKINGS

We had one job in a house where the army wanted me to open up a big safe they'd found in the cellar. This was army HQ, general staff. It was a huge safe, and I was going to blow it, a controlled explosion. First they said, 'OK,' then they said, 'No.' There was stuff in there that was far too valuable to risk any type of explosion. I said: 'It'll only be a mild explosion.' I had quite a good idea how to do it. But no, they wanted a crack welder, and a captain from a REME unit came down to cut it open. That's how important they thought the contents were. What a job it was.

When we got it open all there was in the safe was a tiny pair of kiddies' booties, for a new-born baby, and seven little microfilms. They snatched those away – didn't give us a chance to get hold of those. I don't know what was on these microfilms, but they were desperate to get them.

When we were coming to Luneburg, we picked up Captain Hunter, from the Field Security police. He was after the chap who'd murdered our people in France. Our job was to pick up all the leading lights and put them inside, so we went ahead of the attack. We drove into Luneburg several hours before the army got there. We were picking up all these people, holding them for the army, then we took over the jail and put them in there. We didn't arrest him, but we picked up young Willi Messerschmitt. We went to his place, knocked on the door. He answered it and said: 'One does not know what to do these days, does one.' In perfect English.

We were questioning him, thinking he was a good chap to get well in with, because he was sure to know all the brass. Which he did. We decided we weren't getting enough co-operation from him, so we searched his house, and looked at his jacket, and just under his jacket flap – they used to have a thread put through in a certain manner, which denoted they were one of the dreaded members of the hierarchy of the Gestapo. He was a member. He tried to deny it, then he realised we knew more than he thought. He said he'd been forced into it because of his position in the aircraft industry. We said we wouldn't worry much about that. That sort of thing was honorary at times. But he was giving us information we wanted.

We were after someone called Hauptmann, and Willi told us where Hauptmann's mistress was. So we went along there. There was an old girl there, the landlady. I saw her slip a picture under a cushion in the armchair, and I asked her if she knew so-and-so. No, she didn't have anybody there by that name.

I picked out this photo she'd hidden and said: 'Who is this?' Poor old girl, she wasn't up to that. 'Yes, that was Fraulein Hauptmann.' She was frightened; she didn't want to get into trouble. I said: 'Where is she?' 'She should be coming in for lunch any time now.' We thought we'd pick her up in the street, just outside. So we went out, in sight of the house. We saw her coming along – a very striking woman – and we dropped in as though we were trying to pick her up. Snooty bitch. Telling us to clear off, etc. We followed her into the house and she didn't know what it was all about until we got her inside and started questioning her.

Hunter had a Scots sergeant with him. He was Highland Light Infantry in the '14 war, and married a French nurse and never came back to Britain, lived in France, had a son. He decided at Dunkirk that he'd come out and join the forces, wouldn't stop in occupied France. Left his wife and young son behind. He joined the Field Security police – spoke fluent French and German – and went back to France. When he went to his home village, his wife had been in the concentration camp and had just been released. The son was seventeen at the time, and greeted his father with Heil Hitler. His wife threw her arms round his neck and she died in his arms. He was so bitter about this; an ideal man for the job he had.

But this woman was tough. He stood her up against a wall, put bullets alongside of her. She wouldn't flinch. No way did she know this Hauptmann. We didn't know whether to arrest her, but we thought no, we won't. We told her she'd be watched, and we thought that would be enough. Then I had a brilliant idea. We had a German photographer, a chemist, who was developing films we took in Belsen. He was a nice old boy, and according to him, dead against the

Nazis. I believe he'd had a rough time. So I said had he got any photographs of any pretty women? He thought we wanted something naughty. I said: 'No, I've got a reason: I want one showing plenty of leg, or in a bathing costume.' He found this gorgeous blonde. I said: 'Now can you fake up this picture of Hauptmann as if she's being very intimate, sitting on his lap?' 'Oh yes, I can do that.' Then we went back to this girl with the photo and started questioning her again. I said: 'You mean to tell me you don't know this man?' And I showed her the photograph. She blew her top and we quickly knew where he was. She let it out before she realised.

So we went off to the village where he was hiding, and knocked on the door of this big place. A chap answered the door. He'd been ambassador for the Reich overseas. He was very jaundiced – not the type of man to stand up to much punishment. Johnny spoke to him, and he was very casual and hoity toity in his answers. So I hit him, whang: 'When you address a British officer, stand to attention, address him in a proper manner.' And hit him again. That was enough for him, and he told us that this man was in his gardener's place. We went along there and another blonde answered the door. I asked her if Hauptmann was there. No, there was no such man there. 'I've information that he's here.' 'No, nobody here, except my husband.' And this chap came to the door. Silly bugger, he'd left his jackboots on. Denying all knowledge of being in the SS and wearing jackboots.

Then we went on another job – peculiar work for SAS. We'd picked up rumours from agents and others of the treasures reputed to be buried at Luneberg. We heard they were at the airport somewhere, and we spent days measuring walls, checking out everything. We didn't have time to finish that before we got another call to carry on to Lubeck. Not long after we left they found all those treasures.

Things would have been over much quicker if the Russians would meet us, but they wouldn't even take our radio vehicle across there. You stay your side, we'll stay ours.

So it was stalemate. We could have been in Berlin days before that, and saved a lot of lives. Because I do believe the Germans would have surrendered to us. They were surrendering at that time. Make no mistake, the Germans didn't fight hard once we got well into Germany. For the simple reason – the rumour went round that we'd take up weapons, they'd come and fight alongside us, and we'd all take on the Russians. They were most upset when they had to give up their weapons.

In Lubeck, I had a German staff colonel come up to me in the street: 'You are SAS?' 'That's correct.' 'My CO wishes to surrender to you.' I said: 'Good God. There are some redcaps over there, you go to them.' 'No, he was the commandant of this town, he does not wish to surrender to mere redcaps, he prefers to surrender only to the elite – you are the elite.'

He said: 'My commandant insists.' 'Alright,' I said, 'where is this man?' And these two gaunt old boys were standing there, one in a scruffy overcoat. I thought: That can't be the commandant. Then he whipped open his overcoat, and you've never seen so many medals in your life. He'd got his No. 1 dress on underneath this old coat. So I had to take him along and hand him over. He was most upset because we handed him over to the MPs.

When we got to Luneberg, we were picking up different people. One was the Gauleiter. The army had got him quite late in the day. There was a major of this yeomanry crowd, and this Gauleiter was arguing the toss about what seat he would take in the vehicle – he reckoned he took precedence over the colonel. I said to the major: 'Why don't you kick his arse?' He said: If I do that, that's my crown gone.' I said 'Don't be ridiculous' and turned to this chap: 'Hey you, in there.' I did kick him. 'You get in there, don't bloody argue with me.' The major said: 'I wish I could do that, Sah Major.' So we whipped them off and put them in jail.

Next morning I was told to get them out and hand them over to the special police detachment. It was one of those jails where you pull a lever and clang, all the doors open. So we lined them up, and you couldn't miss this Gauleiter, he was the spitting image of Himmler – monocle and the lot. But he was missing. I said: 'Where is he?' 'He's doing his ablutions.' I walked in, and there he is in his underpants, having a wash. So I told him to get dressed immediately. He said, 'I demand a servant,' and started quoting the Geneva Convention conditions for an officer. I said: 'I'm giving you five seconds to get changed and get outside.'

Did I kick him up the arse. He jumped in his stuff, he had two portmanteaux with him, carried them outside, marched them all out, and he gets to the gate. I don't know whether a rumour had gone round town or not, but the square was full of people, waiting. The Gauleiter saw them and turned the colour of fire. He put down the cases, and said: 'I refuse to go one inch further. I will be treated as an officer and a gentleman. I'm not going to be belittled in front of these people.'

I took off my beret and said: 'What is this?' He said: 'You are SAS.' 'That's right. What order did Hitler give?' He said: 'I know of no order.' I said: 'You're a lying bastard.' I put the beret back on, took out the Colt .45, and put a round up the spout.

I said: 'I would rather shoot you than march you across that square, so what is it going to be?' He picked his cases up, and you ought to have heard the crowd – they jeered and booed him to hell. He must have been a bad bastard, even amongst the German people. They gave him a rough time.

They couldn't do enough for me. I wanted a camera but they said they hadn't got any Leicas at that moment. The army orders over the radio was to hand in all cameras and binoculars, wherever we went. As I was driving away, an old police sergeant came tearing after me. He had a Leica, brand new, you couldn't get it anywhere else in the world at the time, and he pushed it into my hand.

Then we had jobs like raiding brothels, because that's where the SS hid. We picked up a lot of them in brothels. German houses were connected up in the ceilings. We used to go there quietly, slip in, then get up in the roof, quietly spread the chaps around, then drop into the rooms and grab them. We bashed into one place – a girl was in there in a hell of a state. A Waffen SS lieutenant had just gone through the window, and before he left, do you know what the bugger had done, real animal, he'd bitten off both her nipples.

The 5th Division had had no communication for three days. They were on the Dortmund-Ems canal, about seventy miles from us. We'd just done a job for the Cherrypickers, blasted some resistance out of a barn, and some mortars got on to us and we were ducking and dodging, running around – quite hilarious, anticipating where the next mortar was coming down. We were outfoxing each other on this flat land. We broke through the mortars, got back and the major in charge of the squadron was waiting for us. Dempsey was on the phone, wanting me.

He told me that 5th Div had gone astray, and he wanted me to proceed with utmost urgency to this place. He said: 'I don't like asking you to do this, because it'll most probably be the last trip you ever make. But I want that bridge taken, and I want it defended to the last man. You're the only person I think is capable of doing the job. I'm sorry, Sergeant.'

He said: 'Load up with every bit of ammo you can get. The Cherrypickers say they can supply you with mortars, anything you need. They will follow up as fast as they can. Hit the bridge, straddle it, and hold it at all costs.' Johnny was there. As the General wished me good luck, I said: 'One final point, can Captain Cooper come with me?' He said: 'I suppose you'd better take your last ride together. You have my permission.'

I picked up a bugle (I'd been a bugler in the Cambridgeshires) and that was the way my squadron went in. When we got a call on the radio anywhere, I used to come out playing tally-ho. The boys used to respond to that and we'd really go to town.

Off we went; John was driving. I was handling the guns because I was better on them, and it was my usual job. We had three or four jeeps with us, and we just motored, ignored everything on the way. Every now and again, I've give a blow as we saw emplacements coming up. The Jerries couldn't make it out: what the hell's going on, look at those crazy so-and-sos. Who are they? I'd blow the bugle, and we never had a shot fired at us. Bloody hilarious. We belted along, and arrived in this place on a Sunday morning. We hit the bridge, no sign of anybody, civvy or military. Out the jeeps, up with the mortars, look around. Nothing happening, no shots. We thought we'd better try and find someone to see what was happening. We couldn't see anybody.

We told the chaps to keep their eyes open, forget about us, if they saw Germans, open up, and we took a jeep and as we got near the church we could hear the church organ going and singing. And this is where we found the commander of 5th Divison. In church. What had happened, they were camped just a bit further back, but because of some fluke with conditions, their radios were out of commission for three or four days. We went and introduced ourselves, told them what had happened. I don't remember what we did then. But it was such a relief: we thought we'd have to defend to the last man.

CHAPTER TWENTY-SEVEN

The Originals were accustomed to operating twenty-four hours a day. Early in May, 1945, they were woken in the early hours. By this stage, they had been fighting behind the lines for a full five years.

REG SEEKINGS

I was called up in the middle of the night to go to Kiel. We actually were the first in to Kiel, me and Johnny Cooper. Our job was to go to the town hall, take possession, quick check of the docks, etc. Bob Bennett's lot started at the same time. We were on the way before first light, and as we went past all the gun emplacements all the way along, and on the road back to Lubeck, Germans were coming out and surrendering,

An SAS jeep entering Kiel.

BOB BENNETT

We were about sixty miles south of Kiel at that time, and we were lying up in a farmhouse, and we had the order to go straight to Kiel, and we thought: what is this, we've done some crazy things – because we didn't know the war was finished yet. So off we went in the jeeps. We had a race with the Russians to get in to Kiel, and we just beat them in. There were no planes firing at you and we sort of clicked that something had happened.

JOHNNY COOPER

Kiel was an absolute laugh all the way. Nobody fired a shot at us. We ended up in the town hall with the mayor. Anything with a swastika on we were breaking; destroyed all the photos of Hitler.

BOB BENNETT

We drove along the quay, and there was a German boat trying to up anchor and get out. We opened up with the twin Vickers, and the boat came back in. It was full of people. I spoke to two Norwegians that came off the boat, and apparently the Germans had been shackling these prisoners all the morning, putting them in irons, and dropping them off in the Kiel canal. So they were happy that the SAS had got there.

REG SEEKINGS

We checked the docks, then Johnny and I found a nice suburb, some girls, and were having quite a party, but I left a chap at the wireless on the jeep.

BOB BENNETT

We had a naval officer, an intelligence officer, with us. We drove right into Kiel, and Major John Tonkin and Captain Riding, and this intelligence naval officer went in with the object of meeting Donitz and saying: 'Well, this is it, the war's over.' I sat outside with the squadron, the lads were looking round to see what was going, then Captain Riding came running back, and said: 'For God's sake, don't let them start anything – they don't know anything about the war being over.' They'd said to John Tonkin: 'We accept it is, but the SS are still over the other side of the Kiel canal and they won't believe it.' So we were pulled.

REG SEEKINGS

The chap on the wireless called me saying Paddy Mayne wanted to talk to me. He said: 'Where are you, what's going on? Get the hell out of there fast, don't argue, they're sealing the place off. There's been a cock-up. If you don't get out quick, you'll never get out.'

Bob's lot had taken the surrender of the naval place and pretty near got wiped out there. The naval commander rang up the German command – because they'd knocked out a German sentry as they went across the bridge and every gun in the place was turned on them – and this chap said: 'The war may have ended that side of the canal, but it's very much in existence here. You have so many seconds to get off our premises. I've just spoken to – I think it was Keitel – and no way is the war finished. There is a truce and you've broken it, gentlemen, get back quick.' John and I dropped the booze and girls, and hared off back to Lubeck. Then they threatened me with a court martial and Christ knows what. We'd broken the truce, you see. I said: 'Well, I received this call in the middle of the night.' 'Did you know who it was – do you just follow anybody's instructions? Did you recognise the voice?' I said: 'Yes.' 'Who was it?' 'I don't know.' 'You just told us you did.' I said: 'I'm not telling and that's that, finish.' So I thought I was in big trouble, but I never heard any more.

BOB BENNETT

We drove from Kiel and got orders to go to Belgium – Ostende – and the next day we were twelve miles outside Brussels, sitting in a cafe. There was a radio playing.

REG SEEKINGS

I had a staff car, a BMW, and that could motor. After the incident at Kiel, we went down to Poperinge, outside Brussels. I went like the clappers. I took a few minutes off and went into Hamburg; it was still burning, a terrible mess. Then I got back on to the autobahn but was running short of fuel, and I pulled in at a garage just a mile outside Brussels.

I was getting filled up and debating whether to go into Brussels overnight and then go to Poperinge the next morning, when a young girl came running out and said: 'The war is finished.' I said: 'I've heard all that before.' She said: 'No, it's true, your Prime Minister Mr Churchill is speaking now.' So I ran into the garage and heard Churchill declare that the thing was over.

And I don't know – a fantastic sort of feeling – you're a bit amazed that you got through. We knew full well that immediately the European thing was over, there was already talk that we would be going out to Japan. But there was a relief – and a big relief – that the war there was over and we'd come out on top.

BOB BENNETT

That was it . . . straight into Brussels to celebrate. And you can imagine – the armoured jeeps of the SAS driving right up the steps, into bars in Brussels, and we had a terrific night in Brussels, before we came back. But the news still came as a shock. Sitting there having a drink, and to suddenly hear Churchill.

REG SEEKINGS

We stopped and had coffee with them and decided we wouldn't go into Brussels, we'd go down to Poperinge, and we took part in the celebrations there. I was glad I did, because it was just as my old man had described it, hadn't changed at all. They were all sitting out on the pavements, having a drink and all these old girls were out there, and we kept running out to the gents, and we heard this old girl say: 'They're just like their fathers – drink-drink-drink, piss-piss-piss.' When I told Dad that really tickled him.

When we left home – my young brother gave a false age to get into the army – my father said: 'I shall never be able to give you much of material wealth, but one thing I have given you, honesty and hard work. Both are hard to come by, easy to lose, and once lost you never get 'em back. So treasure them.'

When we came home, we didn't let the parents know. It had been cancelled so many times, we decided to just drop in on them. So they had no idea we were coming home. My father was home. I said, 'Wait a minute,' and knocked on the door – because he'd told us in this little talk we'd had: 'Never darken my door if you're dishonest.' Dad came out and of course nearly had a fit. He said: 'Well, come on in.' I said: 'Well, I've got to warn you of one thing – I've not been exactly dishonest, but I have been by your standards.' He said: 'Bloody good show, glad you're not stupid.'

My sister had been on night shift, and was upstairs asleep. Mum shouted up: 'Come down, your brothers are home.' She said: 'Don't be stupid, what did you wake me up for?' So I shouted up: 'Come on, get a bloody move on!' And to see her face when she came down. She'd been in hospital when I left, tuberculosis, and I hadn't seen her for years. She'd sent me a photo of herself to Italy and she was a grown-up girl. She said: 'You've been writing to me as though I'm a little child – I'm a grown woman now.' And she also said our parents wouldn't let her go to dances, and I wrote and said I'd take her to her first dance. And that's what we did.

David Stirling, meanwhile, was in Colditz.

During the interview with him, he did not refer in any great detail to his period there; on another occasion, however, he did make mention of a system of cooperating with the local resistance outside Colditz, in order to protect the POWs inside should anything happen to the castle, but again he skipped over the issue. In fact, what he established in Colditz was as incredible and challenging as his plan to launch a guerrilla army from Marisch Trubau – even though most people did not know of it.

It was not an escape attempt. In the closing stages of the war it might be considered more important, and would have affected the lives and well-being not just of a handful of men, but of all the men held there.

Shortly before Christmas, 1944, the SBO, the senior British officer, a Scot named Todd, called Stirling in 'for a chat'. Todd had been informed that command of Colditz was to pass from the Wehrmacht to the SS, the suggestion being that the Colditz inmates would be held as hostages in a last-ditch ploy by Hitler. Among the Colditz POWs were a number of especially interesting individuals – including relatives of the Queen, the Prime Minister, and the American ambassador to London. In order to plan, the SBO needed information. The problem was that this would have to come from outside Colditz.

With Pringle and a small inner group, Stirling set out to achieve this.

Within Colditz, and because many of the prisoners there were long-term inmates, there had developed an informal black market, with individuals selling items from spare Red Cross parcels. Stirling, and his inner team (including, of course, Jack Pringle), persuaded everyone that this should be centralised, with two 'sole traders' – who were working for Stirling. Everyone therefore benefited, but through this Stirling and his team were also able to recruit guards with contacts and families on the outside who could pass them the information Todd wanted. Stirling also established direct connections with people on the outside, including a signal system (via coded movements of men visible on a road from Colditz itself) by which a local contact would inform them of what was happening outside.

The system worked. In May 1945, Todd was ordered by the camp commandant to assemble the POWs to be moved. Because of the intelligence system Stirling and Pringle had established, Todd already knew this and had prepared his response. He not only refused, he also demanded that the commandant surrender the castle, which was done. Stirling and the others then sat on the Colditz castle walls and watched the Americans advancing.

In fact, Stirling and his intelligence cell met the Americans.

Then David Stirling came home.

DAVID STIRLING

We arrived at an airport outside London from Colditz – the Americans flew us back – on April 15, 1945. That was interesting; there were elaborate measures; it was too ludicrous. The psychologists – the trick cyclists, etc. – were getting quite a grip within the medical circles in the UK, and they assumed anybody who came out of Colditz required treatment before they were safe to be allowed back into normal circulation. We had to be examined and talked to by the psychoanalyst. We were put inside a camp which had a wire perimeter and so on – it was a prison camp again.

They had all the official nannies there. We were told we had to be there for two days, and they patronised us rotten – what they were going to do for us, etc. But naturally when we got there, we had dates that very evening in London, and so the moment the official nannies disappeared . . . I don't think there was anybody left in that camp at all by eleven o'clock, we were all in London, or gone home. Twelve o'clock that evening I was in a nightclub. By 2am I was having my first roger for years.

CHAPTER TWENTY-EIGHT

As the war in Europe tailed off, 1 SAS were sent to Norway. Already, thoughts in Whitehall were turning toward the reorganisation of the army in peace-time – and the disbanding of regiments. In London, however, Stirling was up to his old tricks.

DAVID STIRLING

I'd devised the Chungking project in Colditz, which I presented to Churchill when I came back. The idea was to use the SAS in the war against Japan, which was still going on.

I also saw Bill Donovan, who'd founded the American OSS, the Office of Strategic Service, the forerunner of the CIA. I also saw the American ambassador in London. Churchill handed me on to his Chief of Staff, Pug Ismay. Churchill was convinced that the atom bomb – about which I knew nothing – would bring the war with Japan to a quick close. Pug Ismay on the other hand was much more pessimistic, and he wasn't so sure it was going to work.

The whole idea of the Chungking project had been worked out on SAS principles, even though it was on brigade scale. We had three main targets. One was to cut off supplies to the Japanese in the area of responsibility under Field Marshal Mountbatten, mopping up the Japanese there. The second was to help establish landing areas for the Americans, had it been necessary for them to crow-step up the coast, nearer to Japan, so they could mount their final assault against Japan there. And the third one was to sabotage the Manchurian industrial heart of that part of the world, which the Japanese had at their disposal.

The proposal was for me to accept American overall command and they would accept my command of a brigade, which included a regiment of the OSS, Bill Donovan's boys, and one regiment made up of mainly prisoners of war, plus the cavalry, plus two or three other special units which I was able to put on the list for recruiting purposes. I would have the cream of the cream. In China I would have given them all basic SAS training. Plus, of course, I was leading the

2 SAS regiment. I didn't want to interfere with Paddy's 1 SAS regiment, which would have gone to the Far East under Field Marshal Mountbatten.

One of the aspects which I emphasised with Winston Churchill was the great need to maintain an effective British connection within China – all of which had disappeared and given place to an American presence. The Americans didn't know too much about China, and were not as knowledgeable about that sort of situation as the British were in those days. This aspect of it appealed to Churchill very much. I remember the first time I had lunch with him to discuss it, I had Fitzroy Maclean there as well. Fitzroy was going to take on Formosa while I went to Chungking – that was before it became Taiwan and so on. So quite a few of the SAS, as the war in Europe ended, were beginning to think of the political implications while there was still an initiative to be taken, while the Japanese war went on.

I would have had a certain amount of room for taking something of a political initiative as well. It certainly was the part of the proposition that I think Churchill was more interested in than the military aspect, because he was convinced that the bomb would blast the Japanese out of the war.

I was well under way by the time the bomb did in fact explode appallingly successfully. Therefore the whole of my project was at an end.

REG SEEKINGS

We got back from Germany and within a few hours we were sent to Norway, to take the surrender and clean up the German troops there. We went out by Dakotas, took our jeeps with us. They flew us into Stavanger, and then we motored across the peninsula.

Stavanger was important, it was the centre for the new U-boats, so they were particularly keen to get in there. The Werewolf organisation was there. There were some diehard Waffen SS people there, who intended to start a resistance movement of their own. I think a lot of them used the U-boats and got across to South America. It was known there was a big collection of snorkel subs at Stavanger – that's why we had to be there.

We took command of the base at Stavanger. There were one or two nasty incidents there; it was a bit rough at times. We were using rifle butts and fists a lot of the time, because those chaps were crack crews on the U-boats and they didn't take calmly to Englishmen appearing. Then we moved up to Bergen.

BOB BENNETT

I'll always remember that trip. It was supposed to be eleven miles, and we kept driving and driving – a Norwegian mile is eleven English miles, so it was over a hundred miles. We got into Bergen, made base there, then we spent the next few months taking everything off the Germans, all their loot and putting them on boats back to Germany. The two things I remember about Norway are champagne and 4711 eau de cologne.

REG SEEKINGS

In Bergen we didn't really do much at all, just checked on the German army stores, took them over, saw they were dismantled, and passed the personnel back to appropriate places, and tried to maintain decent relations with the local population. In lots of ways it was flag flying, but we got into quite a lot of trouble there.

BOB BENNETT

The feeling against the Grey Shadows, the collaborators, was very, very high in the SAS. They were the power men, in charge of police, the whole administration – people that had been brainwashed by the Gestapo. We went into the cells they'd used. Lots of our chaps were being done up all over the place by these people. And 1 and 2 SAS went down – no officers involved whatsoever, just other ranks – and had this battle. Thank God there were no shots fired. But we threw the chief constable in the lake, did a few Grey Shadows up. But they were not only bad against the SAS, they were bad against other people who'd left the country to fight the war. They were shocking people. Then a signal came – get the SAS out of Norway.

JOHNNY COOPER

We knew the writing was on the wall as soon as the war was over.

BOB BENNETT

After Norway there was nothing left for SAS to do. At that time there were still a lot of people didn't like SAS, there were still a lot of high-powered people had no time for it, and of course the Labour government came in – Attlee and his gang of merry men – and they couldn't get rid of it quick enough. So everyone was going to be sent back to their parent regiments. Well, you can imagine – people being away from their regiments for years and all this comradeship in SAS, it was frightening.

JIM ALMONDS

The SAS had proved themselves financially very good. If you take the amount of damage that was done to the enemy for the number of men employed, we were very good. The number of aircraft destroyed in the desert alone. But I don't think it was ever really liked.

REG SEEKINGS

It was a bad time. There were all these new chaps, who seemed to be gloating that it was all over, and us big gunner boys, we were out of it now. They took great pleasure in giving you the posting back to your parent regiment. I told Colonel David what was going on and he said: 'As soon as you're established get in touch with me and let me know where you go.' I applied to go back to the Suffolks.

JIM ALMONDS

There were a lot of wild hopes. When you went in the sergeants' mess, there were a lot of murals round the wall of people coming down by parachute, and the people on the ground were obviously Oriental – Chinese. That was Stirling's project. If the chance had occurred I would have gone on that. I bought an atlas to check up on that part of the world, to see what the terrain was like, and the people. I think Mike Sadler was with me when I bought that atlas. We went and we checked on all sorts of facts, checked up on all those place names – they still stay with me. I can think of them all now – I could have walked that journey. Then they dropped the atomic bomb, and that finished it.

REG SEEKINGS

It's like the bottom dropping out of the world. You were lost. Because I can tell you that the staff wallahs came into their own. I asked for a favour and I was told: 'Your day is over. You're not a blue-eyed boy now.' And I said: 'Well, I'll stand on my two feet, I'll survive where you won't, you so-and-so.' Colonel Stirling had got out of the cage, and he'd rung me up to ask us – Johnny, myself and our two wives – up to London. I'd already put in for a posting to our holding battalion, the Suffolks, and I asked for that to be cancelled for a day or two, whilst I went up to London, otherwise I'd got to travel all up from Dover to London, mess about. But that wasn't allowed. I was told my day was over. That was the way we were treated by staff wallahs.

JOHNNY COOPER

We were at Highlands Park, the home of Lady Hanbury – Buxtons the breweries people. The officers' mess was in the house even though she still lived there.

JIM ALMONDS

I remember the final days. One or two wild parties. We had a last party that went on till the early hours of the morning.

JOHNNY COOPER

We got a jeep up the central staircase, a huge marble staircase, on to the top landing, then we couldn't get it down. How it got up I don't know. We were all very pissed. That was the night we rang up Atlee, the prime minister. Pote was second in command, myself and our motor transport officer, a Scotsman, all a bit pissed, and we rang up and got through to Atlee's private secretary. We said: 'If you cut our bacon ration, we'll cut a slice off your arse.' Then the security thing went down.

JIM ALMONDS

Paddy said: 'I want everyone on parade in the morning, properly turned out, at 8am or 9am.' So everybody had to forget their hangovers quick, get smartened up, and get outside.

JOHNNY COOPER

Next day we were there. Paddy rang up the fire brigade and said: 'Highlands Park's on fire.' And as the firemen arrived all our mess waiters were out with trays of drinks. We got the whole of Chelmsford fire brigade pissed. One engine arrived, then another, then another . . . pandemonium.

There were officers there from HQ who were quite pleased to see it wrapped up. It was a very tragic day. These huge lawns, with the open part in front of the hall, and there was the whole regiment on parade. I think it was Monty who came down. I remember him bullshitting me. I had met him once before and he used the same old trick as he was going around. Paddy said: 'This is Captain Cooper.' Monty said: 'I know his name's Cooper. What's your Christian name again, I've forgotten it.' Lying bugger. The old PR stunt.

We were all in red berets, that we had since we came back to Europe for D-Day. But Paddy was in the sand-coloured beret, from the first days in the desert.

JIM ALMONDS

We had the parade. A photograph was taken of the regiment.

JOHNNY COOPER

Then the SAS was disbanded.

AUTHOR'S NOTE

It was not the end of the SAS, of course. But the reason it was not the end was not because of decisions made in Whitehall. It was not the end because of the SAS themselves. And especially of one man.

In 1945 Brian Franks, who had taken over 2 SAS from Bill Stirling, ordered his intelligence unit to the area of Moussey, in France, the site of Operation Loyton, to find out what had happened to SAS men still missing, and to track down those responsible and bring them to justice. The unit finally came home in 1948, three years after the wartime SAS had been disbanded.

At the same time, however, Franks also played a key role in resurrecting the SAS, at first as a Territorial Army unit, combining it with the Artists Rifles to form 21 SAS (Artists), which provided the basis for SAS to survive in the future.

But what of The Originals?

JOHNNY COOPER

We were all sent back to our parent regiments, and I was shipped straight off to Cyprus, where I was adjutant of the 6th Battalion Green Howards. I stuck it for a time, but I think that I was rather spoilt being with 1 SAS and with L Detachment, so I decided to leave the army. But at that time Brian Franks was forming the territorials – 21 SAS (Artists) and I joined as a lieutenant. I finished the war as a captain, and I joined the TA as a lieutenant, and went to the first camp. I went back to my wool trade. I was working in Bradford, where it had all started, then the firm decided to send me out to Australia.

PAT RILEY

I went back to the police but I became a bit restless. I suppose I missed all the activity. I was back on the beat again which didn't work out as far as I was concerned. I went off to the police college to sit my exams for promotion, and I passed, but there was no promotion coming. So getting a little restless I met up with Jim Almonds, who put an idea into my head, but that didn't work out, so that unsettled me more. In fact I'd packed my job in, so I had to go and ask them could I have it back again.

BOB BENNETT

When the SAS was disbanded, I went along to the orderly room and found that there was a job going in Greece, with the Greek military mission, and I immediately volunteered for that. I spent the next four years in Greece with what used to be the Greek SAS, the Sacred Squadron, that were then called raiding forces. I was with a Major Alastair McGregor, from 2 SAS. It was quite a war that was going on there, it was a lot worse than people thought. Although the SAS had been disbanded, Major McGregor and myself carried on wearing the SAS gear – the beret, the badge, the breast wings – which we were entitled to, and we never took them off. We thought that as long as us two were out in Greece, SAS was still alive.

JOHNNY COOPER

I was only in Australia about a year and I realised that civilian life wasn't for me. I'd kept my contacts – I was still a TA officer – so I got back home, and this movement had started, designed to go to Korea, but then the Americans didn't want us.

BOB BENNETT

I came back from Greece in 1949, and decided that this was the end of the road as far as Special Air Service was concerned, and left the army. I was out about three months. By that time I'd had enough of Civvy Street, and decided to go back in the army. I enlisted with the Royal Artillery, and they said: 'We'll take you as a bombardier, a corporal.' Well, you know, I'd come right down from sah major.

REG SEEKINGS

I'd been running a pub some considerable time. They were demolishing pillboxes all around the place and there was a young lad, Nobby, who had served with me, he'd got a job with one of these firms, and he said: 'I've got somebody I want you to meet. I'll bring him in at lunchtime.' In came this chap – good-looking, blond – and Nobby says to me: 'This is Reg Seekings.' I said to this chap: 'Oh yes. How do you do?' I said: 'Do you know Johnny Cooper?' 'Oh yes, I know Johnny Cooper.' I said: 'I believe you had some good times together.' He said: 'Yes, I knew Stirling and I knew Paddy Mayne.' I said: 'Oh yeah.' And a little plaque which I had hanging up in the bar caught his eye, and he said: 'Oh, you know something about the SAS?' I said: 'Look, mate, before you go any further, you're not very observant for Reg Seekings. Go outside, cast your eyes up. And if you can read, just read.' I've never seen that man from that day to this.

BOB BENNETT

I spent a few weeks up in Wales with the Artillery, and I was sent for one morning by the CO, and he said: 'You've got to go to Aldershot and report as soon as possible. What's it about?' I said: 'I haven't got a clue.' I got to Aldershot Station, and who should be waiting but Major Greville Bell, who was 2 SAS, Major Alastair McGregor and Jock Easton. And they said: 'What's all this business, two tapes – get a crown up.' And this was the start of the squadron that they were calling 'K' Squadron that was going be sent out to Korea.

There was only two regulars in it – the rest were from the SAS Territorial Army. Then it was decided the Americans didn't want SAS out there, and so people were given an option to go back to Civvy Street. But there was a thing they could volunteer for, in Malaya, a unit called the Malayan Scouts. And so we proceeded to Malaya.

JOHNNY COOPER

I found myself out in Malaya with what they called the Malayan Scouts (SAS), which was a peculiar sort of unit. Slowly we took over and it became SAS (Malayan Scouts). Then it was decided that as we had the 21st, the 22nd Regiment was formed. I stayed in Malaya right the way through to the end of 1958, and finished up commanding a squadron. I went to the Jebel Akhadar campaign, that was the winter of '58-'59, then SAS came home and we were based at Malvern. We were cut down by the powers-that-be to two squadrons. My head was due to fall; I was offered a job as G2 SAS in the War Office. I'd never sat at a desk – I don't think I'd be capable of doing so anyway – and I volunteered to go out to the Oman again, which still had a little bit of a show going.

PAT RILEY

I was still restless, so I decided I'd go back to the Services. I went back and I joined the Gloucesters. The first posting I got was Jamaica which was very nice, and from there on I got seconded to various governments and was moved around. I went to Central America, to Belize; then I went to Malaya and I fought the communists there. You know, led the Malays. That was a wonderful experience, just one white person with all the Malays. They're very, very good fighters. Next I went to Accra, some frontier force. Then I went up to Gambia – that was marvellous. I was very fortunate in all this moving around to have my wife with me.

Moving around like that, I suppose we saw the sun set on the Empire.

Then I came back to England, did some cross-Channel stuff, going across to the continent quite a lot. Finally time caught up, and I decided to retire from the

Services. I took a hotel on, did various jobs, worked for a timber company. Then I got in on the ground floor with Securicor. I was landed with the opportunity of helping to expand the company, and I was moving right around, with many things that happened there. That was very exciting – it was just like being in the SAS.

JOHNNY COOPER

So I disappeared to the Oman. I'd only been there a short time and David Stirling once again upset my plans. He said: 'I want to lead a British-French contingent to the North Yemen, to ascertain whether it's a puppet government; also I want you to take a regular unit in.' So under the pretext my mother was dying, I was flown home, went to France on my birthday, June 6, D-Day, and met certain officials. David was behind the whole thing. We assembled in Chelsea and we were all due to go over there, then the Profumo affair broke. David got a message: 'You'd better pull back on this one.' But David, as usual, said to the boys: 'Let's go.' So we went. I'd collected the regular boys; I picked up two Deuxieme Bureau from the French, who were excellent, and two French colonial officers.

We landed in Aden, and we were told to stay on the plane. Then (X) came on board and said: 'Major Cooper, you're in charge of this party?' I said: 'Yes.' 'Give me your passports. Stay on the aircraft.' The next thing, a DC-3 chunters alongside – everything was quiet on the Aden airstrip – and we were pushed across into the DC-3. We were flown up to the North Yemeni border, and that night we went across on camels. I was told I would be there three months. Three years later I came out.

After that I had a little excursion, once again for the club, into Chad. We got together twelve of the boys, and did all different shapes of things. We even had helicopter experts brought, and we built an airstrip just outside of the old Fort Laramie. It was quite an experience. Then, coming back through the French Cameroons, they locked us up, just for good measure. And that was my last job. . .

REG SEEKINGS

Later, I went to Rhodesia, against the guerrillas. When the government changed, I was at the airport when the new government flew in. The man whose people I had been fighting came up to me. 'You're Seekings,' he said. I said: 'That's right.' He said: 'You're good. I want you to work with me now.'

But not all the activities of The Originals were connected with military matters, even with the SAS.

JIM ALMONDS

Whether they bring it to the fore or not is a different matter, but every human has the thing of survival, and they all have the desire to create. It's probably just a question of make-up, or it's a question of opportunity to do these sort of things. I consider I was very fortunate in having that opportunity.

I'm no sailor; I didn't know anything about sailing. I had a fair idea of direction and things like this.

I was in West Africa, doing a four-year stint, and the wood is beautiful – mahoganies, African teak, and all that sort of thing. And seeing all this delightful wood lying about, it was a great chance to do something. So I built this ketch, a 32-footer. I did it all by hand. I made the sails by hand, most of the rigging by hand, made my own blocks and pulleys and everything.

Then the great day came. We put it on a low loader and took it down to the sea, lifted it off with a crane into the water, and it floated. There was no time to really try it out, because my stay down there was up, and I'd already broadcast what I was going to do – there was a notice on the board in the departure lounge saying that Major Almonds was going home in his own boat. So I couldn't really back out.

Originally I was going to go alone with a cat, but two other chaps signed on. One was a tea planter from India, who'd heard from someone through the post that this trip was going to be made; he came and asked if he could have a berth. And the other was a district commissioner in Ghana.

So we piled aboard and set off.

And I then began to discover the little things that had to be overcome. Neither of them were sailors, they'd never done anything like this before, and nor had I. When we got well out, seasickness began to show itself and I found that I was on duty just about twenty-four hours a day, until they got over it. Then we started taking watches. We'd do a four-hour watch round the clock. There were only two bunks inside – we had to carry a lot of provision and things – and two would be asleep down below and one on watch. The one on the watch did the cooking, sailed the ship, altered the sails if they had to be altered and things like that. Then he woke the next man up, gave him a cup of tea and he went to bed, in the bed the other man came out of.

The first port we put into was on the Ivory Coast – this is travelling northwards, out of the Bight of Benin and up the western seaboard of Africa.

And we went from there to Liberia, and from Liberia to Sierra Leone and on up the coast as far as Port Etienne. There we struck the Atlantic current which runs in a clockwise direction and runs fast down the west coast of Africa, plus the north east tradewinds. We were passing one spot sometimes three or four times before we got clear of it, on account of when the wind dropped at night, you'd go backwards, and then the wind gathers again in daylight and you go forward.

We weren't making any real progress, so we decided to turn and make for Bermuda, get out across the Atlantic, until we could pick up the westerly winds, which brought us back into the Azores, then from the Azores we made for the Channel, and brought the boat up the east coast in at the Wash and up the Witham to my home.

A lot of people wouldn't understand that. It's quite understandable, to me anyway. Other people might think it odd, but I live in the same house my father lived in and my grandfather and so on. It's a tradition to live in that cottage, and so that's where I live.

And what of David Stirling himself? Much has been written about his escapades and exploits. There was one project, however, in which he firmly believed, and which shows another aspect of the man, but about which little has been written.

DAVID STIRLING

I was well under way with the Chunking project by the time the bomb exploded; therefore my whole operation was at an end. So I went out to Africa and started the Capricorn project.

Capricorn's intention was to go back to Africa as a continent, and rationalise it as a continent, and have a political philosophy which was emotionally valid for all races and all religions. For twelve years I worked towards creating a contract between all the great religions of the world – for all the blackamoors, the white-a-moors, the brownamoors, the in-between-a-moors – to regard this philosophy as emotionally valid to all of them. You had to have the Africans themselves feeling it, because it was their continent.

I had eighty-five or eighty-six citizenship committees up and down the continent, reporting on what we called the Capricorn Contract. In London, I had a headquarters which dealt with the religious leaders of the world. Also Laurens van der Post, with whom I used to campaign in Africa.

It was a very exciting project. We didn't have the do-gooder Africans. The Africans we had were those who later fought the Europeans – they were real nationalists – and they were the ones that I suppose we would have been, had we been Africans. They're the front-line boys. They weren't likely to subordinate themselves to the Europeans, any more than the Scots did to the English.

This was a total political plan. But one had to arrive at that in a way in which the Africans themselves were emotionally involved in its success. They had to believe in the concept that Africa could be a vastly rich continent if all the boundary lines, which were drawn up from London, Berlin and elsewhere, could be overcome. For instance the Kapriwi Strip – the Germans wanted to give a Christmas present to Queen Victoria, or the other way round – but the Kapriwi Strip was totally false. It came right across German South West Africa onto the Zambesi. It was characteristic of how boundary lines were drawn up.

But we were done in by two factors.

The Africans felt by that time they'd been dominated by the European, and had to go through the process of creating their own record of throwing the European out, or mastering the European, before they could feel a nation.

But it was the Colonial Office operating their own ridiculous policy, based on these more than idiotic land divisions within the continent, and wanting to establish Whitehall type of constitutions – totally irrelevant to the African continent – which overrode us.

I came back from Rhodesia for a mission to Vienna during the Hungarian uprising. I felt it would be an enormous help to the Russians to put spies in Europe. I put my proposal to Andy Head and he backed it, and appointed me to carry out the mission.

Bill Donovan was appointed by Eisenhower. When I first met him on this mission and we decided what we would do, it was at the time of the Suez crisis, so we knew there would be no American tanks rumbling down Hungarian roads to rescue anyone.

The refugees would include spies, so I said we ought to apply a filter from Vienna to catch what we could, and we'd try to create another sieve behind that.

When I arrived in Vienna to meet Donovan, he'd got the beginning of a brain tumour and was already halfway down the hill. I went to our ambassador and he said: 'They won't allow you to talk to any American, because of Suez.' I thought I'd go and see Donovan. It was very sad, because Donovan was a great guy. His manservant told me that poor old Bill wouldn't even recognise me. He was so far gone the tumour was as big as his brain.

Anyway, Capricorn didn't come off. You don't make much money as an agitator, so I came back and for a brief period I had to work like hell. I set up about fourteen television stations round the world, mostly based on the need for the younger countries to acquire television, as it was very important from an educational standpoint. But those didn't make very much money. I had the biggest collection of the most bankrupt television stations in the world. They were hanging on, just economically viable and no more.

I was quite professional in the game by then, and I went out to Hong Kong and set up HKTV, in competition with Rediffusion which was out there. But their outfit was in English, and something under two per cent of the population was English. So mine was set up primarily in the Chinese language, and of course it took off. It's worth £140 million today, and because I set it up and put the whole thing together, I got my shares for free. So I did make money out of that, and therefore was able to go into all the other things I've been doing.

POSTSCRIPT

In June, 1984, David Stirling officially gave his name to the SAS headquarters in Hereford. The headquarters has since moved, but retains the name. Stirling's words that day are typical of the man:

What a magnificent gathering. It moves me to conclude that our regiment has a special magic in generating for itself an intense loyalty in all who have served it. Indeed, we are more than a regiment – we are a family.

In the SAS it is a tradition never to be heard in public boasting about our regiment's past or present performances. Today, because this is strictly a family occasion, I am going to break that rule – in a modest way.

Almost to the day forty-three years ago, as a second lieutenant and known to be something of a 'cheeky laddie', and of dubious value to the army, I submitted to Field Marshal Auchinleck's chief of general staff a paper setting out in my own nearly illegible handwriting the SAS proposition. Within days I was authorised to raise and command a sixty-five man unit to be called L Detachment SAS Brigade; and within minutes of getting that favourable nod, the SAS was underway.

Most survivors of the original SAS foundation unit – and I understand we are known in the regiment as the Dirty Dozen – are here today (and in spirit alongside me). Perhaps you can understand our astonishment, and how proud we are, looking around this mighty throng.

After L Detachment's first disastrous parachute operation on a moonless and stormy night, in November 1941, L Detachment was reduced to only twenty-seven men; but it was more than enough to get on with proving the SAS role.

In January 1942, during our drive for recruits, we were joined by Georges Bergé and his Free French Unit. From this group eventually was born the French SAS regiments. Bergé's men were of superb quality and they were the bravest of the brave.

In those early days we came to owe the Long Range Desert Group a deep debt of gratitude. The LRDG were the supreme professionals of the desert and they were unstinting in their help. Here among us today is David Lloyd Owen, long a wartime commanding officer of this magnificent unit. We are proud to regard the Long Range Desert Group as honorary members of our SAS family.

By February 1943, L Detachment had prospered at the enemy's expense and had become the 1st SAS Regiment. By then we had acquired our full establishment of jeeps and supply vehicles, and we had consolidated our maritime capabilities by incorporating under George Jellicoe the Special Boat Squadron. Thus, sub-units of the regiment could arrive at a selected target area by air, by sea or by land.

Shortly after I was nabbed by the enemy and after a hiccup or two the command of the 1st SAS regiment passed to the great Paddy Blair Mayne.

In the meantime the 2nd SAS regiment had been formed by my brother Bill and commanded by him until he had a bitter quarrel with the High Command, who insisted on his regiment being used in a semi-tactical role for which it had not been trained. Although he had to resign he won the argument. He was succeeded by Brian Franks, who was allowed to revert to the true SAS strategic function – of operating deep behind the enemy lines. At the end of the war, Paddy Mayne was still in command of the 1st SAS and Brian Franks of the 2nd SAS, and the SAS Brigade from the end of 1944 was under the command of Mike Calvert; while in the Middle East George Jellicoe had been succeeded by David Sutherland in command of the Special Boat Squadron.

You will all know of the prodigious range of SAS operations carried out in the Western Desert, Italy, France, Norway, Germany and the Eastern Mediterranean. A senior general, Miles Dempsey, who commanded 13 Corps, in writing to the commanding officers of the 1st and 2nd Regiments, summarised his view on the SAS as follows:

> *In my military career, and in my life, I have commanded many, many units, but I have never met a unit in which I had such confidence. And I mean that.*

Surely a marvellous accolade coming from such a famous soldier.

After the war, the anti-climax – we were disbanded. Had it not been for Brian Franks we should have been consigned to oblivion – just a meagre footnote in the history of the Second World War. With admirable tenacity of purpose he persuaded the military establishment to form the 21 SAS as a territorial unit. By 1951 the 22nd SAS was being formed in Malaysia, and the regiment soon thereafter regained its proper status.

With John Woodhouse and his successors in command, there began the post-war heyday of the regiment. Campaigns were fought in Malaysia, Borneo, Aden, The Oman, Northern Ireland, South Georgia and the Falkland Islands – campaigns often operationally complex, and each of them studded with episodes demanding the full range of SAS skills.

During the post-war period, the SAS family was further enriched by the forming of the Australian, New Zealand and Rhodesian SAS squadrons. Each of them have merited splendid chapters in the history of their own countries. The Australian and the New Zealand SAS retain the strongest of links with Hereford. The Rhodesian SAS, sadly now disbanded, had its roots in 22 SAS as 'C' Squadron. Their roll of honour stands alongside that of 22 SAS within these lines.

At this point I want to emphasise that I have always felt uneasy in being known as the founder of the regiment. To ease my conscience, I would like it to be recognised that I have five co-founders: Jock Lewes, Paddy Mayne of the original L Detachment; Georges Bergé, who started the French SAS; Brian Franks, who re-raised the SAS flag after the war; and John Woodhouse, who created the modern SAS during the Malaysian campaign by restoring to the regiment its original philosophy.

There are so many others who have played vital parts in the SAS story, like Mike Calvert, Ian Lapraik, Eddie Blondeel who raised and commanded the Belgian SAS, Christodoulos Tzigantes and his Greek Sacred Squadron Brigade, a squadron of which fought gallantly alongside the SAS in the Middle East, Pat Riley, Bob Bennett, Johnny Watts, George Jellicoe, Peter de la Billiere, Fitzroy Maclean, Reg Seekings, Johnny Cooper, Jim Almonds, Tankie Smith, Tom Burt, Roy Farran and Mr SAS himself, Dare Newell – but to mention them all would be almost like calling the roll.

I must specially commend to you the wise words of Neville Howard on the standard of the SAS man. I would go further. The very survival of the regiment, in a society wary of elitism, depends on the calibre of each individual man recruited. This was, is and must remain the cornerstone. I know the regiment believes in this and must always do so.

There is a further imperative which the SAS has traditionally imposed on itself. The regiment must never regard itself as a corps d'elite, because down that road would lie the corruption of all our values. A substantial dash of humility, along with an ever-active sense of humour, must continue to save us from succumbing to this danger. Only then can we be sure of consolidating the foundations of these splendid new lines, and shielding the spirit and integrity of those setting out from here on their exacting tasks.

The sum total of all that has been accomplished in all those campaigns waged during the regiment's forty-three years, the sacrifices of all those who have died, been disabled or wounded – from the time of our first casualty in the Western Desert to the last just two months ago on Mount Everest; the grief and anxieties caused to the wives and families throughout those years; all this must be added together for us properly to grasp the scale of our investment in the regiment as it stands today. We are deeply proud of our regiment. And we are confident that in the crucial years ahead, as we advance towards our fiftieth anniversary, the SAS will further enhance that standing and thereby its ability to serve our Queen and country.

And now, on behalf of the entire SAS family – with a chest fit to burst in sheer pride – I declare open the Stirling Lines.

INDEX